52 Activities for Successful International Relocation

52 Activities for Successful International Relocation

Patricia A. Cassiday, Donna M. Stringer

INTERCULTURAL PRESS

an imprint of Nicholas Brealey Publishing

BOSTON • LONDON

First published by Intercultural Press in 2015.

20 Park Plaza, Suite 610
Boston, MA 02116, USA
Tel: + 617-523-3801
Fax: + 617-523-3708

3-5 Spafield Street, Clerkenwell
London, EC1R 4QB, UK
Tel: +44 (0)20 7239 0360
Fax: +44 (0)20 7239 0370

www.nicholasbrealey.com

Printed in the United States of America

20   19   18   17   16   15   14   1   2   3   4   5   6   7   8   9   10

ISBN: 978-0-9839558-8-7
E-ISBN: 978-0-9839558-9-4

Library of Congress Cataloging-in-Publication Data

Cassiday, Patricia A.
52 activities for successful international relocation / Patricia A Cassiday, Donna M. Stringer.
pages cm
ISBN 978-0-9839558-8-7 (paperback) -- ISBN 978-0-9839558-9-4 (e-book) 1.   Cross-cultural orientation--Activity programs. 2.   Visitors, Foreign--Life skills guides. 3.   Students, Foreign--Life skills guide. 4.   Foreign workers--Life skills guide.   I. Stringer, Donna M. II. Title. III. Title: Fifty-two activities for successful international relocation.
GN345.65.C37 2014
303.48'2--dc23
2014013197

Contents

Section A Pre-Departure

Section B In-Country

Section C Reentry

Appendixes

Acknowledgments

This book has evolved from the successful and challenging experiences of international transition and travel shared by the authors, their colleagues, and their many friends. These personal and professional experiences have led us to appreciate the importance of effective training during pre-departure, in-country, and especially during the reentry period. Training issues become even more critical as organizations and individuals strive to develop cross-cultural insights and competencies.

This book is possible because of the generosity of our colleagues and friends, who have kindly shared their ideas, their writing, and their research. We are especially grateful to the three individuals who wrote introductions to each of the sections of this book: Stephen T. Duke, who introduces readers to pre-departure training; Joyce Osland, who helps readers think about in-country training; and Bruce LaBrack, who outlines why and how reentry training is important. This collection of introductions and exercises is truly a collaborative effort, and we thank everyone who participated.

We owe much of our education and intercultural insights to our years of work with the Intercultural Communication Institute in Portland, Oregon, and the Society for Intercultural Education, Training and Research; both organizations are central to the ongoing development of leading-edge ideas in the intercultural field and have been central to forging both our understanding and application of intercultural practice.

We also thank the editorial and production team at Intercultural Press for their expertise and careful editing. As always, no book can be done without a team like we had at the press.

We hope this book is useful to you. Please modify the activities to meet the needs of your audience—as we have through the years.

The authors have made every effort to cite and acknowledge all those from whom research, lecture material, or activities have been adapted.

Classification of Activities

	Title	Time in Minutes	Purpose	Risk
A	**Pre-Departure: The Importance of Pre-Departure Preparation**			
1	Personal Reflections for Transition	75–95	P, R	M
2	Build a RAFT: Sailing Off to a New Place	50–65	P, R	L–M
3	Postcards from the Heart	30–45	P, R	L
4	(Country) at a Glance	40–60	P, I	L
5	Different Days—Different Ways	50–65	P	L–M
6	Country Rally: A Family Project for Discovery, Growth, and Adaptation	45–60	P, I	L–M
7	Involvement to Re-Involvement: Moving You from Here to There	45–60	P	L–M
8	Culturally Self-Aware?	65–95	P, I	M
9	The Name Game: More than an Icebreaker!	60	P, I	L–M
10	Cultural Sense-Making	240–480	P, I	L–M
11	The 5Rs of Culture Change	75	P, I, R	M–H
12	Crafting My Future	55–75	P, I, R	L
13	International Transition Bingo	80–100	P, R	L
14	Hats: Worn, Re-Worn, Torn, Born	55–85	P, I, R	M–H
15	Entering "Right"	40–55	P	L–M
16	Safe, Savvy, and Secure	75–100	P	M
17	Role Throwaway	75–120	P	M–H
18	Exploring Values and Behavior	80	P, I	H
B	**In-Country: Training Importance and Characteristics**			
19	Neighborhood Mapping	30	I	L
20	Getting Involved: The Second Ninety Days	40–50	I	L
21	Organizing the World	30–35	P, I	L
22	Who Am I? Echoes of Culture	60	I	M
23	Transition Cube	45	P, I	L

	Title	Time in Minutes	Purpose	Risk
50	Job Reentry—Coming Home	85–125	R	M
51	Returning "Home"	120–145	R	L–M
52	Expatriate Debrief	80–115	R	M

Purpose	Risk
P = Pre-Departure	L = Low
I = In-Country	M = Medium
R = Reentry	H = High

Introduction

"Living in a foreign culture is like playing a game you've never played before and for which the rules have not been explained very well. The challenge is to enjoy the game without missing too many plays, learning the rules and developing skills as you go along.

You'll learn a great deal, though much of it will be intangible and difficult to define. In negotiating the unfamiliar and uncharted territory of another culture, change and growth occur at deep levels, leaving you more competent, more self-assured, and more knowledgeable about yourself and how the world works."

—*L. Robert Kohls (2001, p. 131)*

Change

Change is the antecedent of transition!

When circumstances in our life change, we must accommodate the change in some way. Change may occur intentionally, because of something we choose, or as the result of something beyond our control. Change may be viewed as either positive or negative, depending on the external effect it has on our life and/or a more subtle internal influence. Change frequently results in a symbolic ending of "what was." When something ends, there is groundwork for new possibilities, new realities, and even a new way of being and/or a new way of living.

Transition

Transition is the process of letting go of the past and moving into the new circumstances resulting from change. Transition offers the opportunity for personal growth, self-renewal, and enhanced creativity. The transition process requires time. When the transition process involves an international move, the individual has an opportunity to expand his or her worldview while exploring the cultural paradigms that influence perceptions and assumptions, learning how to survive and succeed in a "foreign" culture.

Self-Awareness

Each culture has both explicit and implicit values, beliefs, and assumptions that define the culture's frame of reference and form the foundation for that culture's socialization process. Members of the culture learn to depend on these norms for consistency in "how things are done" in the world. When individuals travel to another culture, they encounter new frames of reference, and for many people this encounter challenges the assumptions, values, and beliefs that have been framing the foundation of their own identity.

Janet Bennett (1998) suggests that "culture shock" is actually a subcategory of the transition experience. The challenge of cross-cultural adaptation has the potential for being a positive as well as a negative experience. Cultural transition, as a life-changing experience, offers the opportunity for personal growth and increased self-awareness. As an individual seeks to establish effective communication and build meaningful relationships under new cultural rules, introspection becomes a necessity.

International Transition

As pre-departure trainers consider international transition, they need to recognize that the participants' fundamental needs for survival must be met before their other needs can be addressed. Pre-departure programs too often attempt to deal with cultural differences and language skills at a time when the primary needs and anxieties for those departing are focused on questions of day-to-day living.

Logistic concerns include the passport, visa, and work permit requirements for the receiving country. Other questions that require answers include: When will we travel? How will we travel? What is the weather like? What type of clothing is needed? Are there restrictions to the type of dress for women/men? What are the housing accommodations? Should furniture be shipped or stored? Will there be public transportation? Should a vehicle be shipped, stored, sold? How about large and small appliances? Is there electricity? 110 or 220? What access will there be to technology, banking, health care? Are there safety concerns to be considered at the new location?

Families in transition have additional concerns for meeting the appropriate educational needs for the children. Partners may also be anxious about employment opportunities for the accompanying spouse, who may be displaced from a lucrative and rewarding career.

PRE-DEPARTURE TRAINING

The main components of pre-departure training are (1) logistical information and (2) cultural information. Efficient, well-organized training design is essential, as time is of the essence. When participants are offered logistical insights first, they will be able to more fully participate in the cultural learning components.

The specifics of cultural information included in the pre-departure training will depend on the experience of the participants. Culture-general information should be introduced if the participants are embarking on their first international transition. Culture-specific information should be included for both new and experienced travelers. Pre-departure training should be designed in an effort to reduce initial culture shock and also to raise the participants' awareness of the subtle expectations for appropriate behavior in the new country.

If participants were not screened for cultural sensitivity/adaptability during the selection process, pre-departure is a good time to do a formal assessment using an instrument such as the Intercultural Development Inventory (IDI), the Cross-Cultural Adaptability Inventory (CCAI), the Intercultural Sensitivity Inventory (ISI), or other cultural orientation self assessments. A formal assessment creates an initial benchmark of intercultural competency and provides specific information for the in-country training design. When the same instrument is administered at the time of reentry, data from the two assessments can be compared as a measure of training effectiveness and personal growth.

Employees and students who have lived abroad are often willing to lend a helping hand to those beginning their journey. Trainers may wish to invite expatriates to participate in a section of the pre-departure training. If possible, also encourage the establishment of an in-country contact or "mentor" for the employee or student prior to departure. Cultural mentors can provide sojourners with accurate and insightful culture-related information, as well as offer moral support during times of frustration and loneliness.

In his introduction to the pre-departure exercises included later in this book, Steven T. Duke, Ph.D., Executive Director of Global Student/Faculty Development, Research, and Risk Management at Wake Forest University, outlines the importance of preparation for departure and describes five key elements that instructors should consider for such training.

IN-COUNTRY SUPPORT

Prime time to provide additional intercultural training occurs three to six months after participants have started working or studying in the international environment. By this point, individuals have had an opportunity to apply the cross-cultural information they learned during pre-departure training, and the "honeymoon period" is likely over. At this stage, they are learning that "how we do things here" may be very different from their expectations and prior experience. The challenges of the first few months serve as the framework for applying theory to actual life events. The relevance of day-to-day experiences can enrich the training and enhance the learning.

As Kelly (1963) argues, "A person can be a witness to a tremendous parade of episodes and yet, if he fails to keep making something out of them or if he waits until they have occurred before he attempts to reconstruct them, he gains little in the way of experience from having been around when they happened" (30). The cognitive dissonance created from living internationally, combined with an individual's willingness and ability to learn, offers opportunity for significant personal growth and development. Training should be designed to enhance understanding of what is "really" happening and the cultural underpinnings of why.

Much of how we behave and how we expect others to behave is based on implicitly learned cultural values. Until we encounter another way of being or doing or thinking or perceiving, we have no need to question what is "true." The difference in cultural value preferences becomes more evident after a few months of living, working, or studying in the new environment. Exploring the realm of cultural values along orientation continuums of time, relationship, and activity preference will be more meaningful for those experiencing the differences in real-time.

Many misunderstandings can be avoided if there is an opportunity to provide support from a cultural mentor for the sojourner. The cultural mentor should be a native from the host culture who has knowledge of all the subtle nuances of verbal and nonverbal communication. To be effective, the cultural mentor needs not only a clear understanding of the host culture's implicit and explicit expectations, but also a deep understanding of the employee's or student's culture of origin. With a deep understanding of both cultures, the mentor can assist in the navigation of unforeseen social and relational expectations.

IN-COUNTRY TEAM BUILDING

Living and working internationally allows individuals to explore the breadth and depth of cultural diversity. In the international setting we have the perfect incubator for the development of effective multicultural teams. Multicultural team building is most effective in a transitional space away from the work site, where a less formal environment can be established. This change of location encourages authentic participation, free from position and role bias.

Culturally appropriate experiential activities for values exploration and cross-cultural communication take on new meaning in this setting. These activities can be very effective for developing trust and building relationships. The debriefing of experiential exercises provides insight into behavioral motivation and differing cultural perspectives.

Intercultural communication skills are essential for prevention of misunderstanding and are necessary for the development of cohesive working conditions. Intercultural negotiation skills, conflict resolution skills, and culturally appropriate employee evaluation procedures are important components that can be effectively addressed during in-country training.

Joyce Osland, Executive Director, Global Leadership Advancement Center, School of Global Innovation and Leadership, College of Business, San Jose State University, offers an overarching framework for in-country training design and methods in her introduction to the in-country exercise section that appears later in this book.

REENTRY PREPARATION

Reentry support, provided to returnees, demonstrates a commitment on the part of the organization to the individual and helps to promote a sense of employee loyalty toward the organization. Reentry support for students is crucial to programs designed to promote cross-cultural learning through an international experience.

A "shock" when returning home is rarely anticipated. Individuals who have lived, studied, and worked internationally have grown and changed in ways they may be unaware of. Too often, after a brief "honeymoon period," those returning "home" realize things are not exactly as they remember. Not only has the international experience shaped the way they see the world, but also, during their absence, "home" has been shifting and changing.

Reentry preparation should begin approximately three months prior to departure from the host location. Cultural components for saying "good-bye" and transition information preparing individuals for the possibility of "reverse" culture shock should be included. Logistic support for the move "home" needs to include many of the details provided during pre-departure.

During the reentry, it is important to facilitate individual and group conversations and reflections on the international experience. Reentry support has proven to be a fertile resource for the organization as well as for the individual. The insights garnered from creating a space for reflection, in this world of "thirty-second sound bites," allows the organization to maximize on its investment of both time and money.

A reentry "refresher" should be offered three to six months after return. If an assessment such as the IDI, CCAI, or ISI was given pre-departure, a post-assessment, using the same instrument, can provide important insight into personal growth and additional data relevant to organizational knowledge and training/teaching design.

Organizations hoping to retain expatriates need a strategic plan for their placement on return. Employees and students who have survived and thrived in international settings have learned to face complex problems and meet day-to-day challenges effectively. Placing these individuals in a position that maximizes "lessons learned" while offering new challenges and a degree of autonomy will enhance the possibility of retaining the expatriates' intercultural insight and talent.

In his introduction to the reentry section of this book, Bruce LaBrack, Professor Emeritus and Former Director of the University of The Pacific Institute for Cross-Cultural Training, outlines the challenges of reentry, as well as strategies for managing the potential culture shock experienced when returning home.

Why This Manual?

This book is unique in its singular focus on transition exercises. Trainers and educators supporting the international transition experience will find this collection of exercises valuable. We offer consideration of an integrated program designed to enhance the richness of the international experience.

We have collected and adapted existing transition activities from many sources as well as developing many of our own. We have included activities appropriate for the various stages of transition, including pre-departure, in-country, and reentry experiences. No matter what your situation, we hope you will find an appropriate exercise to meet your objectives.

How to Use This Manual

The introductions to each of the three sections in this book can be used to prepare employees and/or students for international assignments. Individuals who are responsible for designing pre-departure, in-country, and reentry programs will find these exercises useful; they have all been "field tested" with individuals who have experienced international learning, working, and living.

We have divided this book into three sections: pre-departure, in-country, and reentry. While some exercises may be used in more than one type of training, we have placed each exercise in one of the three sections so that trainers or educators can go directly to the section most relevant to their audience or training content. The Classification of Activities chart is a primary resource: it helps to identify the setting in which each exercise might be most useful and also identifies the level of potential risk for participants. Risk is defined as how psychologically challenging an activity might be for the participant. High-risk activities could create distress for some participants and should not be attempted too early in a training program or by trainers who do not have the ability to manage strong emotional reactions.

A Note About Adult Learning Styles

David A. Kolb's (1983) approach to learning styles serves as a framework and guide for our development of these activities. Kolb discusses four types of learning preferences:

a. Concrete Experience
b. Reflective Observation
c. Abstract Conceptualization
d. Active Experimentation

We have attempted to include as many types of learning preferences in each activity and its debriefing as fit the activity conceptually. Following is a brief description and example of each type of learning preference:

Concrete Experience requires learning by relating to other people and identifying feelings. Small-group discussions regarding personal experiences and feelings about an issue or experience make use of this preference.

Reflective Observation requires people to observe what goes on around them, think about what they have seen, and explore their observations from a range of perspectives. Even though this preference is the most difficult to address in training because of the length of time it can take, it can be included through a journal-writing activity or through debriefing questions. There is a wealth of journaling opportunities in the activities included in this book, and international transitions lend themselves to this learning style.

Abstract Conceptualization involves systematic planning, logical analysis, and intellectual understanding of a situation or theory. This is addressed through lectures or problem-solving activities such as case studies.

Active Experimentation is the "doing" preference. It includes completing self-assessment instruments and participating in role-plays, simulations, and other activities. Nothing involves more active learning than international experiences!

While many will ask, or demand, that your training design be primarily experiential in preparing for international transitions, we caution you to balance all four styles. Too much "doing" can result in little or no understanding of the underlying reason that a behavior or action may or may not be effective cross-culturally. Preparing for effectiveness in all three arenas (pre-departure, in-country, and reentry), as well as making sense out of lessons learned for a lifetime of application, requires that all four learning styles be utilized.

Pre-Departure

The Importance of Pre-Departure Preparation

Steven T. Duke, Ph.D., Executive Director of Global Student/Faculty Development, Research, and Risk Management at Wake Forest University, Winston-Salem, NC

In recent years, hundreds of thousands of U.S.-based workers have traveled overseas for work assignments, and hundreds of thousands of U.S.-based students have traveled abroad to study, serve, do research, or complete an internship. At the same time, more than a million foreign students and workers have traveled to the U.S. for similar activities. We live in a time of increasing globalization—not only of the world economies, but also of the educational and transportation systems. It is likely that this cross-border travel will increase as globalization expands its reach and as countries in Asia, Africa, and Latin America continue to modernize and increase international trade.

Corporations, nonprofits, colleges, universities, and governments that send their students or employees abroad have a vested interest in the quality of interactions in which their travelers engage. Many of us have heard "horror stories" of corporate representatives who have traveled to another culture only to offend their hosts, commit cultural faux pas, or completely ignore culturally held values and beliefs. Many U.S. students travel abroad and remain in a cultural "bubble" with their U.S. American counterparts. There is a huge need for these individuals to be prepared for their overseas experiences, to be guided on cultural norms and values in their host country, and to be aware of how individuals typically act in the local context. Those traveling to multiple cities or countries need to learn about the variations or differences among those locations, in addition to similarities with their own culture.

Preparing your employees, students, and volunteers for their particular assignments, projects, or studies is important for numerous reasons, including the five key reasons detailed below.

1. Prepare for effective interaction with others.

When getting ready to travel abroad or work with individuals from other cultural contexts, it is important to anticipate the forms and situations in which communication will take place. Teach your students or employees about methods of communication, keeping in mind that body language and nonverbal behavior are critical parts of how people communicate. Help your travelers understand both direct and indirect forms of communication, how people in the host culture say "no," the social norms for how people greet each other, and the expectations of both host and guest in the target culture. Where possible, your travelers should learn as much of the local language as possible, even if that is just a few dozen words of "survival" language. Being able to communicate as much as possible in the local language is viewed as a sign of respect, and it will give your travelers additional insights into the people and their culture.

2. Learn about the country's infrastructure, political structure, economy, and history.

Knowing who leads the government, how the government is structured, and at least some of the historical influences that have brought the country to its present state will provide travelers with added insight into the people and their culture. Learning about the infrastructure, including transportation networks and how most people get around on a daily basis, will also help travelers understand the people they will interact with while abroad.

3. Learn about cultural values, expectations, and socially acceptable behaviors.

As you prepare your students or employees for effective communication, it is also essential to help them learn about what "drives" the culture. Much of what individuals see on a daily basis are behaviors and social expectations that are communicated throughout the culture. Keep in mind that most countries have multiple subcultures or groups of individuals who share different things in common. The expectations, habits, and beliefs they hold in common are cultural values. It often takes time and many conversations with "cultural informants" to identify and understand what values underpin the way people behave and act in a culture. Most of the activities in this volume are geared toward discovering and understanding cultural values.

4. Prepare for cultural adjustment and "culture shock."

Numerous models have been developed over the last few decades to describe how individuals crossing into another culture experience the transition. Cultural adjustment is essential for both short-term stays and long-term sojourns. Help your travelers understand that adjusting to a new culture is different for each individual. One person might struggle with issues that do not bother others. Another might have a moment of crisis or panic when his or her expectations or experiences are not as expected. Although the "U-curve" model of adjustment (initial excitement followed by irritability, then adaptation, and ending in adjustment; Lysgaard, 1955) might capture the experiences of many travelers, it does not recognize that many individuals experience culture shock immediately, while others adjust readily and with fewer difficulties. Help your travelers understand that each person adjusts individually to new experiences. Explain that many travelers find that reflecting on their own experiences and then speaking with others about these challenges are key steps to successful adjustment abroad.

5. Travel safely.

Teaching about the host country, including its infrastructure, history, and cultural values, will help your students or employees better understand the environments in which they will live and travel. One of the keys to being safe abroad is to learn about social interactions, specifically the widely held attitudes regarding the roles of men and women and social norms for how they interact, including gender and sexuality. Identifying common risk factors and common challenges of social interaction will help your travelers take control of their own interactions and prepare them for more effective interactions with their hosts.

You or your organization may have additional needs or justifications regarding why you should organize pre-departure preparation workshops, events, or seminars for your students or employees. The overriding imperative here is that they are prepared to interact effectively with the individuals they meet. It goes without saying that the elements of any particular training program will vary depending on the length of time abroad; the type of assignment or project; the technical, social, and cultural knowledge base of those traveling; and the location or locations abroad. Use these concepts and principles to guide you in developing the kinds of training structures that will enable your organization and travelers to be successful.

The ultimate goal of pre-departure preparation is to help your students or travelers take charge of their own planning and interactions and to make the most of opportunities for interacting effectively with their hosts. Although your students or employees may commit cultural faux pas or feel awkward in various situations, preparation can help them to recognize cultural values, communicate effectively with the individuals they meet, and enjoy learning more about themselves and their hosts.

Personal Reflections for Transition

Time Required:

75–95 minutes (5 minutes for setup; 20–30 minutes for completing worksheet; 20–30 minutes for small-group discussion; 30 minutes for debriefing)

Work
X–X
X, X, X, X

Objectives:

1. For participants to engage in reflection, initiating the process of letting go of their current location and moving on psychologically to their new location

2. For participants to recognize that transitions are a process, not distinct events, and that they can facilitate their transitions with conscious intent

3. For participants to relax and get additional perspective and inspiration during what is typically a challenging time

Materials:

Transition Worksheet, Parts I–IV (one copy per participant)

Process:

1. Introduction

   - Pre-departure is a very, very busy time in any person's transition. It can be tempting to focus on the thousand-and-one logistical decisions and to overlook the emotional aspects.

   - Transition experts, however, emphasize that the quality of a traveler's leaving will directly influence the quality of that person's arrival—and that the quality of the leaving is directly influenced by the person's attention to the emotional dynamics of transition.

2. Distribute the Transition Worksheet. Advise participants that their worksheets are for them; they will not be showing the worksheets to anyone else. Explain that while they will be

discussing their reflections with others, they will decide for themselves how much they actually disclose.

3. Give participants a generous amount of time to complete the worksheet. If your location makes it possible, invite participants to relocate from the training room to comfortable seating in nearby breakout rooms.

4. After participants complete the worksheets, encourage them to discuss their responses together.
   - Place participants into small groups.
   - Invite them to discuss the four parts of the worksheet (expectations, ending, neutral zone, new beginning).
   - Suggest they use these questions to guide their discussion:
     a. What surprised you?
     b. What challenged you?
     c. What pleased you?

Debriefing Questions:

1. What was it like to reflect on these aspects of your upcoming transition?

2. How was it to discuss these aspects of transition with other people also about to relocate?

3. What stands out to you from your reflection and discussion?

Debriefing Conclusions:

1. Transitions are a fact of life.

2. No matter how many transitions we've experienced, and no matter how much we understand transitions conceptually, when we are in a transition we have to do the psycho-emotional work that transitions demand of us.

3. Completing the worksheet was just the first step—please follow through on the things you identified as potential ways to support yourself during each of the three phases.

4. When we engage the reflective work of transitions, and put in place structures we think will support us in our transitions emotionally, transitions can open wonderful new possibilities in our lives.

Optional Processes:

- When working with a couple in pre-departure, ask them to more specifically disclose to one another their responses on the worksheet. Give them the opportunity to do some joint strategizing about how they will support not only themselves but also each other and the relationship.

- Just as when working with a couple in pre-departure, a family can also be served when members communicate about these topics and discuss how to support each other through the process. Young children may not be able to use the worksheet, but many of the key categories can be posed to them through conversation and/or play.

This activity was created by Barbara F. Schaetti, Ph.D., Owner/Consultant, Transition Dynamics (www.transition-dynamics.com).

Transition Worksheet Part I: Personal Expectations

Transitions have phases. They overlap, but they're also distinct. William Bridges, in his book *Transitions*, identifies three phases: (1) ending, (2) neutral zone, and (3) new beginning. The following pages of this worksheet invite you to reflect on each of these phases as part of your personal preparation. First, however, please take a moment to think about some of your general expectations.

Leaving _____

1. I will miss:

2. I will be happy to leave behind:

Going to _____

1. I look forward to:

2. I am concerned about:

Created by Barbara F. Schaetti, Ph.D., Owner/Consultant, Transition Dynamics.

Transition Worksheet Part II: Personal Plan for the *Ending*

Two of the most important tasks during the Ending phase of a transition are to say "thank you" and "goodbye." Please take this opportunity to think about your life in _____ . Who are the people who have been important to you? What places have had special meaning for you? What activities have you particularly enjoyed? Are you also leaving behind beloved pets and meaningful possessions?

Make a list in the spaces below of the people, places, activities, pets, and possessions with whom and to which you need to say thank you and goodbye. For each, decide how, when, where, and with whom you will do this before you leave.

As you make your list, remember to include not only the people, places, and activities you most enjoyed, but also the ones you simply saw or went to or did on a regular basis. Sometimes it's the everyday kinds of people and things that we miss the most after we've left. And sometimes what we actually need to say is "I'm sorry" and not just "thank you." If that's the case for you, make a note of that below as well.

Saying Thank You and Goodbye (How / When / Where / With Whom)

People

Places

Activities

Pets

Possessions

Before I leave _____ . . .

1. I want to go to _____ one more time.
2. I want to buy _____ to take with me.
3. I want to take pictures of _____.
4. I want to exchange contacts with _____.
5. I want to apologize to _____.
6. I want to say "thank you" to _____.
7.
8.
9.
10.

Created by Barbara F. Schaetti, Ph.D., Owner/Consultant, Transition Dynamics.

Transition Worksheet Part III: Personal Plan for the *Neutral Zone*

Now is your chance to reflect on the second phase of transition: the neutral zone. This can be the most confusing phase because it's the "in-between" time. You're no longer living where you were and doing what you did, but you're not yet established where you're going next.

The most important thing about the in-between time is to let it be in-between. That means not hanging on to what you are leaving behind and not reaching out to what is approaching. The in-between time can be a period of great personal insight, if you can just let yourself be in-between.

1. Think of a past transition—especially the part of it where you were "in-between." What was it like? What was hardest about it? What was best about it?

2. What are some creative ways to respond to people when they ask you, during this in-between time, where you live or what you do?

3. Being "in-between" can be stressful and uncomfortable. How do you know that you're under stress? What are some of your own personal "tells" that let you know you're feeling stress?

4. What stress management techniques serve you best?

5. What kinds of support do you think would be useful to ask for from your family and from your friends?

Created by Barbara F. Schaetti, Ph.D., Owner/Consultant, Transition Dynamics.

Transition Worksheet Part IV: Personal Plan for the *New Beginning*

What do you already know about the place you're going? Think about the geography, history, foods, holidays, sports, fashions, cultural values, and beliefs.

Are you going back "home"? How recent or out-of-date is your experience there? Remember: having a family vacation in your passport country is not the same as living there year-round!

How can you learn about the country you are going to and what your life there will be like *before* you arrive? Please customize the list of things you want to find out about. The list will vary depending on if you're moving to an(other) international posting, moving home to your passport country, moving away for college or university, etc.

Things to find out about	How you'll find out
Where will you be living?	
What logistical matters need to be arranged (e.g., driver's license, bank account)?	
What kinds of things will you be doing that you haven't done before, or have not done recently (e.g., hiring and managing household staff or, vice versa, doing your own cooking, cleaning)?	
What recreational activities do you enjoy? Where can you do them (or similar activities) in your new location?	
Write down additional "Need to Know" questions from the group.	

Many of the skills you've learned by moving from one country to another will be valuable to you in this next move, even if you're going "home." Think about the skills you've gained and their component parts. What do you do *step-by-step* when you put each skill to work? Again, please customize this list depending on your particular circumstances.

Skill	Step-by-Step
Example: How do you start a conversation when you do not know anyone in the room?	**Example:** Take a breath. Choose a candidate and approach. Ask an opening question. (E.g., "How do you know the host?" or "How did you learn about the event?")
How do you take care of yourself when you are lonely, confused, or uncertain?	
How do you choose and make new friends?	
How do you find your way around a strange, new, and unfamiliar place?	
How do you figure out the "right" way to do something in a given situation?	
How do you keep an open mind when people do things in ways that surprise you?	
How can you relax and recharge in the face of all that needs to be done?	

Created by Barbara F. Schaetti, Ph.D., Owner/Consultant, Transition Dynamics.

Build a RAFT: Sailing Off to a New Place

Time Required:

50–65 minutes (15 minutes for introduction; 20–30 minutes for group discussion; 15–20 minutes for debriefing and synthesis)

Work

X–X

X, X, X, X

Objectives:

1. To identify feelings associated with the "leaving"
2. To heighten understanding of challenges inherent in "leaving"
3. To provide techniques/tools for "healthy closure"

Materials:

- Chart paper, markers
- Handout of lecturette found in Appendix A: Building a RAFT (one copy per participant)

Process:

1. Introduce the topic of leaving by using language such as the following:

   This activity was designed to help you understand the motivation behind various detachment/separation behaviors and then explore more positive choices for "leaving." Positive choices can protect and encourage ongoing relationships with those you love and respect even though you are physically leaving them behind.

   Consciously or unconsciously, travelers begin to loosen emotional ties as they prepare to leave. Detachment, a natural part of the transition process, is intended to make leaving somewhat less painful, but it is not always the best strategy.

   Researchers have found that although the goal of detachment is to reduce the pain of leaving, it can actually increase that pain. If you start to become angry with your friends and family, creating distance in your relationships, you may experience deep sorrow for your misbehaviors when you finally get on the airplane. Detachment behavior, designed unconsciously to protect you, can actually make you feel worse. Staying connected until the end is ultimately far less painful than pulling away.

2. Distribute the Building a RAFT handout.

3. Place participants in groups of four or five and ask them to discuss the following questions. (Grouping options: Each group answers all questions; one group is assigned to each topic; or people form groups based on the topic of greatest interest.) Be sure the groups have enough time to thoroughly discuss these key points.

   - *Reconciliation:* Why might this step be a challenge for the sojourner? For those staying behind? What are some possible cultural aspects to consider in the reconciliation process? How might reconciliation look differently for family members? Children? Accompanying spouses? Identify three strengths and three challenges in taking this step.

   - *Affirmation:* Who should be considered for inclusion in the affirmation step? Describe several ways to show appreciation to someone who will be left behind. How might this step differ depending on cultural preference? Gender? Age?

   - *Farewells:* Pollock and Van Reken (2009) include people, places, pets, and possessions in the farewell process (the four Ps). Why would each of these be important to include in closure? Describe two or three ways to "say" farewell to each of the "Ps." What special considerations should be given to cultural preference? To age and developmental needs of family members?

   - *Think Destination:* Identify several questions to ask about the new location: personal/professional/logistical/for accompanying spouses/teens, etc. Why might you need to ask questions when you are returning "home"? How can this step be helpful in easing the transition? Share any guidance/insight about cultural preferences to consider.

4. Provide an opportunity for each group to share answers and solutions.

Debriefing Questions:

1. How easy was it for your group to identify choices and challenges? Cultural preferences? Considerations for family members?

2. How did you feel during the discussion of detachment behaviors? Were there any personal insights or aha moments?

3. What happened as your group heard the answers offered by other groups? Were there any surprises?

4. What did you learn from this activity? How might you use this in the future? Personally? Within your organization?

Debriefing Conclusions:

1. Expatriates frequently experience a sense of loss/grief for what is being left behind: friends, stimulating environments, a sense of autonomy, etc. (This is true even when the move is desired and sought after.)

2. Ignoring or avoiding these feelings and associated detachment behaviors can have long-term consequences (loss of friendships or one's professional reputation).

3. Preparing an appropriate goodbye strategy is an important step in closing out unfinished business and preparing for a smooth start at the new destination.

4. Leaving in the right way is an essential step to entering in the right way.

This activity has been adapted from David C. Pollock and Ruth E. Van Reken's work in *The Third Culture Kid Experience: Growing Up Among Worlds* (2009). The RAFT concept was originally developed by David C. Pollock in the late 1980s.

3

Postcards from the Heart

Time Required:

30–40 minutes (5 minutes to select cards; 15 minutes for small-group discussion; 10–20 minutes for debriefing)

Work
X–X
X, X, X, X

Objectives:

1. To identify the travelers' personal concerns about their new location (pre-departure) or about reentering their home country
2. To openly share those concerns in a way that helps individuals identify and explore their concerns

Materials:

A stack of postcards (three to four times as many postcards as potential participants) with a wide range of pictures (e.g., landscapes, people, locations, abstract images, etc.)

Process:

1. Spread postcards on a table so that participants can walk around them and see the entire set of cards.
2. Ask participants to look at the postcards and select one that is representative of something they are either concerned about or excited about with their upcoming transition. Note: Based on the content of the session and what you know about the group, select to discuss *either* challenges or excitement.
3. Place participants in small groups of four to six and give them fifteen minutes to share their postcards with each other, telling their small group why they selected the card they chose.
4. Bring the groups together. Ask people to choose one person to introduce. The person making the introduction should share their partners' postcards and *one* interesting thing about each selection.

5. Tell participants to keep the postcard they have selected as a reminder of what they discussed and/or learned from this session.

Debriefing Questions:

1. What was your first reaction when asked to select something that represented a challenge or something you are excited about?
2. What did you notice when the small group began sharing stories?
3. What did you notice when the large group began sharing stories?
4. How can you use this information as you plan your transition?

Debriefing Conclusions:

1. The concerns/excitement people have about transitions tend to be very similar. Knowing that concerns/excitement tend to be universal reduces the sense of being alone or isolated.
2. When travelers recognize their own concerns/excitement, they can focus energy on preparing to manage those feelings.

This exercise was developed by Sandra M. Fowler, Intercultural Consultant and Trainer.

(Country) at a Glance

Time Required:

50–60 minutes (30 minutes for placing Post-its; 20–30 minutes for debriefing)

Objectives:

1. To become familiar with the host country's history, economics, political system, people, geography (and sometimes religion, attitudes about sexual orientation, or other relevant topics)

2. To develop an understanding of how the country's history—and its regions—has been influenced by factors such as wars, migration and immigration, inventions, its basis of economy, trade patterns, neighboring nations, population, and cultural/ethnic/religious groups in the society

3. To make a connection of the development of the country with the primary or fundamental values and beliefs of its people (e.g., how freedom has become an important cornerstone of the United States, or how monarchies influenced the hierarchy of French society)

Materials:

- A large map of the host country (a laminated map works best if the map is taped to a wall, window, or door)
- Masking tape or stickpins and about thirty three-inch-square Post-its

Process:

1. Prepare each Post-it with one or two historical events or facts from very early history to today. Include significant discoveries, economic progress, important national legislation, wars, development of the political system, development of cities, and current events.

| Work |
| X–X |
| X, X, X, X |

2. Give the Post-its to the participants and instruct them to stand in front of the map.

3. Ask them to take turns reading aloud one Post-it at a time and placing it on the location/section of the country where the event occurred, originated, or had an impact. (No more than three or four Post-its should be stacked on each other in one area, like the capital, or they may fall off of the map.)

4. After participants have placed about half the Post-its on the map, ask a couple of questions to analyze what they are learning. For instance, if they are studying the history of Switzerland, you might ask the following:

   a. What is significant about the history of Switzerland by the early 1800s?

   b. Where did the interest in forming a confederation originate?

   c. How does the growing desire for neutrality influence its future?

5. Expound on a few events, customizing to the interests and needs of the participants. Keep the pace lively to prevent having to rush through the last few Post-it notes of history and current events.

6. Lead a discussion/report-out. Ask the participants to identify two or three things they learned about the country that they didn't know before starting the exercise. If time permits, ask the following:

   a. Did anything surprise you?

   b. Did you change your image of the country and its people?

   c. How might this information impact your approach to people when you get there?

Debriefing Questions:

1. From what you have just learned, what would you say are important values that people hold? About family? Education? Employment?

2. [If applicable] What cultural dimensions, such as Individualism-Collectivism or Hierarchy-Egalitarianism, did you learn about today?

3. What behaviors has anyone observed that support these values in this country?

Debriefing Conclusions:

1. Having knowledge of a host country's history, economics, geography, political system, and religion is helpful in both personal and organizational contexts.

2. Factors such as war, migration, immigration, trade patterns, influence from neighboring nations, pressure from various cultural/ethnic/religious groups, and so forth have both explicit and tacit influence on the culture.

3. The fundamental values, beliefs, and assumptions of the people in the host culture have been influenced by the history and development of the country.

This activity was created by Carolyn Feuille, President, Esprit Global Learning, Expatriate Trainer and Global Leadership Coach.

5

Different Days—Different Ways

Time Required:

50–65 minutes (10–15 minutes to complete daily schedule; 15–20 minutes for group discussion; 25–30 minutes for debriefing)

Work
X–X
X, X, X, X

Objectives:

1. To identify similarities and differences in daily life when entering a new cultural context
2. To heighten awareness of mental and behavioral alterations that might be necessary when adjusting to new realities
3. To provide insight into cultural/social values reflected in day-to-day preferences

Materials:

- Worksheets: Typical Days' Schedule (one per participant)
- Schedule that shows what a typical day might look like (Use the sample that follows the worksheet to create your own.)

Process:

1. Ask individuals to work independently to complete the worksheet.
2. Place travelers in groups of three to five participants. Discuss various aspects of daily life that may be different in a new cultural setting (e.g., meal times, staple foods, transportation, bathing times, use/cost of utilities, recreational opportunities, use of "free time"/"alone time," family expectations).
3. Ask each group to share one or two of the differences discussed and key concerns.
4. List the differences and then facilitate a large-group discussion about which might pose the greatest challenge or biggest personal adjustment. Why?

Debriefing Questions:

1. Did you discover some of your "unconscious" cultural assumptions about "typical" daily life? Describe.

2. How might day-to-day expectations differ depending on location? How could you verify the accuracy of your expectations?

3. Have you seen someone from another culture behaving in a way you did not understand? What did you see? What cultural difference might be motivating the behavioral difference?

4. How might your personal preference in communication style, need for privacy, and so forth have affected the way you felt during this process? How do you feel about your ability to adjust in a new cultural setting?

5. How might insight from this activity help you improve your international experience?

Debriefing Conclusions:

1. The daily routines differ considerably across cultures. These routines often do not feel "real" until the traveler is in the new culture. Based on how deeply these differences touch a person's value system, the differences can be stressful.

2. "Normal" activities in the home culture may not be possible and could even be inappropriate in another culture.

3. Each country's history, economics, demographics, aesthetics, geography, religion, politics, and so forth contribute to the shaping of behavioral patterns and communication preferences within the culture. Learning about these cultural influences offer added insight into the values, beliefs, and assumptions underlying the cultural behavior.

Note: This activity can also be used by agencies assisting refugee/immigrant populations to stimulate conversations about the salient differences between their clients' former life and their new circumstances. This activity can also be adjusted for in-country and pre-reentry reflection. With appropriate alterations, this exercise can be adjusted for participants who are facing any form of significant transition (change of employment, domestic relocation, retirement).

This activity was developed by Bruce LaBrack, School of International Studies, University of the Pacific.

Worksheet: Typical Day's Schedule

Typical Day's Schedule	Home Culture	New Culture
12:00 A.M.		
01:00		
02:00		
03:00		
04:00		
05:00		
06:00		
07:00		
08:00		
09:00		
10:00		
11:00		
12:00		
13:00		
14:00		
15:00		
16:00		
17:00		
18:00		
19:00		
20:00		
21:00		
22:00		
23:00		

Created by Bruce LaBrack, School of International Studies, University of the Pacific.

Sample Schedule: Comparing "Typical" Days in the U.S. and in Japan

Schedule	Typical U.S. American Student	Typical Japanese Student
12:00 A.M.		
01:00	Sleep	Sleep
02:00		
03:00		
04:00		
05:00		
06:00		Wake up with family; no shower (showers or bathing are done at night)
07:00		Breakfast with family
08:00		Commuter train to university
09:00	Long hot shower Eat breakfast (alone or on the go) Drive to school	At school
10:00	At school	
11:00		
12:00		
13:00		Commuter train home
14:00		Study; homework
15:00	Recreation (soccer, running)	
16:00	Drive to a friend's house and visit	
17:00	Dinner alone or on the go	Dinner with family

Schedule	Typical U.S. American Student	Typical Japanese Student
18:00	Study; homework (alone)	Study; homework
19:00		
20:00		
21:00	Watch TV; play video games alone	Watch TV with family
22:00		
23:00		Bath or shower Retire to bed

Created by Bruce LaBrack, School of International Studies, University of the Pacific.

Country Rally: A Family Project for Discovery, Growth, and Adaptation

Time Required:

45–60 minutes for each of two pre-departure sessions and at least one in-country follow-up (face-to-face or virtually)

Work
X–X
X, X, X, X

Objectives:

1. To build a mind-set of adventure and enthusiasm
2. To provide a discussion framework for learning about the host country and culture, and to facilitate the emergence of personal perceptions of that country
3. To encourage initiative, autonomy, and connection with the country
4. To foster sharing within the family (noting similarities and differences)
5. To provide a platform to address concerns in a relaxed manner

Materials:

- A map of the country (to define the areas to be visited)
- A calendar
- A folder for collecting information and photos
- An idea sheet where everyone can add pictures of places/things/foods/objects (e.g., cuckoo clock, sari)
- A large blank piece of white construction paper to build a collage

Process for Session I:

1. Introduce the Country Rally with a simple discussion to see what is already known about the destination country. Then discuss what family members would like to know before

leaving, and what they hope to discover once they have arrived.

2. Facilitate a discussion where excitement and concerns of individual family members about the relocation can surface. (e.g., perhaps one family member is fearful based on a preconceived notion about the host country's culture, while a second family member hasn't even considered safety; surfacing this difference provides an opportunity to increase family members understanding and supporting each other, etc.).

3. Help family members reframe challenges into possibilities. "What are the main concerns (challenges) being faced right now?" (E.g., dealing with the children not wanting to leave their friends or teachers; what might they put into place to stay in contact, such as using Skype, creating a blog, and/or opening an online account to share photos?) How will the family maintain communication with grandparents, cousins, and friends? Is the partner leaving behind a professional position?

4. Encourage individual family members to commit to taking on one or two elements of "country research," such as checking out Wikipedia, finding a book about the country, searching the Internet, discovering films or music from the host country, and so forth. Even small children can participate by drawing pictures of what they hope to see once they arrive. Add ideas to the idea list and information collected in the folder.

Process for Session II:

1. Ask the family to share what has been discovered since the last session. Begin to trace their planned trip onto their map, defining the "treasures" to be collected along the way. These treasures will form the basis of the collage once they have arrived. What are family members most looking forward to? What do they hope to experience?

2. Facilitate a discussion highlighting some of the differences between cultures, environments, and people. Individual members can each draw up a list of things they want to discover depending on the host country (e.g., different foods or sweets, neighborhoods, monuments, markets, cities, leisure options, etc.) Do they want to discover lions or monkeys in India? Special shells from the beach in a coastal area? Lederhosen from Germany?

Process for Arrival:

1. Ask the family to begin the rally upon their arrival, using the first planned adventures and filling in the map with the routes used and the objects and memories accumulated. This structure provides the positive basis for a debriefing focused on learning.

2. Set up a relatively early time for a first debriefing. This allows the trainer/coach to help diffuse any eventual surprises or strong negative experiences and highlight the positive experiences while building a mind-set of adventure.

3. Schedule follow-up sessions to help members bridge their culture gaps and come to terms with the differences. Provide coaching to offer a safe space for participants to express their difficulties, build resilience, and foster a mind-set of growth and learning.

Debriefing Questions:

1. What did you learn on this trip/outing about the local culture? About yourself?
2. What did you like best?
3. What didn't you like at all? What was hard for you?
4. How do things work differently in the host culture? How can you adapt to how that is? How could you learn more about those differences?
5. What would you like to do again?
6. What would you do differently next time?

Debriefing Conclusions:

1. Building family enthusiasm and establishing a framework for adventure when relocating internationally can contribute to a smooth transition.

2. Discovering similarities and differences across cultures can increase understanding, ease anxieties, and enrich learning.

3. Addressing family concerns (individually and collectively) in a relaxed manner can open lines for honest communication and thus enhance the solidarity of the family unit during the shared transition experience.

Note: This activity can be introduced to a large group or an individual family. Follow-up to the introductory session can be face-to-face or virtual. If the activity is introduced in a coach/mentoring format, the path for individual/family goals and objectives can be "discovered" and a plan for action identified. This activity could also be adapted in an educational setting for new students at an international school or a study abroad program.

This activity was developed by Patricia Comolet, ACC, Intercultural and Professional Transitions Coach (www.camcomcoaching.com).

Involvement to Re-Involvement: Moving You from Here to There

7

Work
X–X
X, X, X, X

Time Required:

45–65 minutes (15 minutes to introduce a five-step cycle and discuss "Involvement"; 15–30 minutes for three rounds of group work; 15–20 minutes for debriefing)

Objectives:

1. To define a five-step cycle for successful relocation
2. To explore highlights/rewards/benefits of Involvement
3. To identify individual abilities, skills, and talents
4. To recognize future application

Materials:

- Chart paper, markers
- Handout of Appendix B: A Five-Step Cycle for Successful Relocation (one copy per participant)

Process:

1. Introduce the topic of international relocation in terms of a five-step cycle. Distribute Appendix B and briefly review the five steps.
2. Explain to students that this activity will focus on the Involvement phase of the cycle. Use phrases such as the ones shown here:
   a. We are going to explore the stage of "involvement." This is a stage where we feel like we are "in the know." Involvement is usually a comfortable stage where we know what is expected of us personally and professionally. We know how we fit into the community. We have established

routines and favorite places. We take many day-to-day activities for granted. There is no need to prove ourselves or build credibility, because those around us already recognize our talents and skills. We have a social network.

b. One of the best ways to appreciate the real "feel" of involvement is to think back to a time when you were starting a new job, moving to a new location, starting out in a new school, etc. Much of the comfort of involvement—knowing where you fit in—can disappear during these transitions. It takes time to regain that "familiar feeling." The comfort with "the familiar" is one of the main reasons our friends and family members may never choose to move.

3. Break participants into groups of three to five and ask them to brainstorm answers to the following questions.

Round 1:

- Think of a time when you felt you were in this state of Involvement. What are some of the things you most enjoyed? Special activities, special places, special people/relationships? Important/meaningful aspects of your career/school involvement?

- What does it feels like to be involved? How does it feel to know you can find your way around? Have an outlet for your special interests? To work with people who know and respect you? Are you more or less likely to take risks, be creative?

Round 2:

We have shared many personal things about Involvement, including what we most appreciate and what makes us happy. There is a saying, "Wherever you go, there you are." Let's think about our stories and use them to identify some of our personal strategies and collective strengths and talents.

- If this is what Involvement feels like, how do you think relocating to a new place might change your sense of involvement? Why? Or how?

- What have you learned about yourself in the Involvement stage that you will be able to use no matter where you go? What strengths and skills do you have to draw on?

- As you think about your "beginning" in your current community/career assignment/school, what were some actions you took to "get started"? How and why did you begin to feel connected? If you are preparing to reenter, which actions will be most important to your success in the reentry process? How is this different from entering a place you have never been before?

- When you run into a confusing challenge, what are the three skills you can count on to help you through?

Round 3:

Now with these shared experiences fresh in our minds, let's generate a list of skills we can fall back on when we experience the challenges of transitioning to a new location and again seek to become part of the day-to-day routines of an organization, a community, or a school environment. Please list the following:

- Various approaches to coping
- Dependable talents/skills for survival
- New discoveries to apply when navigating new territory
- Important action steps to take

4. Ask each group to share their charted answers. Offer to consolidate the lists and e-mail them to participants for future reference, or engage one of the participants to do this. This step allows participants to take responsibility for their own learning and begin or continue networking with each other.

Debriefing Questions:

1. How did you feel during the discussion of the five steps? Was it helpful to hear about the steps? Was there any information that was a surprise for you? That sounded or felt familiar?

2. How easy was it for your group to generate a list of special activities, places, and people? Rewarding aspects of the community and/or career assignment? Identifying individual skills, talents, coping strategies? Were there any cultural challenges to answering some of these questions? Are you willing to give examples?

3. What happened as your group began to list your findings on the chart to share with the larger group? What are your thoughts or feelings about the information listed?

4. What did you learn from this activity? Which strengths, strategies for coping, or identified actions will you use as you move into the relocation process?

Debriefing Conclusions:

1. International transition can be understood in terms of a five-step cycle.

2. Every person has had some prior experience with adjustment: to a new location, a new school, a new organization, a new career, a new relationship/roommate.

3. Recognizing the talents, skills, abilities, and coping techniques used in prior adjustments can help people deal with the challenge of international relocation.

4. The Involvement stage has many clues about what makes people feel happy/fulfilled, what makes a place feel like home, and what needs to be considered and/or adjusted when relocating internationally.

5. The ultimate stage of transition is Re-Involvement, which allows people to once again feel a part of a place and connected to people. So when people are in the middle of chaos or confusion, they must remember that since they have been Involved before, they can be again. The key is to allow enough time.

This activity has been adapted from David C. Pollock and Ruth E. Van Reken's work in *The Third Culture Kid Experience: Growing Up Among Worlds* (2009).

Culturally Self-Aware?

Time Required:

65–95 minutes (10–15 minutes for lecturette; 20–30 minutes to complete assessment; 20–30 minutes for activity; 15–20 minutes for debriefing)

Objectives:

1. To understand the Cultural Orientations Framework (COF)
2. To become aware of personal preferences on each continuum
3. To gain insight into the cultural preferences of others
4. To experience similarities and differences among members of the same group

Materials:

Appendix C: Cultural Orientations Framework (one copy per participant)

Process:

1. As an introduction to the activity, explain that our perception of a particular cultural orientation or value preference and our understanding of what it "really" means has been influenced by a variety of personal factors, such as parental and/or group flexibility in relation to the preference, our experience with the actual behavior we associate with the preference, our exposure or lack of exposure to those with a dissimilar preference, and so forth.

2. Distribute Appendix C and initiate a general discussion about cultural orientation using the information provided.

3. Ask participants to complete the COF assessment by marking their personal preference on each continuum.

4. Select the continua that are most relevant to the group. (You need not go through all seven continua). Taking one

<table>
<tr><td>Work</td></tr>
<tr><td>X–X</td></tr>
<tr><td>X, X, X, X</td></tr>
</table>

preference from the COF at a time, ask people to physically place themselves in a line with the far right, far left, and center reflecting the continuum. Give participants the following instructions: "We are going to create a human continuum for a few of these cultural preferences." (Acknowledge that cultural preferences may vary depending on the context.)

5. When you describe a continuum, ask participants to physically go stand where your personal preference lies as indicated by your answers on the COF.

6. Encourage participants to engage in conversation with those on either side of themselves regarding the degree of their preference. This conversation will assure they are standing in the appropriate place. (I.e., I strongly believe you should clearly state the exact "truth" vs I strongly believe you need to speak the "truth" in such a way that the listener can save face.)

7. Ask participants on the far right and the far left and the persons in the center to share the strength of their preferred approach. This allows each group to begin thinking about the "positive" aspects of other cultural positions.

8. If you are working with a culturally similar group, explore how the continuum might differ with members from both the host country and home country participating. How might the difference in cultural preference influence the following: Relationships? Teamwork? Productivity? Problem Solving?

Debriefing Questions:

1. How did you feel making your preference known to others? Did you feel pressure to alter some of your choices? If so, why?

2. Did you find yourself on the continuum with the same group of people for many of the cultural preferences? Why do you think that might occur? What might that mean for your team? Your organization? Please share both the positive aspects and possible challenges.

3. Was there anything that made this activity more or less challenging for you? If it was used in a different setting, would you have felt pressured to answer differently?

4. How could you use this activity or something similar in the future? How might it benefit members of a multicultural team or organization?

Debriefing Conclusions:

1. An understanding of the Cultural Orientations Framework provides insight into personal and cultural bias.
2. Cultural self-awareness is the first step toward cross-cultural competence.
3. Our personal understanding of a cultural preference has been affected by our personal life experience and our "cultural upbringing."
4. Similarities and differences exist between members of the same group. We cannot truly understand "the other" without asking questions and listening to their answers

Note to Trainers:

The Cultural Orientations Framework is available free electronically to individuals at www.philrosinski.com.

Appendix C includes a very brief description of the orientations. You will need a deeper personal knowledge of the orientations to effectively facilitate this exercise.

This activity was adapted from the work of Philippe Rosinski, *Coaching Across Cultures* (2003). Also see www.GlobalCoaching.pro and www.philrosinski.com.

The Name Game: More than an Icebreaker!

Time Required:

60 minutes (10 minutes for introduction; 15 minutes for activity; 15 minutes for report-out; 20 minutes for debriefing/application)

Objectives:

1. To establish an open atmosphere and build rapport for the training
2. To introduce the concept of "cultural identity"
3. To heighten awareness of objective and subjective cultural influence

Materials:

- Sample Name Game Story to use as a model for your own
- Flipchart and variety of colored marking pens
- A chart with these four questions:
  - Who named you?
  - Why was this name selected for you?
  - What does your name mean to you?
  - What does your name mean to other people?

Process:

1. Introduce the activity: Begin by generating a brief discussion about cultural identity; be sure the participants understand some key points related to cultural influence as related to identity. Possible points:
   - Language is intrinsic to the expression of culture. Language offers a means to communicate values, beliefs, and customs and helps to foster feelings of group identity and solidarity.

- Cultural identity refers to the influence culture has on an individual's identity. Cultural identity helps us frame a bigger picture of how we belong to the group and how we belong in the world.
- Names (first, middle, last, nicknames, chosen names, etc.) frequently hold some cultural identification clues.
- Individuals may choose to "embrace" or try to "erase" the cultural identification in their names.

2. Model the activity by briefly sharing a story about your own name. (See the sample Name Game Story as an example.) Your openness and energy when sharing your story can heighten interest and encourage openness in participants. Implicitly include as many sources of your cultural identity as are relevant (family, gender, religion, age, nationality, region, ethnicity, class, profession, language, music, film, sports, aspects of popular culture, etc.)

3. Uncover and use the four questions from the flipchart.

4. Ask participants, "What were some of the sources of my *cultural identity* that you heard in my Name Story?" Write responses on chart paper. (Option: List possibilities from the suggestions in #2 and circle the ones identified as relevant to your story. This list can be helpful to participants in framing possibilities for their own Name Stories.)

5. Give participants a minute or two to formulate their stories. Tell them they can talk about any part of their names: first, middle, last.

6. Ask participants to select a partner they don't know very well—and who might appear to be different from them. Give each person seven minutes to tell their story (Give a two-minute warning after five minutes, and announce a switch at seven minutes.) Repeat for second set.

7. Reconvene the larger group. Ask for someone to share an interesting name story he or she just heard. Following the story, ask the group to identify various sources of cultural identity revealed in the story. Place a checkmark next to the applicable source on the cultural identity list. Repeat for two or three stories. (Use a different-colored marker to check off sources from different stories.)

8. Close the activity by asking participants to review the cultural identity list and discuss any emerging patterns they observe: similarities, differences, missing items, and so forth.

Debriefing Questions:

Note to Trainer: The process and questions here are from both David Kolb's (1983) central concept of "learning around the learning cycle," and debriefing style of questions developed by Sivasailam "Thiagi" Thiagarajan. Please choose one or two questions from each of the five groups below.

1. *How did you feel?* (Reflect on and explore feelings during the activity.)
   - How did you feel when you heard you would be sharing a story about your name?
   - How did you feel when you were listening to your partner's name story? Stories from the larger group?
   - If you had any negative feelings during the activity, what might be at the root of those feelings?

2. *What happened?*
   - What happened while you were telling your story?
   - What similarities or differences did you notice in either the content of your stories or the way you told your stories?

3. *What did you learn?* (Uncover/identify principles or hypotheses.)
   - Given this experience, what important information have you learned about names, culture, and identity?
   - Share something about the ways cultural heritage/context, family experience, age, gender, religion, etc. can influence perception, choice, or action.
   - What were some cultural insights that were uncovered during this "simple" name game? Professional/personal preferences? Age or gender insights?

4. *How does this activity relate to the real world?* (Note the relationship to day-to-day activity, personal/professional life.)
   - What insights from this activity can you apply to your day-to-day life? When meeting or greeting someone from another culture?
   - How could this experience be helpful in your international transition?

5. *What Next?* (Gather insights for application and next steps.)
   - Given this experience and what you have learned, would you tell your name story differently, if you were to tell it again? Would you choose to share a different part of your name? Would you like to discuss your name in more depth with parents/relatives?

- How might this activity be useful in your international transition?

Debriefing Conclusions:

1. Our names can offer insight into our cultural identity.
2. Telling our name story allows us to reflect upon our name, heightening our awareness of
   - How we relate to our name and the meaning(s) attached to it;
   - How others may attach meaning to our name;
   - The cultural underpinnings and implications of one's name.
3. Names are an important part of personal and cultural identity. Remembering, correctly pronouncing, and correctly spelling someone's name can be foundational for us when we are hoping to establish rapport.

Note: The trainer should be aware of the cultural preferences in the cultures where they are training. In formal cultures, participants may (a) include titles as an integral part of one's name, and (b) be more comfortable discussing family names than given names. Many rich Name Stories are to be found in the experiences where the difference in Formal/Informal communication style preference is confronted.

This exercise was developed by Michael Vande Berg, Ph.D. (mvandeberg@ MVBAssociates.com).

Sample Name Game Story

My first name is "Michael," but all of my friends and most of my colleagues call me "Mick." My parents always told me that they started calling me "Mickey" soon after I was born, but I remember that some members of my mother's family called me "Michael" when I was young.

My mother was Roman Catholic, and I was baptized as Michael. Catholic children are normally baptized with the name of a saint or angel—very good beings who, in the Catholic belief system, live with God in Heaven. I was named after Michael the Archangel, who plays a very important role in that belief system: a very wicked and powerful angel, Lucifer, rebelled against God, and Michael, serving as God's champion, fought and defeated the wicked Lucifer.

My relatives on my mother's side sometimes told me how important the Archangel Michael was, and how important I was since I had his name. But I never felt comfortable being associated with the Archangel. I just didn't see myself fighting the wicked, or protecting soldiers—and some of my earliest memories include people around me calling me "Mickey." I think this is because my father liked the name. It was popular at the time, associated with people like the movie star Mickey Rooney and the famous New York Yankee baseball player Mickey Mantle.

My father came from a very Dutch family and was raised in the Dutch Reformed Church. His grandparents were born in Holland, and even though he was born in northwest Iowa, he spoke Dutch as a first language. While my father had agreed to raise the children as Catholics, family tradition says he was concerned that my mother wanted to name the first two children "Pat" and "Mike," the most stereotypically Irish names that existed in the U.S. at that time. And I think he may have thought that good names were not the ones named after Catholic saints, but those that seemed friendly and playful, like Mickey.

But as I grew up, my nickname Mickey created problems for me: our family moved a lot, and by the time I was thirteen, my sister and I had changed schools seven times. The kids at each new school would meet and check us out. As you know, children can be very judgmental, and when they would find out that my name was "Mickey," they would begin to sing the song that all children knew, the Mickey Mouse song, which was played at the beginning of the Walt Disney Show, the most popular kid's show on TV during those years. It went like this:

"Who's the leader of the club/ that's made for you and me/ M-I-C-K-E-Y M-O-U-S-E. Forever let us hold our banner high! High! High! High!/ Come along and sing a song/ And join the jamboree/ M-I-C-K-E-Y M-O-U-S-E," and so on. I got tired of fighting with other boys in the playground over my name, so when I was twelve, I started telling people my name was "Mick."

This created a different sort of problem. My mother and all of her relatives were, as I say, of Irish ancestry, and when the Irish came to the U.S., they were often the target of cruel and sometimes violent discrimination—for a long time, during the nineteenth and well into the twentieth century, they were treated as a poor and worthless minority group. And people often called them "Micks" to insult them. My mother, who had grown up having some children call her and others of Irish heritage "dirty Micks," simply would not allow my friends to call me by that name. She and I went round and round about my name for years—when I was a freshman in high school, so fourteen years old, she was still telling my friends who came to our house, asking for "Mick," that "Sorry, but there's nobody by that name living here."

I guess my friends understood by that point that my name had quite a story behind it!

Exercise developed by Michael Vande Berg, Ph.D. (mvandeberg@MVBAssociates.com).

Cultural Sense-Making

Time Required:

Half day or full day of training. Can be broken into shorter sessions depending on setting and accessibility.

Objectives:

1. To introduce participants to the paradoxical nature of culture and the importance of context

2. To encourage participants to move beyond sophisticated stereotyping to a more complex understanding of culture

3. To provide participants with a model to make sense of cultural behavior and paradoxes

Materials:

- Worksheet: Common Cultural Dimensions
- Worksheet: Cultural Sense-Making Model
- Paper with pen or pencil
- Short culture-related video clips and/or cultural case studies
- Modeling clay, craft paper, crayons, pipe cleaners, or other craft material for each participant (optional)

Process:

1. Adapt your training to the amount of exposure your audience has had to other cultures and the degree of motivation they have for understanding cultural behavior. Introduce the concept of stereotyping. Here are some ways you might do this:

- With a regional audience (great with study abroad groups), you could begin by passing out clay and asking participants to create something that captures the essence of _____ (target) culture. Optional materials should allow participants to use a creative process to demonstrate

---

Work

X–X

X, X, X, X

---

their perceptions of the target culture. Participants then explain their creations and discuss whether their work portrays a stereotype or a reality. This leads to the discussion of stereotypes, where stereotypes come from, and their implication for cross-cultural interaction.

- With more culturally experienced participants, you can begin with cultural value differences and the associated theories. When working with executives, it is important to focus on practical application. Using case studies or current and previously experienced cultural difficulties is important.

2. Ask, "Are stereotypes ever helpful?" or, "How might stereotyping be helpful?" Encourage participants to draw the following conclusions from the discussion:

- Stereotypes can be beneficial for making comparisons *between* cultures rather than in trying to understand variations of behavior *within* a particular culture.

- Helpful stereotypes should be
  - Consciously held;
  - Descriptive rather than evaluative;
  - Accurate in describing a behavioral norm;
  - Used as the "best first guess";
  - Modified based on further observations and experience.

3. Explore the concept of "cultural paradox," which occurs in situations where the observable behavior appears to contradict expectations based on the observer's knowledge of a particular culture. For instance, U.S. culture has a historical value for equality and is seen as a "low power distance" culture, yet many U.S. CEOs are extremely autocratic. This autocratic behavior is perceived as acceptable in the role and context of the CEO's position.

4. Ask participants for other examples of "cultural paradoxes." List them and then ask, "What might explain some of these paradoxes?" Draw from the discussion possibilities such as role differences, unresolved cultural issues, individual rather than group behavior, real vs. espoused values, "value trumping," and so forth.

5. Explain that "value trumping" is the recognition that in specific contexts certain sets of values take precedence over others. When trying to comprehend cultural differences, it is best to take "a holistic, contextual view of culture in which values co-exist as a constellation, but their salience differs depending on the situation. . . . A true understanding of the logic of

another culture includes comprehending the interrelationships among values in a given context" (Osland & Bird, 2000).

6. Share this metaphor for cultural learning:

- Cultural learning is like putting together a jigsaw puzzle. You may use the picture on the box top as a guide, but making sense of each individual piece and understanding where it fits is exceedingly difficult.

- If we accept cultures as paradoxical, then we can learn about culture in a dialectic fashion:

  – Thesis = hypothesis involving a "sophisticated stereotype."

  – Antithesis = identifying an oppositional cultural paradox.

  – Synthesis = making sense of contradictory behavior by understanding why certain values are more important in certain contexts.

7. Introduce the cultural sense-making model. Explain that behavior appears less paradoxical once the "foreigner" learns to frame situations with an understanding appropriate to the perspective of the members of the host culture. The cultural sense-making model conveys a holistic understanding of culture and explains how culture is embedded in context. Cultural sense-making involves a series of steps: framing the situation, making attributions, and selecting a script. These steps are undergirded by both the patterns of cultural values and cultural history. Distribute the Cultural Sense-Making Model worksheet and the Common Cultural Dimensions worksheet. Discuss the following key points.

- *Framing the Situation:* The process begins by identifying the specific context where the behavior is observed and then indexing the behavior (noticing or attending to stimuli that provide cues about the situation). In determining what to attend to and what to ignore, we can "frame the situation." For example, to index the context of a meeting, we might consider characteristics such as these: prior events; the nature of the organizational relationships usual for this type of business setting (are relationships informal or formal? is communication direct or indirect?, etc.); the specific topic under discussion; and the location of the interaction. (Trainers may wish to share an example from their own experience to "frame" for discussion.)

- *Making Attributions:* The next step is attribution, a process in which contextual cues are analyzed in order to match the context with appropriate schema. The matching process is moderated or influenced by our own social identity (e.g., ethnic or religious background, gender, social class, organizational affiliation) and our own history (e.g., experiences and chronology). Consider this question: "Who is this person, and how does he or she view the situation?" (The Common Cultural Dimensions worksheet can be helpful here.)

- *Selecting a Script:* Schemas are cultural scripts. They involve a pattern of social interaction that is characteristic of a particular cultural group. Schemas are accepted and appropriate ways of behaving, specifying certain patterns of interaction. Growing up, we learn appropriate vocabulary and gestures that are likely to elicit a fairly predictable response from others. At work and in school we watch and learn the "culturally appropriate" behavior for each environment. We then develop scripts for how to act as we assume our roles in our new setting. From personal or vicarious experience, we learn how to select schema. Cultural scripts or schemas reflect an underlying hierarchy of cultural values. For example, in the U.S., managers tend to have a more relaxed and casual style, openly share information, and provide opportunities for employees to make independent decisions. The configuration of values embedded in this management style consists of informality, honesty, equality, and individualism. At a certain point, however, these same managers may withhold information about a sensitive personnel situation because privacy, fairness, and legal concerns would trump honesty and equality in this context. This "trumping" action explains why the constellation of values related to specific schema is hierarchical. It also helps us understand why cultural decoding for employees from various other cultures can be difficult.

8. *Cultural History:* When decoding schema, we may also find vestiges of cultural history and tradition. Mind-sets inherited from previous generations explain how history is remembered (Fisher, 1997). For example, perceptions defining organizational loyalty, a strong work ethic, characteristics of a strong leader, and so forth may differ within the U.S. culture, where three and even four generations of workers can be found in one organization.

9. Provide participants with an opportunity to apply the cultural sense-making model in a variety of contexts. Depending on group size, you may decide to stay as a whole group or divide into smaller groups for practice with individual case studies and/or video clips. Explore how this sense-making model takes abstract, sometimes vague notions of culture and cultural dimensions and gives participants a way to focus on the

not-so-vague and less-abstract beliefs and behaviors of individual actors in specific situations.

10. Play a short video clip or present a case study with problematic cross-cultural interactions. Ask the participants to assume the perspective of one of the characters and graph the observable behavior of their character. Then encourage further discussion by saying, "In light of our knowledge of the cultural values framework and the sense-making process, explain how your character framed the situation, what attributions he or she made, and why the script was not effective." Continue in this way: "Now reframe the situation using your knowledge of cultural values within this situational context. What attributions can you make from this new perspective? How might you create a script that is more effective?" Allow time for several participants to share their cultural case and their two analyses with the group. You may wish to ask questions such as: *What are your hypotheses for why _____? How can you find out if your hypotheses are correct?* (You may wish to refer back to the previously discussed cultural paradoxes in step 2 and explore these shared paradoxical examples more deeply.)

Debriefing Questions:

1. What did you think when you heard about useful stereotyping? When you heard the descriptions of various cultural values and the concept of cultural paradox?

2. What did you observe during the video/case study activity? How easy or difficult was it to index the behavior? To make attributions? To explore the impact of your own social identity on your perceptions?

3. Were you surprised by anything you saw or heard? Experienced?

4. What challenges might you face in using this model? How might you counteract some of those challenges?

5. How do you feel now that the activity is complete? What did you learn about working across cultures? About yourself?

Debriefing Conclusions:

1. To work successfully across cultures, it is necessary to decode cultural behavior with an understanding of cultural values.

2. Cultural behavior can best be understood within the context in which it occurs.

3. Sophisticated stereotyping can be helpful when making comparisons between cultures but is not as useful when trying to understand variations of behavior within a culture.

4. The cultural sense-making model provides an effective framework for better understanding cultural behavior.

This activity has been adapted from the work of Joyce Osland, professor at the Global Leadership Advancement Center, San Jose State University, and Allan Bird, professor at Northeastern University.

Worksheet: Common Cultural Dimensions

Subjugation to Nature	Harmony	Mastery of Nature
Past	Present	Future
Being	Thinking	Doing
Evil Human Nature	Neutral or Mixed	Good
Hierarchical	Collectivistic	Individualistic
Private Space	Mixed	Public
Monochronic Time	Polychronic Time	
Low Context Language	High Context Language	
Low Uncertainty Avoidance	High Uncertainty Avoidance	
Low Power Distance	High Power Distance	
Short-Term Orientation	Long-Term Orientation	
Collectivism	Individualism	
Femininity	Masculinity	
Universalistic	Particularistic	
Neutral	Affective	
Diffuse	Specific	
Achievement	Ascription	
Inner-Directed	Outer-Directed	
Long-Term	Short-Term	
Hierarchy	Egalitarianism	
Embeddedness	Autonomy	
Mastery	Harmony	

Adapted from the work of Joyce Osland, professor at the Global Leadership Advancement Center, San Jose State University, and Allan Bird, professor at Northeastern University.

Worksheet: Cultural Sense-Making Model

This model presents a process-oriented way for people to understand culture and focus their attention on being more effective in intercultural interactions.

Expectations

What type of situation am I entering?

- An initial meeting?
- A conference call?
- An informal conversation?
- Reporting on completed tasks?

Framing the Situation

- We develop expectations about a situation before entering into it. These expectations are based on past experiences and on what we think we know about the situation.
- Upon first entering into the situation, we take in the scene, scanning for relevant cues that confirm our expectations.
- Based on the initial scan, we quickly establish a frame for the situation.

Making Attributions

- We make attributions about the situation and about the "other" based on the frame we built and cues we perceive.
- Our attributions are influenced by our self-identity, our ethnicity, religion, social class, past experiences, etc.
- Attributions about the "other" are influenced by our attitudes and beliefs about their identity, ethnicity, religion, social class, etc.

Selecting a Script

- Based on the frame and the attributions we have made, we select a script to get us through the situation.
- We select a script from a repertoire of past experiences.
- The selection of scripts is influenced by our ability to draw similarities between this situation and past experiences.

Adapted from the work of Joyce Osland, professor at the Global Leadership Advancement Center, San Jose State University, and Allan Bird, professor at Northeastern University.

11

The 5Rs of Culture Change

Time Required:

75 minutes (5 minutes for set-up/introductory lecture; 15 minutes for activity; 40 minutes for discussion/report-out; 15 minutes for debriefing/application)

Objectives:

To help participants:

1. Understand the five key changes typically faced when transitioning to another culture.
2. Recognize the stress these changes can create for themselves and others.
3. Develop strategies for managing the associated stresses of cultural transitions.

Materials:

- Easels
- Pens or markers
- Worksheets: The 5Rs of Culture Change (one per participant)
- Worksheet: The 5Rs of Culture Change—with Sample Answers (one per participant) Optional—see Process Step 6.

Process:

1. Set up two easels at each of five stations around the room. For each pair of easels, label one easel with an "R" (Routines, Reactions, Roles, Relationships, Reflections About Yourself) and leave the other blank. (Make sure to use all 5Rs.) Alternatively, attach easel pages to the walls to create five stations.
2. For the introduction, provide a brief overview of the 5Rs of Culture Change:

- Explain that travelers face many changes when they transition to another culture.
- Note that five of these changes, called the 5Rs of Culture Change, will be explored in more depth in this workshop.
- Provide a brief description of each "R": Routines, Reactions, Roles, Relationships, and Reflections About Yourself. (See the handout for sample language.) If appropriate, also give a *brief* example of each R to stimulate the group's thinking.
- Explain that these changes have many positive aspects, but they also can create transition stress.
- Note that transition stress is normal, natural, and will surface in different ways for different people.
- Explain that knowing some of the stressors travelers may face and planning to manage these stressors is a key step in a constructive transition process.

3. Put participants in five groups and assign each group to one of the "R" stations. Alternatively, have people go to the station that interests them. If this results in uneven groups, you can let that be (it may signal where the group predicts or is experiencing stress) or ask a few people to relocate to another station to even out the groups. Groups that contain more than six individuals tend to interfere with full participation.

4. Pose a question to be answered at each station, based on the "R" of focus.

- **Routines:** *What routine changes are you likely to face in the move abroad?*
- **Reactions:** *In what situations are you likely to face different reactions? What are the differences you may face?*
- **Roles:** *How will the roles you play change? What new roles will you take on? Which old roles will be harder to live out in the new culture?*
- **Relationships:** *Which relationships will be easiest to maintain? Hardest? What will you need to do to develop new relationships?*
- **Reflections About Yourself:** *In what ways might you change in this experience?*

Note: Adapt these questions for pre-departure, in-country, and reentry. For example, the question "What routine changes are you likely to face in the move abroad?" changes for in-country and becomes "What has changed in your routine?" while for reentry, the question becomes "What changes will you face when you return home?"

Give the groups time to discuss the question at their station and record their ideas on the flipchart. After five minutes, ask them to take three minutes to write answers to this question: *How are you likely to feel when you face this change?* Again, adapt the question for use in-country and reentry. Ask the group to record the feelings and stress reactions that these changes could create or are creating. Go around the room and have each group share what they have discussed and recorded on their easel page. Now ask the groups to rotate to the next "R" station.

On the second flipchart paper (on the blank flipchart), ask them to record strategies for managing this change. After five minutes, have each group report the top strategy they identified to help manage this change. As you do this, ask the others to listen with curiosity to the various strategies. If they have other ideas, encourage them to share them (time permitting).

5. Conduct a final debrief of the process using the questions below.

6. Pass out the worksheet as a takeaway and have people add and star the strategies they want to remember and commit to doing. (NOTE: At this point the trainer can decide whether to distribute the worksheet with or without sample answers based on what she or he feels will be most useful to participants.)

Debriefing Questions:

As a group:

1. What was it like to discuss all these possible changes with others?
2. What did you learn from the process?

Pair discussion or individual reflection:

1. Which of the 5Rs do you think will most impact you?
2. Which strategies will make the biggest difference in helping you manage the stress of the transition?
3. What three things will you commit to doing to help manage this stress?

Debriefing Conclusions:

1. It can be helpful to have open discussions around the changes we face when we move across cultures and the impact these changes may have on us.

2. Different people may react differently to these changes—including the desire and ability to discuss them.

3. Moreover, we may be impacted by these different changes at different junctures in our transition.

4. Being aware of these changes can help us plan to manage the stress they may create.

Optional Processes:

- When all participants are going to or living in a particular culture, plan to offer culture-specific information for each "R" (and therefore plan for more time for the exercise). For example, with a group in or going to Spain, talk through the common routines, give examples of key ways to engage effectively given different reactions, discuss the role of being a family member in Spain, etc. This exercise is also well suited to conduct after you have covered culture-specific information. The exercise then helps people review what they have learned about the changes they will face and then process more personally how they will likely react to these differences.

- There are essentially three rounds of discussion (recording what changes you will face, how you will react to this change, and then what you can do about it). With more experienced groups, have them rotate after each round so they give input on three of the five Rs by the end of the discussion. For less experienced groups, you can choose not to have them rotate at all, working the entire time on one R.

- To adapt this exercise for working with individuals and couples, introduce them to the 5Rs and then hold a coaching discussion with them to help them understand: (1) which of these changes are most likely to impact them; (2) how the stress from these changes is likely to manifest for them; and (3) what strategies they can develop to best manage the changes and related stress. Have these discussions end with action planning around what each person can and will commit to doing to take care of themselves and assist the other during the transition.

- In cultures where openly discussing feelings is not culturally acceptable, ask the group to develop a story or parable about someone facing that particular "R" so the issue is explored without personalizing it.

Activity created by Kate Berardo, founder of the Culturosity Group, LLC (www.culturosity.com). Adapted from "The 5 Rs of Culture Change" by Kate Berardo in Berardo, K., and Deardorff, D., *Building Cultural Competence: Innovative Activities and Models* (Stylus: 2012).

Worksheet: The 5Rs of Culture Change

What Changes	Common Reactions	Strategies to Manage This Change
Routines Schedules, meal times, how you travel around, how much free time you have and what you do with it, even the basics like how to turn on a faucet or light switch.	• Tired or stressed, without a clear cause • Not anchored or grounded	• • • •
Reactions How people interact and communicate, including greetings and facial expressions, to what is considered appropriate behavior in different situations.	• Confusion and uncertainty • Less confidence • Withdrawing or isolating • Criticizing host culture	• • • •
Roles Roles you play (being a career professional, a student, a family member) look and feel different in your host culture. You may assume new roles ("the foreigner," "the European").	• Mixed emotions! • Excitement for new desired roles • Defensiveness for unwanted roles • Sadness for lost or lessened roles • Confusion for changed roles	• • • •
Relationships You may drift apart from certain relationships back home. You may also experience a deeper connection with some friends and family despite the distance. You have to invest energy in creating new relationships.	• It takes a lot of energy to build relationships—but it is also satisfying • A sense of loss, often initially, with less communication back home	• • • •

What Changes	Common Reactions	Strategies to Manage This Change
Reflections About Yourself You change in subtle and not so subtle ways. You may adopt new behaviors, clothes, and a different lifestyle. You may learn a lot about what you value most. You are growing and developing, becoming more aware of who you truly are.	• Confusion and uncertainty • Sometimes adopting, sometimes rejecting host culture ways of being or doing • Questions like: Who am I? What's most important to me? Where do I feel at home?	• • • •

Activity created by Kate Berardo, founder of the Culturosity Group, LLC (www.culturosity.com). Adapted from "The 5 Rs of Culture Change" by Kate Berardo in Berardo, K., and Deardorff, D., *Building Cultural Competence: Innovative Activities and Models* (Stylus: 2012).

Sample Answers: The 5Rs of Culture Change

What Changes	Common Reactions	Strategies to Manage This Change
Routines Schedules, meal times, how you travel around, how much free time you have and what you do with it, even basics like how to turn on a faucet or light switch.	• Tired or stressed, without a clear cause • Not anchored or grounded	• Expect things to take more time and energy, especially at the start. • Prioritize activities that help you to relax and take care of yourself (exercise, sleep, etc.). • Proactively create new routines.
Reactions How people interact and communicate, including greetings and facial expressions, to what is considered appropriate behavior in different situations.	• Confusion and uncertainty • Less confidence • Withdrawing or isolating • Criticizing host culture	• Focus on learning about the culture and keys to understanding different reactions. • Be curious toward differences you experience. • Find a cultural bridge to help you understand appropriate actions and reactions. • Start to build needed skills to interact effectively in that culture. • Set realistic expectations for the time and energy it will take to learn these skills. • Remind yourself of what you are good at.
Roles Roles you play (being a career professional, a student, a family member) look and feel different in your host culture. You may assume new roles ("the foreigner," "the European").	• Mixed emotions! • Excitement for new desired roles • Defensiveness for unwanted roles • Sadness for lost or lessened roles • Confusion for changed roles	• Expect roles to be different. • Hold discussions to gain clarity (as much as possible) on your new roles and responsibilities. • Strategize how to live out the same roles in a different location (e.g., taking care of parents who remain in your home country). • For roles you no longer play, reflect on what you gain from that role and where and how else you might experience that.

What Changes	Common Reactions	Strategies to Manage This Change
Relationships You may drift apart from certain relationships back home. You may also experience a deeper connection with some friends and family despite the distance. You have to invest energy in creating new relationships.	• It takes a lot of energy to build relationships—but it is also satisfying • A sense of loss, often initially, with less communication back home	• Know it will take time to build new relationships. • Take initiative: reach out, join a club, and build new connections. • Create rituals to keep relationships back home going (Sunday Skype calls, a blog, online photo album). • Keep dialogues open about hopes, needs, and concerns in existing relationships.
Reflections About Yourself You change in subtle and not-so-subtle ways. You may adopt new behaviors, clothes, and lifestyles. You learn about what you value most. You are growing, developing, becoming more aware of who you truly are.	• Confusion and uncertainty • Sometimes adopting, sometimes rejecting host culture ways of being or doing • Questions like: Who am I? What's most important? Where do I feel at home?	• Acknowledge that these changes are natural during transitions. • Note your feelings. Write in a journal and reflect on what you are learning about yourself. • Share and seek support from others who can relate to your experience.

Activity created by Kate Berardo, founder of the Culturosity Group, LLC (www.culturosity.com). Adapted from "The 5 Rs of Culture Change" by Kate Berardo in Berardo, K., and Deardorff, D., *Building Cultural Competence: Innovative Activities and Models* (Stylus: 2012).

12

Crafting My Future

Time Required:

55–75 minutes (5 minutes for setup; 20–30 minutes for activity; 20–30 minutes for discussion/report-out; 10 minutes for debriefing/application)

Objective:

To allow participants an opportunity to consider their concerns and excitement about transition in a nontraditional manner that allows them to engage the right brain

Materials:

- A wide array of craft materials: scissors, glue, yarn, construction paper, magazines (travel magazines are particularly good), stickers, balloons, etc.
- A large page of construction paper (12″ × 18″) for each participant

Process:

1. Place craft materials on a large table to the side of the room. Be sure there is plenty of table space for participants to work on.

2. Ask participants to divide their sheets in half by folding them, drawing a line down the middle, or any other method they choose.

3. Give participants 20–30 minutes to use the craft materials to complete two tasks: (1) create a representation on one side of the page that demonstrates any concerns they might have about their upcoming transition; (2) create a representation on the other side of the page that shows something they are excited about or anticipate will occur during the transition. Be prepared for some reluctance, but encourage participants to try it, even if it means only placing a sticker on each side of the

---

Work
X–X
X, X, X, X

page. Generally, once people get started on this process they get very engaged. If someone simply cannot or will not do it, however, ask that person to quietly observe what they see others doing.

4. After 20–30 minutes, ask participants to share their creations and the meaning with the group. Allow 20–30 minutes for this discussion.

Debriefing Questions:

1. How did you feel when you were first asked to do this activity? Why?

2. How did your feelings shift as you began working on the assignment?

3. What insights have you gained from your own creation as well as from listening to others?

Debriefing Conclusions:

1. Engaging in a process that is more right brain or creative can give us different insights than simply responding to questions via verbal conversations.

2. Many of the concerns and the excitement that people have about transitions are shared with others.

3. When people understand that others share their concerns and excitement, it reduces the sense of isolation.

4. When travelers can isolate their concerns or excitement, they can also focus their attention on how to prepare for the transition most effectively.

Optional Processes:

1. When used with children, the questions can relate to school or playmates.

2. When used with spouses, the questions can relate to how their role(s) in the new setting will differ from those with which they are familiar.

3. When used in employment settings, the questions can relate to workplace skills and/or relationships.

Developed by Donna M. Stringer, Ph.D., Cross-Cultural Consultant, Seattle, Washington (donnastringer42@gmail.com).

13

International Transition Bingo

Time Required:

80–100 minutes (30 minutes for bingo; 20–30 minutes for group discussion; 30–40 minutes for debriefing)

Objectives:

1. To identify various aspects of cultural difference and stages of transition

2. To stimulate discussion regarding the possible impact (personally/professionally) of cultural differences related to transition

3. To heighten understanding of challenges in international transition (both going out and returning home)

4. To further explore the concepts of greatest interest/concern to the group

Materials:

- One International Transition Bingo Card for each team
- One International Transition Bingo Questions and Answers List for facilitator
- One International Transition Bingo Questions and Answers List for each participant (to be distributed after playing the game)
- Something to cover or X out the squares when the team knows the answer
- Optional: Small prize for each "team bingo" (e.g., an age-appropriate item, a country-specific item, candy)

Process:

1. Form teams of four or five participants around a table or hard surface.

2. Distribute the bingo cards, one for each team.

3. Explain the purpose of the activity is to have fun while learning more about cultural differences and stages of transition.
4. Explain the rules:
   - The facilitator will read a definition from the list and the participants will scan their card to find the word on their card that matches the definition. When a team finds the word, they raise one hand. The first team to raise a hand answers the question. (Note: You may want to ask for a volunteer to "spot" the first raised hand. If there are "ties," the facilitator calls on one team OR allows both teams to answer the question and cover a square.)
   - If the answer is correct, the team can cross off the square.
   - If the answer is wrong, the team loses a square cover. If no squares have been covered, they sit out the next round and the second team who raised a hand answers the question.
   - Bingo occurs when five squares are covered horizontally, vertically, or diagonally.
5. Begin the game by reading the questions from the International Transition Bingo Questions and Answers List.
6. Optional: Reward the team for each bingo.
7. Continue playing. End session when all of the items on the question and answer list have been read.
8. Distribute answer sheets to the group. Give the groups an opportunity to discuss the terms on the card. Are any terms unfamiliar? What might be (or was) the greatest challenge for you to deal with personally/professionally? What items would your team like to discuss in more depth?

Debriefing Questions:

1. Which terminologies were familiar? Which require more explanation? Which could have the most impact on your personal transition/professional adjustment?
2. If you have lived internationally, what bingo terms brought back memories? How might understanding these cultural terms/differences help/hinder transition?
3. Why might someone run into a challenge when returning home? Please share something you have personally experienced or have observed in someone returning from an international assignment.
4. How easy was it for your group to shift to identify the most important terms? Share some similarities/differences that came up for your group.

5. What did you learn from this activity? How could you use this information?

Debriefing Conclusions:

1. Moving internationally requires cultural adjustment (personally/professionally).

2. Many cultural aspects are not visible.

3. Moving abroad and returning home presents a variety of adjustment challenges.

4. Understanding differences in cultural preferences can make the transition more manageable.

5. While the experience of living abroad and returning home is a deeply personal experience, discussion of common concerns can enrich the experience, deepen the learning, and reduce the stress.

Exercise developed by Patricia Cassiday, Collaborative Connection, Seattle, Washington (www.collaborativeconnection.org).

International Transition Bingo Card

Formality	Monochronic Time	Individualism	Ethnocentric	Low Context
Minimization	Culture Shock	Worldview	Adjustment Phase	Honeymoon
Intercultural Competence	Cultural Acculturation	Power Distance	Collectivism	Cultural Values
Third Culture	Marginality	High Context	Reentry Shock	Polychronic Time
Cultural Assimilation	Pre-Departure	Informality	Culture	Ethnorelative

Exercise developed by Patricia Cassiday, Collaborative Connection, Seattle, Washington.

International Transition Bingo

Questions and Answers List

1. Acting in hierarchical manner, following a specific set of rules and/or role expectations (Answer: Formality)

2. Underlying assumptions about the nature of reality and human behavior (Answer: Worldview)

3. Belief that one's own ethnicity is most worthwhile and has the "right" way of seeing the world (Answer: Ethnocentric)

4. Tension and anxiety often experienced when entering into a new culture, often combined with a sense of loss, confusion, and powerlessness (Answer: Culture Shock)

5. The ability to adapt one's behavior and verbal/nonverbal communication to the appropriate cultural context (Answer: Intercultural Competence)

6. A type of communication using explicit words and "saying everything that needs to be said" (Answer: Low Context)

7. Process by which families/individuals are "absorbed" into the new culture; taking on the new culture's values and beliefs (Answer: Assimilation)

8. Time orientation focused on involvement with people/relationships and balancing multiple task simultaneously. (Answer: Polychronic Time)

9. Playing down or diminishing difference when it comes to culture or ethnicity (Answer: Minimization)

10. Unexpected feelings of tension, anxiety, and/or confusion experienced when returning to one's "home" after an extended stay in a foreign culture (Answer: Reentry Shock)

11. Time orientation based on scheduled blocks of time, concerns with "running out of time," and being "on time" (Answer: Monochronic Time)

12. Understanding that the different values, beliefs, assumptions, and behaviors in another culture are logically connected to the history and experience of individuals in that culture (Answer: Ethnorelative)

13. A cultural lifestyle "at the edge" where two or more cultures meet; feeling comfortable in either culture but not really a part of either (Answer: Marginality)

14. A euphoric feeling often experienced when first entering a new culture or when first returning home (Answer: Honeymoon)

15. Experienced when persons from different cultures come together and establish relational empathy grounded by their experience with cultural differences (Answer: Third Culture)

16. An accumulated pattern of values, beliefs, and behaviors shared by a group of people with a common geography, history, and language (Answer: Culture)

17. Hierarchical expectation that accepts and expects power to be unequally distributed (Answer: Power Distance)

18. When the group is the primary unit of culture and group goals and the good of the group is valued over the individual (Answer: Collectivism)

19. The period of time spent preparing for an impending international move (Answer: Pre-Departure)

20. Qualities of character, behavior and thought regarded as intrinsically good by members of a society and worthy of emulation (Answer: Cultural Values)

21. Interacting effectively within another culture without losing one's own cultural perspective (Answer: Acculturation)

22. Cultural orientation where the individual is recognized as unique and special: the individual's needs take precedent over the needs of the larger group (Answer: Individualism)

23. A stage of culture shock where individuals seek out information and employ effective problem-solving skills/strategies (Answer: Adjustment Phase)

24. Communication style where the meaning is implied rather than expressed; inference must be made from what is not spoken (Answer: High Context)

25. Treating everyone in a personal, familiar, and/or causal way; treating everyone as "equal" (Answer: Informality)

Exercise developed by Patricia Cassiday, Collaborative Connection, Seattle, Washington (www.collaborativeconnection.org).

Hats: Worn, Re-worn, Torn, Born

Time Required:

55–85 minutes (5 minutes for introduction; 20–40 minutes for activity; 20–30 minutes for discussion; 10 minutes for debriefing/application)

Objectives:

To help participants:

1. Understand how the roles we play change during cultural transitions
2. Recognize the impact of these role changes
3. Plan for the implications of these role changes

Materials:

- Index cards

Process:

1. Distribute stacks of index cards (approximately 10–15) to each participant.
2. For the introduction, set up the activity as follows:
   - Introduce the metaphor of "hats" for the different roles we play in life.
   - Provide or elicit a few examples of different roles we play (e.g., sibling, manager, student, etc.).
   - Note how these roles may look and feel different when we take them into other cultures.
   - Give one brief relevant example for the participants. In educational settings, for example, highlight how being a good student in some cultures can involve diligently taking notes and not asking questions, whereas in other cultures, asking questions is considered a sign of active learning. In

Work

X–X

X, X, X, X

workplace settings, note how a good leader in some cultures imitates a parental figure, carefully guiding and teaching the employee how to engage. In other cultures, a good leader is more like the model of a sports coach—not having to excel at the sport being played, but able to bring out the best in the players and help them solve problems.

- To continue the analogy, note that the roles they have identified can be considered "hats re-worn," even though they may require some resizing to fit.

- Offer a second category of role changes: hats torn. These are often roles or hats that we used to play that we no longer play in our new culture. Provide an example here (e.g., an individual who is giving up his or her job to accompany the spouse or partner).

- Finally, there is a third category of role changes we may face when we move abroad: hats born. Give a brief example here as well (e.g., being labeled suddenly as "the foreigner"). Note this too can present some challenges. What if, for example, individuals don't see or define themselves how others are suddenly labeling them?

- Note how understanding these role changes and planning for them are part of a successful transition, and therefore what the training program will now focus on.

3. Complete the Hats You Wear activity.

- Ask participants to take the stack of index cards in front of them. Have them write down at the top of each index card a key role that they currently play, one per index card. Tell them to stop when they feel they have listed the main roles that define them. For some people, this may be two or three roles. Others may continue to ten or more.

- Ask people to choose no more than five top roles to work with. Have people create two columns on each of these index cards, with one column titled "Gain" and the other titled "Give" (still on the front side).

- Under "Gain," ask them to record the feelings, beliefs, or sense of meaning they gain from this role. Complete one index card with the group as you do this, so they can see an example live. For example, for the role you might write down *intercultural facilitator*, and under *gain* you might write *sense of purpose, satisfaction, hope, etc.*

- Under the "Give" section, ask them then to record what they offer to others or to society at large with this role. For example, as an intercultural facilitator, you might write *knowledge, intercultural competence, care, etc.*

- Give people a few minutes to complete their Gain and Give columns. This helps people to lock into the associated feeling and meaning associated with each role.

- Ask the group now to look at their roles, or hats, and to sort them into two piles: *hats re-worn* for roles that they will continue but in a different form, and *hats torn* for those roles that they will no longer play.

Note: Anticipate and check for torn hats in the group. For example, with students, you may find fewer or none and can skip this step and the hats torn portion of the exercise. In contrast, when you use this with individuals who are giving up their jobs for a move abroad, this will be one of the most crucial parts of the exercise, so you will want to spend good time on the hats torn section.

4. Complete the Hats Re-Worn activity.

- Ask the group to call out the different roles that will be re-worn, and list these on the board.

- To make the instructions clear, use the following questions to complete an example with one re-worn hat that is relevant to many individuals:

  - What will stay the same?

  - What will change about this role?

  - How are these changes likely impact you?

  - What adaptations do you need to make so you can have a similar sense of gain and give with this role?

  - What steps and actions do you need to take now and when you arrive to ensure you are best prepared to wear this hat in a new culture?

Note: Adapt these questions for pre-departure, in-country, and reentry. For example, the in-country questions may become "What has stayed the same? What has changed? What has been the impact of these changes? What steps can you take now to help you to resize this hat to fit in your new culture?"

For instance, you might use the example of being a student. Discuss what may be similar (grading system, amount of work, etc.) and what may be different (teacher-student interactions, attitudes toward students in town, etc.), and help people process the impact of these changes. Then encourage them to think through actions and steps students might need to take (e.g., set up an appointment with their teacher during office hours to clarify expectations on upcoming papers, etc.).

- Ask participants to choose two or three of the re-worn hats they have identified and then go through the questions above. They can record their answers on the back of the index cards. Encourage students to connect back to the "Give" and "Gain" columns as applicable. For example, under *friend*, the participant might have listed under both "Give" and "Gain" "a place to vent frustrations!"

Ask people to work in pairs to discuss their answers. For instance, partners might discuss how travelers can work out a way to gain "a place to vent frustrations" from friends back home, who may not be able to understand their frustrations while abroad, or how to balance this need to vent with new friends without coming across as critical of the local culture.

Give the pairs roughly 10 minutes to discuss the other roles they will continue to wear. After 10 minutes, ask each pair to share one role they focused on, and what actions they will take to "resize the hat to fit." For roles that are common to the group (e.g., being a friend), ask others to add the strategies they developed for keeping in touch with friends back home so they could still serve this role while abroad.

5. Complete the Hats Born activity.

- Ask the group what, if any, new hats they will wear when they enter the new culture. Have individuals create a new index card for any new hats they may wear.

- Then have them complete a "Gain" and a "Give" column for these new roles, or have them simply record how they may feel wearing this new hat (especially if it is not one that they may consciously choose to take on).

- Have people form new pairs and discuss the implications of taking on this new role. Ask them to again record any actions or steps they may want to take as a result. For example, one common new role people often take on is to be defined by their country or region of origin. For example, outside of the country, they may now be seen primarily by others as a U.S. American (or Canadian, Nigerian, etc.). As such, it is important to understand the perceptions and beliefs others in the destination culture may have about them. If one perception is that U.S. Americans tend to be overly loud, then a practical implication—especially if they don't want to be defined by this hat—may be to ensure that their volume of communication is lower and matches more the style of others.

6. Complete the Hats Torn activity.

   Note: This portion can invoke powerful emotions and therefore should be handled with care and by experienced facilitators only.

   • Finally, have people look at any torn hats from their list of roles. Note how natural it is to experience a sense of loss and to grieve the loss of particular roles, so encourage people to honor any feelings that may bubble up as they review this role.

   • Have people focus on the words they wrote in the "Gain" and "Give" columns for these torn hats. Ask them to individually reflect on the following questions:

     – What are the implications of you not having this role (wearing this hat) in your new culture?

     – How can you best prepare for this loss? For example, what other activities can you take on that will give you a similar sense of gain and give?

   • Read the energy of the room. If the group has been openly sharing, encourage people to share the implications of their torn hats, and enable the group to think together some ways to compensate for the associated loss of this role.

7. Finish the exercise with the Pack Up the Hats for the Move activity.

   • Ask the group to turn over all their index cards so all the backs with the strategies are showing. Ask people to star those actions that they feel will make the biggest difference to them. And as appropriate, encourage people to assign a timeline for taking those actions.

Debriefing Questions:

1. What insights or learnings did you have through this process?
2. What steps or actions will you now take to help support yourself during role changes?

Debriefing Conclusions:

1. The roles we play and how we live out those roles can shift when we move across cultures.
2. Understanding which roles change and how they change is critical to understanding the transition process.
3. Having a clear and realistic understanding of role changes is a key step in transitioning.

4. Some roles we have need to be resized to fit in the new culture (hats re-worn), some roles we lose or no longer can live out (hats torn), and some are new roles we start to play in a different culture (hats born).

5. Even if we can't live out certain roles in a new culture, there are other ways to gain a similar sense of satisfaction and minimize what is often an accompanying sense of loss.

Optional Processes:

- Go through the activity first for yourself, as this will both help you understand how to facilitate it and also provide you with good examples to share with the group.

- When all participants are going to or living in a particular culture, you can spend time providing more culture-specific information for different roles. For example, during the Hats Reborn section, for people going to, living in, or returning to Japan, discuss relevant key roles (family member, leader, student, and responsible citizen) and compare and contrast these roles to the same roles in the culture of origin or current location. Plan for more time for the exercise if you choose this option.

- This exercise provides a deeper look at role changes introduced during the 5Rs of Culture Change exercise (see Exercise #11). Consider doing this activity after the 5Rs for those people who are facing significant changes in their roles, especially, for example, accompanying spouses who are giving up their job for the move.

- This exercise is highly powerful with individuals and couples. Follow the general process above, allowing more time for individualized discussion and coaching. Enable a deep discussion around what each person gains and gives to the different roles they play and the implications of role changes in their move abroad.

- Have a large number of actual hats available that people can put on while sharing their roles. This can create a greater sense of reality for a role, and it can add a bit of playfulness to the exercise.

This activity was created by Kate Berardo, founder of the Culturosity Group, LLC (www.culturosity.com). It was adapted from "Hats Worn, Torn, Reborn" by Kate Berardo in *Building Cultural Competence: Innovative Activities and Models* (Berardo & Deardorff, 2012).

15

Entering "Right"

Time Required:

40–55 minutes (10–15 minutes to introduce or review the Five-Step Cycle and discuss "Entering"; 15–20 minutes for group work; 15–20 minutes for debriefing)

> **Work**
>
> X–X
>
> X, X, X, X

Objectives:

1. To define/review a five-step cycle for successful relocation
2. To identify strategies for a positive "entrance" in the new location
3. To develop an individual plan for successfully negotiating the entry stage

Materials:

- Chart paper, markers
- Handout of lecturette Appendix B: A Five-Step Cycle for Successful Relocation
- Paper and pens or pencils

Process:

1. Introduce the topic of international relocation in terms of a five-step cycle. Briefly review the five steps.
2. Use language such as the following to lead the training:
   We are going to explore the Entering Phase of transition today. Your physical arrival at the new location does not mean you have actually "entered" your new community. The more you have consciously planned for this stage, the better chance you have for a smooth entrance. We will discuss a few strategies for a successful entrance and then plan for some strategies that you believe will work for you.

- Be proactive; find information on resources and activities available to incoming employees/students; reach out to those in the new community with interests similar to yours.
- Lean in toward your new community by inviting others to do things or to come over to your home instead of waiting for others to reach out for you.
- Find a mentor, someone who can act as a cultural bridge and help you get acclimated to your new surroundings. Qualities to look for in a mentor:
    - Positive attitude about the people, place, and the organization
    - Knowledge of the local culture and the ins and outs of your organization or school
    - Ability to describe and model appropriate cultural behavioral patterns
    - Understanding of how to access and negotiate for necessities, such as a place to live, transportation services, electric, phone, computer access, etc.
    - A native language speaker with knowledge of the host culture and your home culture
- A word of caution regarding mentors:
    - Many organizations have a mentor or sponsor program in place. Sometimes these mentors are an enthusiastic blessing. Other times these mentors have seen so many people come and go that they have only minimal interest in sharing their knowledge.
    - Mentors who are not positive about the community may have a negative influence on your perspective and even your ability to be effective.
    - If your mentor does not have a positive reputation in the community, your reputation may suffer by association.
    - Not all mentors are a "good fit." If you have been "assigned" a mentor, you may need to scout out a second mentor that would be a better personal fit.
- When someone reaches out to us in the new location, we can easily jump into a new relationship without understanding the ramifications of our decision. Take a little time to evaluate a potential friend/mentor. Some questions to ask:
    - Is this a person who fits into the local community, or is she or he marginalized in one way or another?

- Does this person exhibit the positive attitudes I would like to foster, or does he or she make negative remarks or display poor attitudes toward others or the organization?

- If the person is marginalized in some way, why does she or he want to help me get acquainted with this community?

- Sometimes the person reaching out will be a relative newcomer, looking for a friend. Sometimes the person is reaching out because she or he has available time and an interest in helping you feel "at home," but sometimes the person reaching out may be in trouble with the community and is trying to recruit newcomers to his or her own agenda. Give yourself a little time and trust your instincts.

- If you are moving with a family, it is especially important to explore all of the possible support services available. Some organizations have a formalized mentoring program. Some organizations set up "matching families" and even encourage contact between family members prior to the move. For students, the new school may have a welcoming program, such as "Student 2 Student" or "Big Brothers/Big Sisters."

- Entry, like all of the stages of transition, takes time. Your feelings may range from "Isn't this wonderful!" to feelings of anger and confusion, to finally beginning to "figure out" the answers and begin creating your new life. Knowing that these feelings are a natural part of the transition should help you avoid being too vocal about things you find frustrating in your new situation.

- Bottom line: unpack your bags, plant your trees . . . commit to creating the life you want in your new location!

3. Give participants approximately ten minutes to review the following questions and think through their personal stories:

- Have you had previous experience with entering a new community? Organization? Career?

- What worked well for you in the past?

- What was especially challenging?

- Is there any new information presented here today that offers insight into your past experience? Please share.

- What specific action steps can you to take?

4. Place participants in groups of four or five to share their stories and also their plans for entering the new location successfully.

Debriefing Questions:

1. How did you feel about the request to create and share your story?

2. What happened when your group came together? How did you decide who would share first? Were there common themes or concerns?

3. Were there any surprises in your group? What did you learn?

4. How do you plan to use this activity?

Debriefing Conclusions:

1. International transition can be understood in terms of a five-step cycle.

2. Entering a new community, starting a new job, and/or beginning in a new school can present challenges.

3. Identifying strategies for the new beginning can help make your transition a positive experience, adding to your initial satisfaction and effectiveness.

This activity has been adapted from David C. Pollock and Ruth E. Van Reken's work in *The Third Culture Kid Experience: Growing Up Among Worlds* (2009).

16

Safe, Savvy, and Secure

Time Required:

85–115 minutes (10–20 minute for lecturette, 10–15 minutes for country research; 35–40 minutes for station activity; 15–20 minutes for station reports; 15–20 minutes for debriefing)

Work
X–X
X, X, X, X

Objectives:

1. To provide participants with a safety and security "self-assessment"
2. To help participants develop a personal profile of capabilities, limitations, and expectations
3. To help participants explore a wide range of safety and security issues while living abroad
4. To help participants gain awareness and create balance regarding safety and security issues

Materials:

- Six charts with easels and markers
- Worksheet: Safe, Savvy, and Secure: A Personal Inventory (one for each participant)
- Pens or pencils
- Wi-Fi access for computer with projector and for mobile device access

Process:

1. To begin, share the following lecturette:

   For many of us, the opportunity to travel and/or live abroad sounds like an exciting adventure—an opportunity to experience a new way of seeing and doing. Travel and/or living abroad can be an opportunity to make a real difference in the world, learn new skills, and meet new people.

When considering this opportunity, we can easily be blinded by our own desires. Our hopes and aspirations can obscure our ability to objectively evaluate the risk of living in a new country. We may overestimate the value of the sojourn in comparison to the personal safety and security risk factors, just because we *want* to go.

When we speak about safety and security, we are referring to a desirable state—a freedom from threat. But these words are not necessarily synonymous. Here are some definitions to keep in mind as we proceed. [*Post or project definitions.*]

- *Safety:* Freedom from threats that occur as a result of living in the world, including national disasters, accidents, disease and sickness, natural death, and other sources of unintended but serious potential harm.

- *Security:* Freedom from hostile acts, including crime, war, harassment, intimidation, discrimination, and in the extreme case, genocide.

- *Threat:* Any occurrence, situation, or potential action that puts one's safety and/or security into jeopardy.

- *Risk:* An assessment of the probability and consequences/impact of a particular threat.

- *Behavior:* An individual's specific words and actions in response to stimuli encountered in day-to-day life.

So what is this big deal about safety and security?

Our goal today is not to discourage you from your "adventure" but to make "visible" some safety and security concerns and then offer insight about you as an individual in relation to your new destination. Today's activities will assist *you* in making the right decision for yourself. With this in mind, please take a few moments to complete the worksheet: Safe, Savvy, and Secure: A Personal Inventory.

2. When students have completed the Safe, Savvy, and Secure Inventory, explain that it is important for travelers to learn about their assignment destination. (A valuable U.S. resource for updated country information is www.travel.state.gov; two private security companies without political or diplomatic perspectives can be accessed at www.ci.pinkerton.com and www.kroll.com.) If participants are all headed to the same location, you can use a projector and have a discussion with the whole group. If participants are heading to a number of different

locations, you can divide the participants into country groups for research.

3. Arrange the room into five "stations." (If the room size allows, this can be set up before the training begins.) Each station should have a chart that contains the following questions.

Station 1

1. How might age and gender matter?

2. What key concerns should be considered in health and physical fitness?

3. Does race matter? What impact might race have on this experience?

4. How will you deal with unwanted attention?

Station 2

1. How might your risk tolerance influence your experience?

2. What challenges might a "need for companionship" bring in the new location?

3. How comfortable are you with conflict? What part does your "comfort with conflict" play in your ability to succeed?

4. What is your (safe) plan for social activities? For learning about the culture?

Station 3

1. What importance might the ability to drive or not drive play in your new assignment?

2. How might safety concerns arise around alcohol or drug usage?

3. What are some concerns about money? Enough? Access? Bill paying?

4. What are the greatest sources of threat in this new location? Environment? Health? Corruption? Crime?

Station 4

1. How do you feel about legal concerns? Writing a will? Last wishes?

2. What might be the challenges of living in a rural area vs. an urban area?

3. Are there advantages to speaking a foreign language when many individuals in the host country speak English? Describe.

4. What do you hope to gain by going overseas?

Station 5

1. How can your attitudes toward safety affect your time abroad?

2. Are the police and government officials to be trusted in the new location? How will you understand that relationship in regards to your work?

3. How can you find out more about your organization's emergency preparedness plan?

4. What will be your strategy for staying in contact with family and friends in case of an emergency or natural disaster?

4. Ask participants to form five equal teams. Number each team and send them to the station that corresponds to their number. Give students the following instructions:

Having a deeper awareness of your planned destination and of the safety and security considerations, please move to your station. You will find four questions. You will have five minutes to discuss the questions and two minutes to post a team response to two. At the end of seven minutes, you will move to the next station and repeat the process. After completion of Round 5, the teams will each report out on the key statements at their current station.

Debriefing Questions:

1. What are some of your thoughts and concerns after completing this activity? Do you have questions about particular items? Were there any aha moments? New awareness to contemplate?

2. How do you feel about this information? About your decision to go? What might be an important next step to take? How might you find someone to talk over your feelings with? Someone to provide insight? Support?

3. What did you see happening in the room as the information was provided? As participants were completing the profile? As the group began to discuss the topic? Describe.

4. How can your profile be useful in the future? How might this process benefit members of your family? Team? Organization?

Debriefing Conclusions:

1. There are a wide range of external and internal factors to consider related to safety and security.

2. It is important to be fully informed about the new location prior to making a commitment to go.

3. Not all places are equally safe, or a good "fit" for you personally, for a variety of reasons.

4. Exploring these factors prior to departure allows for informed decision-making.

   Note to Trainers: *This activity includes a very brief introduction to the safety and security concerns to be considered when living and traveling internationally. You may need a deeper personal knowledge of the issues to effectively facilitate this exercise. Deeper insight can be found in the book:* Travel Wise: How to be Safe, Savvy and Secure Abroad" *by Ray Leki. The book contains suggestions for skill development, case studies, and informational resources.*

This activity has been adapted from the work of Ray S. Leki, *Travel Wise: How to Be Safe, Savvy and Secure Abroad* (2008).

Worksheet: Safe, Savvy, and Secure: A Personal Inventory

To understand your threat profile, complete the following questions as honestly as you can. If you are uncomfortable answering a question, leave it blank. If you will be traveling overseas with someone—a family member, friend, close associate—you might want to share your answers and thoughts with them before you travel. Go through this survey element by element and note points or questions you have as you ponder these factors.

Part I: Personal and Interpersonal Skills

PERSONAL CHARACTERISTICS:

1. **Gender:** _____

2. **Age:** _____

3. **Stature:** (Tiny/Small/Average/Large/Immense) _____

4. **Posture:** _____

    Tend to slouch/Droopy shoulders/Average/Erect/Buckingham Palace Guard

5. **Physical fitness:**

    _____ I resent having to bend down to pick up my television's remote control.

    _____ I minimize any activity that might make me sweat.

    _____ I know I should do more exercise, but I am not worried about it.

    _____ I know I should do more exercise, and I am concerned about it.

    _____ I try to exercise regularly but am not regular about it.

    _____ I exercise regularly.

    _____ I am frequently involved in active, competitive sports.

    _____ I compete regularly in events such as marathons, triathlons, or ironman/woman.

6. **Appearance:** Describe yourself as others in an international setting might see you.

    _____

    _____

    _____

    _____

PERSONAL CHARACTERISTICS:

7. **Health:**

    _____ I have significant health problems that require ongoing attention.

_____ I have some problems—usually manageable, but occasionally problematic.

_____ I am of average health.

_____ I am healthy.

_____ I am ready for the international space colonization.

8. **Medical dependence:**

_____ I take many daily prescriptions that I cannot live without.

_____ I take a daily medication that I cannot live without.

_____ I take daily medications that I need but could go a day or two without.

_____ I take a medication when I have a flare-up of a condition.

_____ I rarely take any medication.

_____ I don't take/rely on medication.

9. **Mobility:**

_____ I am not ambulatory.

_____ I am wheelchair dependent.

_____ I use a walking aid.

_____ I can walk without problem but cannot run.

_____ I can walk without problem and run for short periods of time.

_____ I can walk and run fast without problem.

_____ Masai warriors look upon me with awe.

10. **Vision:**

_____ I am visually impaired/legally blind.

_____ I am dependent on eyeglasses or contact lenses; I can't see without them.

_____ I am dependent on eyeglasses or contact lenses but can get along for short periods without them.

_____ I use reading glasses and/or need to wear sunglasses in bright light settings.

_____ I do not need or use glasses.

_____ I have excellent regular and peripheral vision.

11. **Hearing:**

_____ I am hearing impaired/legally deaf.

_____ I am hearing impaired and rely on a hearing assistance device (hearing aid).

_____ I have a slight hearing problem but can function without assistance.

_____ I can hear without problem.

_____ I have exceptional hearing.

12. **Voice:**

_____ I cannot speak without assistance (mute).

_____ I can speak but have a soft voice or a speech impediment.

_____ I can speak and yell when I need to.

_____ My voice can stop locomotives.

13. **Nervous system vigilance:**

_____ I am very calm and can nod off easily if not active.

_____ People tell me it is hard to get my attention when I am focused on something.

_____ I am pretty much middle to average.

_____ I am easily startled.

_____ I tend to be nervous/excited/hyper-vigilant.

PERSONAL CHARACTERISTICS:

14. **Risk tolerance:**

_____ I love to take risks and accept dares.

_____ I engage in extreme sports (bungee jumping, rock climbing, etc.).

_____ I can be talked into stretching my comfort zone and take a risk.

_____ I am somewhat risk averse.

_____ I refuse to take unnecessary risks.

15. **Sex:**

_____ I am sexually active with many different partners.

_____ I am occasionally sexually active with casual acquaintances.

_____ I am sexually active only with a person or people I know well.

_____ I am in a monogamous relationship or sexually inactive.

16. **Companionship:**

_____ I am most comfortable when I am alone.

_____ I am comfortable when I am alone, but prefer to travel with a friend.

_____ I am most comfortable when with others and won't go out or travel alone.

17. **Alcohol/drugs:**

_____ I frequently use drugs or alcohol and experience inebriation/intoxication.

_____ I have used drugs or alcohol and have been inebriated/intoxicated.

_____ I use drugs or alcohol but avoid being inebriated/intoxicated.

_____ I rarely use drugs or alcohol and am never inebriated/intoxicated.

_____ I never use drugs or alcohol.

18. **Comfort with conflict:**

_____ I am an "in-your-face" type of person and enjoy conflict.

_____ I don't seek conflict, but never shy away from it.

_____ I avoid conflict when possible.

_____ I don't deal well with conflict.

19. **Driving skills:**

_____ I have had no accidents and never use a safety belt.

_____ I have had several accidents but rarely use a safety belt.

_____ I have had several accidents and use a safety belt.

_____ I have had an accident or two and use a safety belt.

_____ I have never had an accident and always use a safety belt.

_____ I do not drive.

20. In the past year, have you ever experienced any number of stressful life circumstances that would tend to make you less resilient for the rigors of cross-cultural transition? (These might include the breakup of a significant relationship; the death of a parent, sibling, or close friend; a life-threatening crisis; or a significant depression or stress breakdown.) List of stressors:

_____

_____

_____

FINANCIAL SITUATION:

21. Do you have enough money to easily cover the anticipated expense of travel, plus some extra money for unanticipated costs?

_____ Yes _____ No

22. How much money have you estimated you will need, based on an average daily expense?

Average daily expense in $ or euros _____

Total number of travel days expected _____

Total resources required _____

Total reserve funds available for unexpected expenses in $ or euros _____

23. Have you left a will and power of attorney for your assets, debts, other accounts?

_____ Yes _____ No

24. If you plan to live and work overseas for a good part of your career, where do you hope to retire? Will you have built up social security credit, retirement, and pension along the way?

_____ Yes _____ No

25. Do people depend on you for their personal, emotional, and/or financial support?

_____ Yes _____ No

26. Have you talked to your family members about their wishes and estates, should they pass away while you are overseas?

_____ Yes _____ No

27. Have you left instructions for your wishes to be enacted if you should die overseas, or become incapacitated and/or be unable to make your wishes known (e.g., life support, organ donation)?

_____ Yes _____ No

28. Do you have a communication plan should an emergency arise either overseas or back at home?

_____ Yes _____ No

29. Have you made your peace and said your goodbyes to those you love in the event you don't, for any reason, return?

_____ Yes   _____ No

Part II: Cross-Cultural Skills

30. Urban living experience:

    _____ I have little or no experience living in an urban environment.

    _____ I have limited experience living in an urban environment but feel comfortable.

    _____ I have experience living in an urban environment and feel competent to do so.

    _____ I have experience and feel competent to live in any city in the world (including Beirut, Nairobi, Port Moresby, Baghdad, etc.)

31. International/developing world living experience:

    _____ I have never lived in a foreign country.

    _____ I have some experience living and traveling in foreign countries.

    _____ I have lived in a foreign country for more than a year.

    _____ I have lived in a foreign and/or third world country most of my life (e.g., as a third culture kid).

32. Language fluency:

    _____ I speak only my own language.

    _____ I have studied one or more languages but am not fluent.

    _____ I speak another language fluently.

    _____ I speak several unrelated languages fluently.

33. If you are single and are intending to go overseas, have you thought about the possibility and implications of marrying someone from another country, culture, and/or race on you, your family, your children, your in-laws, your career? What would that mean?

    _____

    _____

    _____

    _____

Part III: Security Skills

EXPERIENTIAL:

1. Self-defense:

    _____ I feel unable to protect myself from physical assault.

    _____ I feel marginally able to defend myself during a physical assault.

    _____ I feel able to protect myself.

_____ I am a martial arts adviser to commando forces.

2. Experience with crime/assault:

_____ I have never been the victim of a crime.

_____ I have survived a criminal assault, attack, or incident.

_____ I have survived several criminal assaults, attacks, or incidents.

3. Attitudes on safety (protection from accidents, hazards, mishaps, disasters):

_____ I don't think about my safety on a daily basis.

_____ I think about my safety when I feel imperiled.

_____ I think about my safety as I plan my day's activities.

_____ My safety is a concern for me, and I base my personal planning on protecting myself.

4. Attitudes on security (protection from hostile acts):

_____ I don't think of my security on a daily basis.

_____ I think about my security when I feel threatened.

_____ I think about my security as I plan my daily activities.

_____ My security is a concern for me, and I base my personal planning on it.

5. Fire safety:

_____ I do not think about fire safety.

_____ I try to remember to change the batteries in my smoke detectors.

_____ I change batteries and have thought through an escape plan for my dorm/apartment/home in the event of a fire.

_____ I think about fire safety because I have experienced a fire.

6. Attitude about police:

_____ I believe police are generally competent, honest, and trustworthy.

_____ I believe most police are basically reliable.

_____ I neither trust nor distrust police.

_____ I tend to distrust police.

_____ I think of police as basically untrustworthy, corrupt, and/or incompetent.

7. Where would you be safest in your life? Where would you live longer?

_____

_____

_____

_____

LOGISTICAL:

8. Do you have health insurance?

_____ Yes   _____ No

9. Have you checked to see if your medical insurance will cover you wherever you go overseas (e.g., declared war zone, disaster area)?

_____ Yes   _____ No

10. Do you have medical evacuation coverage?

_____ Yes   _____ No

11. Have you made a list or record of your possessions in storage?

_____ Yes   _____ No

12. What do you gain by traveling, living, and working overseas?

_____

_____

_____

_____

13. Why are you going?

_____

_____

_____

Taken from the work of Ray S. Leki, *Travel Wise: How to be Safe, Savvy and Secure Abroad* (2008).

Role Throwaway

Time Required:

50–75 minutes (10–15 for discussion of culture shock and Intensity Factors; 10–15 to identify and rank order roles; 10–15 minutes to discard roles; 20–30 minutes for discussion and debriefing)

```
Work

X–X

X, X, X, X
```

Objectives:

To help participants:

1. Identify the significant changes they may experience during a long-term sojourn.
2. Prepare for personal transformation.
3. Recognize the process of loss and transformation that can occur in long-term sojourns.

Materials:

- Ten index cards for each participant
- Handout: Intensity Factors—one per participant

Process:

1. Before beginning this exercise, participants should be aware of culture shock concepts as well as R. Michael Paige's Intensity Factors. Distribute a copy of the worksheet to each of the participants. Review the intensity factors or allow time for participants to review independently.

2. Give each participant ten index cards and the following instructions:
   As you live in another culture, you come to realize that the roles you typically play may change. Please write one important role you play in your life on each index card. When you

have completed that, please rank order the roles, with the least important one on top and the most important on the bottom.

3. When each person has completed this rank ordering, ask the participants to begin to throw away the roles, starting with the top one (the least important role). To allow for reflection, speak slowly, asking them to throw away the top card and to imagine how it would feel to give up that role. Encourage them to consider what part of that role will be most difficult to give up and what part of the role they will not miss. Proceed through the ten cards, giving a minute between each card for reflection. Be aware that some participants may not be able to proceed beyond the fourth or fifth card. Those last cards may contain roles core to the person's identity, such as wife, mother, friend, etc. Withdrawing at any stage is of course acceptable.

4. When you have asked them to throw away all ten cards, ask them to discuss with a partner in the group for ten minutes the impact they felt from this and how it related to their inter-cultural experience. Some may say it mimics a mini-death experience, since when they reach the final card, many of their most significant roles in life have vanished.

Debriefing Questions:

1. How did you feel while you were throwing away your roles?
2. What happens to your sense of yourself as you give them up one by one?
3. Have you ever had to give up important roles before?
4. Do you see any connections to your life in another country? What roles may you need to give up or modify when you move?
5. How can you recreate the role while abroad or replace it with another role?
6. How does this relate to intensity factors and culture shock?
7. Does it make a difference to know this before you experience it?
8. What can you do to make this adaptation more comfortable for yourself?

Debriefing Conclusions:

1. Your important roles in life may change when you move to another culture.

2. It is best to recognize this in advance and realize that there are ways to cope with this transition.

3. It is not uncommon to feel somewhat alienated in a new environment for a period of time.

4. Staying in touch with how the transition is affecting you can help you to respond to the loss.

5. Movement to another culture may also allow you to add roles that you enjoy as much as those you are losing.

Note to facilitators: This exercise is high-impact for those who have lived overseas as well as those who are planning to do so. Therefore, please do not take this exercise lightly. If you do not feel comfortable processing strong feelings or the context is not appropriate to do so, select an alternative activity. Facilitators should also be aware of any grief issues for participants, such as a recent death in the family, divorce, etc., which can heighten sensitivity to loss.

Optional Way to Conduct the Exercise:

Use only five cards, and give a direction to write down five activities you enjoy that you may not be able to do in another culture. This substantially lowers the risk and emotional impact.

This exercise was designed by Janet Bennett, Executive Director, Intercultural Communication Institute, Portland, OR (www.intercultural.org).

Handout: Intensity Factors

Cultural Differences

Psychological intensity is increased as the degree of cultural differences (e.g., value orientations, beliefs, attitudes, behaviors, patterns of thinking and learning, communication styles) increases between the person's own and the target culture. Moreover, the more negatively the individual evaluates those cultural differences, the more stressful the intercultural experience will be.

Ethnocentrism

Ethnocentrism is an intensity factor that expresses itself in two ways. First, ethnocentric individuals find intercultural experiences more intense. Second, some cultural communities themselves are, in general, more closed and resistant to outsiders. Sojourners in those more ethnocentric cultures will find the experience to be more intense.

Cultural Immersion

The more immersed the person is in the target culture, the greater is the amount of stress. "Culture fatigue" is a common problem among persons who are deeply immersed in another culture, i.e., people who are working and living with host culture persons, and people who are spending much of their time speaking in a language other than their own.

Cultural Isolation

Cultural isolation can be obviated to a degree by time spent with one's own culture group members. This allows for cultural reaffirmation and renewal. In some cases, however, persons can be isolated by geography and other circumstances from their own culture group. These individuals will find the experience to be more psychologically intense.

Language

The less target-environment language ability the person possesses, the greater will be the psychological intensity of the experience. Further, the more essential language ability is to functioning in the target culture, the greater will be the psychological intensity of the experience. Because language is the major mechanism by which culture groups communicate and share meaning, language is a means of entry into the culture. The ability to speak the target language is not always essential, nor does it assure effective communication or intercultural adjustment. Lack of language skills, however, can lead to social isolation and frustration.

Prior Intercultural Experience

Intensity is affected by the amount of prior, in-depth intercultural experience. The less intercultural experience the person has, the greater will be the intensity of any new intercultural experience. Those with a great deal of previous intercultural experience will generally experience less stress in the new culture because they will have developed coping strategies, be familiar with the intercultural adjustment process, be able to establish realistic expectations, and will possess intercultural communication skills to help them in the initial stages.

Expectations

The more unrealistic the person's expectations of the host culture, the greater will be the psychological intensity of the experience. Persons who have positive but unrealistic expectations will experience a psychological letdown. This leads to disappointment with the culture, with their experiences, and with their own performance.

Visibility and Invisibility

Persons who are physically different from members of the host culture are highly visible and may become the object of curiosity, which increases the psychological intensity of the experience. On the other hand, when some important aspect of the person's identity is invisible to members of the host culture (e.g., one's religion or political philosophy)—or is concealed because it is not accepted in the host culture (e.g., being lesbian or gay)—it can increase psychological intensity. Concealing something about oneself for fear it could harm one's standing or reduce one's effectiveness (or safety) can cause considerable psychological stress.

Power and Control

One of the most consistent research findings is that persons in cultures other than their own feel a loss of power and control over events and people compared to what they possessed at home. And the more power one is used to exercising, the more disturbing is the loss. Their personal efficacy is diminished, and they feel that things are "out of control." The less power and control the person has in the intercultural situation, the more psychologically stressful the experience will be.

Status

Persons who feel they are not getting the respect they deserve or, conversely, feel they are receiving unearned recognition will find the experience more psychologically intense. Qualities that are valued in the home culture may not be important in the new one and can result in a loss of status. Alternatively, being granted status on the basis of inherited characteristics (e.g., ethnicity, religion, nationality, family background, occupation) rather than personal achievements can result in discomfort.

Excerpted from Paige, R. M. (1993). "On the Nature of Intercultural Experiences and Intercultural Education." In *Education for the Intercultural Experience* , edited by R. M. Paige. Yarmouth, ME: Intercultural Press.

18

Exploring Values and Behavior

Time Required:

80 minutes (10 minutes for introduction; 20 minutes for round 1; 20 minutes for round 2; 30 minutes for debriefing)

Work

X–X

X, X, X, X

Objectives:

1. To explore participants' own cultural values and behaviors in contrast to those of the host culture (Canadian/U.S. Sample)
2. To identify specific values and/or behaviors that might challenge or confuse participants during their transition
3. To recognize differences in cultural behaviors used to exhibit similar cultural values

Materials:

- Three easels
- Chart paper and markers
- Post-its, or index cards and tape
- Attachment A: Value Cards
- Attachment B: Contrast Behavior Cards
- Attachment C: Core Values Chart (one per participant)
- Attachment D: Overview of Canadian and U.S. values and behaviors

Preparation:

*Round 1: **Contrasting Values***

- Prepare an easel for each team with a column labeled *Canada* and a column labeled *United States*.
- Prepare one set of Values Cards for each team by placing the terms from Attachment A onto Post-its or index cards.
- Prepare a Core Values Chart on the third easel for the debriefing.

*Round 2: **Contrasting Behaviors***

- Prepare one set of Contrast Behavior Cards for each team by placing the terms from Attachment B onto Post-its or index cards.

Process:

1. Take the following steps to provide an introduction to the exercise.

   - Contrast generalization vs. stereotype and note the importance of understanding both national cultural values and behaviors as well as individual differences within each national culture.

   - Point out that similar values across national cultures can result in very different behaviors used to demonstrate those values.

   - Remind participants that similar behaviors can also come from different values.

   - Remind participants of the importance of their own cultural values and behaviors and how these values impact their perception (i.e., if they see a behavior that looks familiar, they are likely to interpret it from their own value perspective, which can be totally incorrect).

   - Emphasize the importance of exploring information about what specific behaviors mean to the individual exhibiting them.

   Note: For additional information, see Appendix D: Culture and Values Narrative and Appendix E: Stereotypes and Generalizations Lecturette.

2. Divide participants into two groups.

3. *Round 1:* Values Exploration

   - Give each group a set of Values Cards and ask them to place the cards on the appropriate place on the chart. (Use tape as needed with index cards.) Caution them that if they are from that culture, they are considering national cultural generalizations and not their own individual value systems.

   - Ask participants to look at each other's charts to identify similarities and differences in the location where the groups have placed the Value Cards.

- Using the third easel, which contains the Core Value Chart, review the results with the group. During this discussion, be prepared to manage:
  - Defensiveness. This may occur if participants don't want to associate with one or more cultural values from their country. Emphasize that these are general patterns in a country and that there are always individual differences.
  - Insistence that this has not been someone's experience. Again, affirm individual differences as well as subculture differences within any country.
  - Past vs. present values. Acknowledge that culture is always changing, but also note that although mobility and technology expedites that process, core cultural values and behaviors tend to change slowly. Acknowledge the experience of those present and use the participants for reference and understanding.
  - Regional differences. These exist and should be acknowledged, again using participants as reference.

4. *Round 2:* Behavior Patterns
   - Introduce this activity by reminding participants that different values can lead to the same behaviors OR different behaviors can come from the same values. When we see someone's behavior, we cannot conclude that we know the value that is causing it. Also remind them that we are looking at patterns of behavior and not stereotypes.
   - Divide the participants into two groups. (Place participants with the original groups or give them an opportunity to work with different people.) Give each group a set of Contrasting Behavior Cards and ask them to place the behaviors on the side of the easel that is most appropriate. Because these are contrasting behaviors, placing the contrasting behaviors across from each other will make the contrast more clear.
   - Have the teams share with each other how they have placed the behaviors.

Debriefing Questions:

1. Which values were more challenging/easiest to place with a specific country? Why?
2. Which behaviors were easier/harder to place into a country column? Why?
3. What was your own reaction to this activity?

4. How do the values of your target transition country compare with those you hold personally?

5. How do the behaviors of your target transition country compare with those you are most comfortable with?

6. How does this activity inform your preparation for transition to your new country? What, specifically, might you do to prepare for this transition?

7. Distribute and discuss Attachment D.

Debriefing Conclusions:

1. There is a wide range of cultural values and associated behaviors.

2. Generalizations about cultural values can be helpful in understanding difference, but it is important not to stereotype individuals within a culture.

3. Some cultural differences in values and behaviors may cause confusion and/or challenge when viewed through the sojourner's perceptual cultural lens.

Optional Process:

1. Rounds 1 and 2 can be debriefed individually after each section, or you can do both activities and then debrief the entire process.

2. Any country of origin or target host country for transition can be used in this process. When doing so, however, it is imperative that current research resources be utilized to avoid outdated value statements and/or stereotyping.

   Note: This exercise is presented with material for two sample countries: Canada and the U.S. These countries are used specifically because some might assume that they are very similar. When we look more deeply into basic values, beliefs, and assumptions, we can see certain values and behavior differences. Without an understanding of these differences, misperceptions and ineffectiveness can result. (Or: "A lack of understanding of these differences can lead to misperceptions and ineffectiveness.")

This exercise has been adapted from the work of Don Rutherford at www.culture-connect.com.

Attachment A
Values Cards

Individualism	Group Rights	Well-Being
Control over Environment	Live in Harmony with Environment	Work-Life Balance
Politeness	Speaking the Truth	Achievement
Progress	Winner Takes All	Pragmatism
Competition	Compromise	Ideals Held High
Egalitarianism	Consensus/Cooperation	Satisfaction with What Is
Patriotism	Status Quo Preserved	More Ambiguity Accepted

Adapted from the work of Don Rutherford at www.culture-connect.com.

Attachment B
Contrast Behavior Cards

CANADA	UNITED STATES
Indirect communication style	Direct communication style
Understatement	Overstatement
The team is important	Focus is on the individual, but cooperation is expected
Professional life is a means to an end	Professional life identifies one's self
Everyone doing well is emphasized	Individual excellence is emphasized
A pragmatic solution is sought	The perfect solution is sought
The result is important, but individual dignity is considered	Focus is on the result
Cautious	Risk-takers
Humor is subtle, indirect	Humor is direct
Laugh at themselves	Expected to take self seriously

Adapted from the work of Don Rutherford at www.culture-connect.com.

Attachment C
Core Values Chart

CANADA	UNITED STATES
Pragmatism	Patriotism
Group Rights	Individualism
More Ambiguity	Status Quo
Work-Life Balance	Achievement
Cooperation	Competition
Well-Being	Progress
Egalitarianism	Winner Takes All
Harmony with the Environment	Control over Environment
Compromise	Ideals Held High
Politeness	Speak the Truth

Adapted from the work of Don Rutherford at www.culture-connect.com.

Attachment D
Key Points for Discussion

A few reasons to explore the values that underlie behaviors:

- Learning about one's personal values and those of one's own culture is the perfect starting point for studying the values of another person and his or her culture.
- There are thousands of behavior differences between cultures; in fact, there are too many for us to know. Important behaviors can be understood more clearly by examining six to twelve key underlying value differences.
- A grasp of key cultural values helps us not only to understand the salient differences between cultures, but also to predict behavior arising from a cross-cultural situation.
- Values learning can provide a lens for more effective comparisons of multiple cultures.

Exploring Values and Behaviors:

Many of the values represented in this exercise comparing Canadians with U.S. Americans make sense only in this context. For example, U.S. Americans are frequently ranked as the most individualistic people on the planet. Canadians are ranked only a bit less. So, nationals of most other countries of the world will find Canadians very individualistic. If you ask a Canadian to choose between "individual performance is not emphasized" and "individual performance is emphasized," most Canadians would choose the latter. Only in relation to U.S. Americans do Canadians seem less individualistic. Again, it is important to use this information as generalizations within context. (E.g., among Western countries, Canadians appear more indirect, but when they are compared to the citizens of most other countries, such as Asia, Canadians appear more direct.)

Adapted from the work of Don Rutherford at www.culture-connect.com.

In-Country

In-Country Training Importance and Characteristics

Joyce Osland, Executive Director, Global Leadership Advancement Center, School of Global Innovation and Leadership, College of Business, San Jose State University

There is no substitute for real experience. For that reason, in-country training is designed to help people understand and take best advantage of their international experience. It is difficult to prepare people for everything they will encounter in another country, and it is hard to predict how individuals will react to a cross-cultural experience. Many in-country training programs are based on the same principles that Steve Duke outlined in the introduction to pre-departure training in the previous section. The focus centers around the following:

- Effectively interacting with others
- Learning about the country's infrastructure, political structure, economy, and history
- Learning about cultural values, expectations, and socially acceptable behaviors
- Preparing for cultural adjustment and "culture shock"
- Safety precautions

In-country training also helps people negotiate the reality of crossing cultural boundaries and how that experience impacts them personally. Challenges can involve failed expectations when the experience does not pan out how they thought it would (e.g., "I thought I would have the same freedoms I do at home" or "I expected them to be more interested in what I can contribute"). Sometimes people need help getting beyond unexpected negative surprises, such as strong affective reactions to their treatment by locals, anxiety over not knowing how to act in certain situations, and so forth. When sojourners cannot decode what is going on or make accurate attributions about why this is occurring, they can develop a negative attitude toward their entire international experience. Thus, in-country training can have a "just-in-time" component when it responds to individuals' specific here-and-now learning and training needs.

The following characteristics of the international experience provide an overarching framework for in-country training designs and methods.

1. The potential for transformation. Cross-cultural experiences have great potential to be transformational. Many people look back on them as one of the most significant crucible experiences in their lives and can readily identify exactly how they were changed. Debriefing and reflecting upon specific experiences can lead to personal change and is often an underlying focus of in-country training. However, trainers must also bear in mind that not everyone is equally open to transforming themselves during an international experience. Sojourners generally get the adventure that they are ready for; transformation occurs when employees and students are willing and ready to be changed.

2. Dealing with paradox and duality. There are many paradoxes inherent in the cross-cultural context. Exposure to paradox is one of the characteristics of an international experience that can trigger personal transformation. Sojourners often come to realize that culture itself is paradoxical and contextual. The way people behave is much more complex than the bipolar value dimensions and communication styles that sojourners tend to be exposed to during pre-departure training. The more familiar participants become with another culture, the more likely they are to observe both poles of these dimensions and styles within a single culture. This level of complex and contingent cultural knowledge comes only with actual experience. Sojourners often come to see as valid the general stereotype of the culture they are visiting, while also realizing that many individuals do not fit that country stereotype. (For example, Indian culture is both collectivist and individualist in certain contexts.)

Seeing the wisdom of both sides in paradox and learning to resolve and live with duality can trigger personal transformation, increased cognitive complexity, and even a change in the participants' identity to include biculturalism. The development of intercultural competence, cultural intelligence, global mind-set, and global leadership results from dealing successfully with dualities. But once again there is a caveat—not everyone is equally well-equipped to perceive and grapple with paradox. Black-and-white thinkers and judgmental people who tend to be rigid may need more help from trainers in in-country programs.

3. The Three Bucket Model and Sojourner Effectiveness. Researchers have done a good job of identifying the competencies that predict sojourner effectiveness. These competencies provide a blueprint for the skill-building components of in-country training programs. The "Three Bucket Model" consists of three components: perception management, relationship management, and self-management (Bird, Mendenhall, Stevens, & Oddou, 2010).

Perception management has to do with how individuals perceive the world around them and its effects on their subsequent learning about that world. It includes

- How mentally flexible participants are when confronted with cultural differences that are strange or new,
- Their tendency to make rapid (rather than thoughtful) judgments about observed cultural differences,
- Their ability to manage perceptions when faced with situations that are not immediately easy to understand because these situations differ from expectations, and
- Their proactive curiosity toward foreign countries, cultures, and international events.

Relationship management assesses how sojourners are oriented toward developing and maintaining positive relationships with people from other cultures. It includes

- How aware they are of others around them, the differences in interaction styles, values, and so on;
- Their personal level of self-awareness and awareness of how their own behavior impacts others; and
- The degree to which they are oriented toward the development and management of interpersonal relationships in a cross-cultural environment.

Self management assesses the participants' natural and learned capabilities to maintain a healthy emotional state when faced with challenging situations. It includes

- The strength of their sense of self-identity,
- Their capacity to adapt and change within the context of a stable self-identity to remain mentally and emotional healthy in a new culture, and
- Their ability to manage their thoughts, emotions, and responses to stressful situations.

4. Facilitating cross-cultural learning. We know that people who are already good learners are more likely to be effective in international assignments because they are good at scanning and gathering information. They are also willing to "unlearn" behaviors that worked well in their native country but are not effective in their host country and elsewhere. They learn to adapt their behavior in a culturally appropriate manner. Ensuring that sojourners learn "how to learn" is another underlying goal of in-country training.

David Kolb's (1983) learning cycle is a good process model to employ given its components:

- Concrete experience (e.g., a puzzling or challenging sojourner experience);
- Reflective observation (analysis of that experience);
- Abstract conceptualization (application of theories or concepts that help explain the experience); and
- Active experimentation (testing the model or lessons learned to see if they work).

If the active experimentation is successful, then knowledge is the outcome. The reflection component of Kolb's cycle is extremely helpful because it promotes self-awareness and perspective-taking. Simply living abroad is not enough—sojourners have to convert their experience into knowledge.

Guided journals and blogs promote helpful reflection, particularly if they are structured to allow room for changing hypotheses as sojourners become more adept at decoding and understanding what they observe and feel. Study abroad research discovered that guided reflection on students' cultural experience was the most important predictor of intercultural development (Paige & Vande Berg, 2012). Cultural mentors are another valuable source of cultural information because of their willingness to answer questions and correct mistaken assumptions. Some sojourners "learn" the wrong lessons; gently correcting misattributions and errors in understanding is another contribution in-country training can make.

In summary, in-country training can help students and employees take best advantage of their international experience when it is based on a deep understanding of the nature and stresses of the cross-cultural experience, and when it is designed to facilitate personal transformation, effectiveness, and learning.

19

Neighborhood Mapping

Time Required:

30-minute introduction, followed by 10–15 minutes a day over the first 2–3 months

Objectives:

For participants to:

1. Become increasingly familiar with their new home, with the region around it, with the people who populate it, and with the geographic relationships between the different locations of their daily lives (home, schools, shops, office, friends, etc.).

2. Mitigate fear of the unknown by making it known, and by heightening the attention they pay to the details around them.

Materials:

- A large surface for drawing and writing (the larger the better; the ideal is butcher paper on a wall, to which additional sheets can be added in all directions)
- Marking pens in an array of colors
- Masking tape
- Pushpins
- Index cards
- Post-it notes
- Colored yarn

Process:

Note to facilitator: This map can be placed anywhere that is readily accessible to the family on a regular basis, including the family home.

1. Begin with the Reflection Activity. Ask participants to reflect on the following statements.

   - It is human nature to fear what we don't understand or what is unfamiliar to us. We can be particularly fearful when we find ourselves in an unfamiliar country or city, surrounded by people whose culture we don't understand and whose language we don't speak. From these kinds of circumstances comes the classic experience of culture shock.

   - The best way to combat culture shock is through culture learning. This activity is designed to help family members learn about the neighborhood around them, starting with the first level of roads and buildings and shops.

2. Build the map. Give participants the following instructions.

   - Start by placing your home (or hotel, if that's where you're first living) in the center of the map.

   - As a family at the end of each day, start drawing out from there—what have family members noticed about surrounding roads, nearby buildings, shops they frequent, friends they visit?

   - Make leaps if you know someplace on the far side of town but you don't know what's in-between; leave blanks where you're missing information, and venture forth the next day to see what you can notice to fill in next.

   - Begin to map not only the roads and buildings but also the "regulars"—which people do you see in the same places every day? What are they doing? (Be as purely descriptive as you can.) What is their positive intent?

   - Use the additional supplies (tape, pushpins, cards, Post-it notes) to layer stories onto your map. For instance, what intercultural adventure did you have at that intersection, in that shop, with that person? What new insight did you gain about yourself or your neighborhood? Use the yarn to make connections between events. Let your map become a living collage of your family's daily lived experience, and of your family's culture learning.

3. Encourage participants to challenge themselves as they discuss their experiences and build the map. Prompt them to do the following:

   - Notice when you are
     - Just describing what you are seeing (the objective facts: there's a shop on the corner that sells food);

- Actually interpreting what you are seeing (the supposed meaning: it must be for the locals only, there are too many flies for expats); and
- Even evaluating what you're seeing (the assessment of good/bad: it's disgusting; I could never eat there).
- When family members fall first into interpretation or evaluation (which is very normal), stop and find the objective language to simply describe what they saw or what happened. Only then start to discuss possible interpretations—and when the family is looking for the meaning, they should be sure to look for the positive intent. For the most part, in 99 times out of 100, people are motivated by positive, values-based intentions.

Debriefing Questions:

1. What have we learned about the neighborhood that surrounds us?
2. What difference does it make to us to have learned these things?
3. What is happening to our sense of belonging in this neighborhood?

Debriefing Conclusions:

1. Belonging, a quality of experience we all need, comes from being familiar *with* the world around us and from being familiar *to* the world around us.
2. An important way to start to feel a sense of belonging when you've moved to a new city or country is to get to know it and to start becoming known by it: get up, get out, and pay attention.

Optional Process:

- Instead of making one big map, participants can make several maps with a different central starting point for each: home, school, office. As the maps develop and expand, they can add paper to the wall so that the separate maps start to connect into one.
- Rather than engaging in this activity as a family, it is possible to engage it as students in a classroom. In that instance, the incoming students generate the map and the questions, with

the continuing students serving as cultural informants. A key role of the teacher when providing cultural information is to focus students on objective descriptions (during the mapping process) and interpretations based on positive intent.

20

Getting Involved: The Second Ninety Days

Time Required:

> 40–50 minutes (5 minutes for introduction; 10 minutes to review objectives; 15–20 minutes for activity; 10–15 minutes for debriefing)

Work
X–X
X, X, X, X

Objectives:

1. Describe a balanced life in the new location; focus on mind, body and spirit.
2. Encourage participants to become involved outside of their familiar community and culture.
3. Explore ways to maximize personal overseas experience.
4. Encourage participants to expand their circle of acquaintances and friends beyond their professional setting.
5. Encourage participants to stretch outside of their comfort zone.

Materials:

- A pen or pencil
- Chart or PowerPoint slide highlighting the relationship between the mind, body, and spirit (interconnected circles)
- Worksheet: The Second 90 Days

Process:

1. For the introduction, explain to the participants that this activity calls attention to the importance of finding personal balance (mind, body, spirit) in the new expatriate life. (Illustrate with the chart.) Expected outcomes are (1) personal growth, (2) improved health and wellness, and (3) increased

social involvement, all while balancing life outside of work. Use language such as the following:

The initial few months are a busy time spent getting established in the new country. Activities include meeting residency requirements, education and family responsibilities, work orientation, finding and settling into a new home, and so forth. Frequently there is a tendency to work "too much." Long hours at work can result in the expatriate assignment not being that much different than the previous life left in the home country. The second ninety days can serve as a great time to start getting involved outside of the expatriate community.

Being an expatriate is an adventure in itself! Getting involved in the host culture allows for new experiences, friendships, and opportunities, thus making the overseas experience as fulfilling and balanced as possible.

Key points to use in continuing the introduction:

   a. Discuss why this activity is designed for the second ninety days.

   b. Answer any questions surrounding the timing and explain that the second ninety-day timeline is flexible given other demands (work, home, family, etc.)

   c. Explain the mind, body, and spirit connection and how it is very important to maintain a focus on this connection, especially during a major transition such as a move abroad.

   d. Gain commitment from the participants about their desire to become involved, meet other people, expand their social network, and have FUN!

2. Distribute the worksheet with the three columns: Mind, Body, and Spirit. Define each section and give participants the following prompts:

   - **Mind.** Think of things that you enjoy doing or have always wanted to do. Now is the perfect time to seek out a new club, activity, and/or other opportunity. Examples include Toastmasters, public speaking, lectures, educational pursuits, personal development, writing, volunteer efforts, etc.

   - **Body.** Your health and wellness are very important. What local activities can you participate in that will enhance your level of physical fitness? Are there any teams, groups, or competitive events you can join? Examples include swim clubs, gym, Pilates, running, bicycling club, diving, skiing, snowboarding, etc.

- **Spirit.** Complete the triad with spiritual balance. What method of honoring your spiritual side will bring you satisfaction? Please consider all. Examples include religious community, meditation groups, yoga, etc.

Have each participant spend approximately ten minutes brainstorming and listing ideas under each heading. Ideally these will be activities and events that they have never done before. Or, they can be continuing with activities from home such as yoga, going to the gym, attending a spiritual service, or joining a club. (The goal is to create a robust list with no limits.)

3. Now pair the participants and have them exchange worksheets:

—Partner A will read the entries from each column of Partner B's sheet. (Hearing our ideas read aloud allows us to notice how we feel when they are read back to us. This also gives Partner B time to add anything that may have been missed.) Partner B then selects one or two top choices in each column and asks A to circle them.

—Repeat the process. Partner B will now read the entries from each column of Partner A's sheet to Partner A. Partner A selects two or three top choices in each column and asks Partner B to circle them.

4. Once this exercise is complete, the worksheets are returned to the authors with the top choices circled.

5. Prompt participants to make decisions: "You have top picks for your Mind, Body, and Spirit activities. Of these top choices, now select the one in each column that excites you the most. Put a star next to that one. This will become your preferred first-choice activity."

6. Ask participants to use the reverse side of the worksheet to list any places, organizations, groups, or events that will allow them to begin getting involved in their top choices. (E.g., embassies, local expatriate publications, fitness clubs, churches, community organizations, online bulletin boards, universities, and expatriate classified websites such as: www.justlanded.com, www.expatexchange.com, etc.)

Debriefing Questions:

1. As you review your worksheet, what stands out for you?
2. Are there any ideas or activities listed that you have wanted to participate in for some time?
3. How did you feel when you heard your ideas read out loud?

4. How is balance created by combining the elements of body, mind, and spirit?

5. Who might be able to help you make contacts with the resources you have identified?

6. How will taking this action impact you and enhance your relationships at work and home?

7. Are you committed to getting involved and making your next ninety days an exciting and fun adventure?

8. If you have had prior expat experience, how might this exercise have changed those experiences? What lessons would you share from those experiences?

Debriefing Conclusions:

1. Balance is important.

2. A new international assignment is the perfect time to redefine ourselves in the safety of a new location.

3. Changing locations naturally shifts our perspective and can result in the discovery of new aspects of ourselves.

4. Getting involved can improve the expatriate's performance skills and assignment enjoyment, thus creating a memorable overseas adventure.

Optional Process:

This can also be done as an individual activity. The person doing this individually may wish to find someone to provide listening and feedback.

This exercise was contributed by Scott Masciarelli, ACC, BCC, at www.clearinsightscoaching.com.

Worksheet: The Second 90 Days

MIND	BODY	SPIRIT

Contributed by Scott Masciarelli, ACC, BCC, at www.clearinsightscoaching.com.

21

Organizing the World

Time Required:

30–35 minutes (10 minutes for activity; 10–15 minutes for debriefing questions; 10 minutes for lecturette and discussion)

Objectives:

1. To explore the influence of values and priorities on an organization
2. To experience organizational strategies from varied perspectives
3. To discuss how and why a "known" situation can cause confusion

Materials:

Prepare a set of four *handwritten* cards for each group as follows:

CARD 1

Write:

> Letter A on upper-left corner
>
> Number 2 on lower-right corner
>
> Text: In the fall, we see the leaves change colors. We enjoy warm meals.

CARD 2

Write:

> Letter B on upper-left corner
>
> Number 3 on lower-right corner
>
> Text: In the spring, we see everything turn green. We enjoy walks in the park.

CARD 3

Write:

> Letter C on upper-left corner

Number 4 on lower-right corner

Text: In the summer, we enjoy having picnics in the park.

CARD 4

Write:

Letter D on upper-left corner

No number on lower-right corner

Text: In the winter, we bake cakes.

Process:

1. Ask participants to form groups of four or five.

2. Give these instructions: "Have you noticed in your daily life how things can be organized differently? Each group is going to receive a set of four cards that need to be organized. You will have approximately two or three minutes to organize the cards. Once you receive the cards, I cannot answer any questions."

3. Distribute the set of four cards to each group.

4. Allow time for each group to organize their set.

Debriefing Questions:

You may have noticed while living in a new culture or working with a person from a different culture that things are organized differently. For example, a person may organize a stack of office documents by date, by the action to be taken, by hierarchy of the person who is signing or giving the instructions, etc.

In this exercise, we have been exploring the different ways in which we can organize our world. It is interesting to note the way we set our priorities. How we decide what is most relevant or important can be very different from what others think or do. This is true, even when we think our way is "obvious" to everyone.

1. How did your group come to a solution for organizing the cards? Were there different opinions? A group leader? Consensus? If there was a group leader, why did you agree to follow him or her?

2. What things were considered in the organization process? What motivated the process of selection? Importance? Relevance? Context?

3. Did the fact that the cards were handwritten influence your perception of this exercise? As simple? Personal?

Unprofessional? Is "simple" good or bad? Or was the hand-written factor irrelevant (high-context and low-context communication)?

4. How did your group arrange the cards? A line? Square? Circle? Other?

Lecturette:

After listening to the various motivations and how the groups came up with a solution, it is important to share with them how other people have sorted the cards and what logic they cited. Use language such as the following.

1. Cards were organized by the letter on the top, putting aside the content and giving more importance to alphabetical order (categorizing, structure, filing).

2. Cards were organized by number, but there was a number missing. Did your group notice the missing number? For some people, it is very difficult to continue with the exercise knowing that there is a missing number because they feel they don't have all the elements (avoidance of risk, avoidance of ambiguity, decision that to follow the numerical order is more important than the text and context).

3. Cards were organized by seasons, but a decision had to be made about which season will come first. Possibilities include: The one that the individual likes the most (emotional). The one that we currently are in (fact). The coming season (future-oriented). The one that coincides with January (calendar)—and if so, does it depend on which hemisphere the individual is thinking about?

4. Cards were organized by the activities and how much they enjoyed them.

5. Cards were organized considering the number of lines in the sentences, and if so ascendant or descendant (detail-oriented).

Debriefing Conclusions:

1. Given the same object or circumstances, we can perceive differently, organize differently, and even conclude differently according to personal values and priorities.

2. Our brain can lead us to perceive that we are in a "known situation" because *some* elements of the situation are familiar. We can then experience frustration when we are unable to figure

out why the situation resulted in a different outcome than the one we had in mind.

3. Based on our cultural background and education, we can have a preference or tendency to look for sequences, for lineal or logic order. Frequently we can be surprised by how much sense another way of organizing makes in a different context.

Optional Process:

Start by asking participants to name some of the things that they have noticed from the new place. In particular, which things have confused them or have been done in a different way or order?

Then proceed with the exercise. Following the exercise, ask them to return to the things they have noticed and ask how they might reinterpret their observations—or how they might identify an interpretation from the local perspective.

This exercise was developed by Ximena Reyes, international consultant and trainer at linkedin.com/in/xareyes.

Who Am I? Echoes of Culture

Time Required:

60 minutes (5 minutes for introduction; 15 minutes for each of the three discussions; 10 minutes for debriefing)

<table>
<tr><td>Work</td></tr>
<tr><td>X–X</td></tr>
<tr><td>X, X, X, X</td></tr>
</table>

Objectives:

1. To help participants understand how identity is shaped and reinforced by the cultural discourse that has been internalized.

2. To help participants understand and accept how culture shapes us as individuals and distinguishes us when we find ourselves in new cultural circumstances.

3. To encourage participants to listen for the cultural discourse that has shaped and continues to shape the people in the new culture and environment where they find themselves.

Materials:

- PowerPoint slides or flipcharts stating the objectives of the exercise and providing question sets for discussion of each stage of the activity

- Notepaper and pens or pencils for the participants

Process:

1. Present a lecturette that calls the participants' attention to the fact that they are always talking to themselves and that this inner conversation is the voice of culture and their interaction with it. Explain that the group is going to explore this self-talk in terms of how it contributes to personal and cultural identity.

   Provide an overview of the activity—We will be reflecting and discussing three sets of questions: one regarding our names, one regarding the stories that have been important to us, and one about the sports or games we have engaged in. Share this quote:

"The stories people tell have a way of taking care of them. If stories come to you, care for them. And, learn to give them away where they are needed. Sometimes a person needs a story more than food to stay alive. That is why we put these stories in each other's memory. This is how people care for themselves." —Barry Lopez, *Crow and Weasel*

2. Engage participants to personally reflect on the first question set about "naming" (see Discussion I below) for a few minutes, encouraging them to make notes should they like to do so. Model some examples of your own name, which will also model comfort with sharing.

3. When the moments of personal reflection are over, ask participants to form in small groups of three or four persons to discuss the first question set.

4. Repeat steps 3 and 4 using Discussion Questions II and III below.

   a. Discussion I: You Are Naming Me What?
      - How did you get your name(s)?
      - What do they mean?
      - What did they mean to those who gave them to you?
      - What nicknames do you have? How did you get them? Why?
      - What personal/cultural impact do these names have on you?

   b. Discussion II: Stories and Songs
      - As a young child, what stories were you told? What songs were sung?
      - What do you remember about them?
      - What did they tell you about how you are and how you should be?

   c. Discussion III: Play and Sports
      - What games did you play growing up?
      - What messages about life did they teach you?
      - What was the personal, gender, and/or cultural impact of those games on you?

Debriefing Questions:

1. What aha moments, discoveries, pain, or pleasure did you experience in the process?

2. How might you use such reflection and discussion to explore how cultural discourse builds as well as challenges your identity in other ways, in your past history? How might this be different and perhaps challenging in your present environment, particularly if you have or work with children in their early formative years?

Debriefing Conclusions:

1. The stories we are told, the songs we listen to, and the sports we play, or watch, all impact our identity. Awareness of this can help us understand our reactions when we are in new settings.

2. Understanding the stories, songs, and games of the new culture in which we find ourselves can help us understand the attitudes and behaviors of people in this new culture.

This exercise was developed by George F. Simons, Founder and Editor in Chief at diversophy.com.

Transition Cube

Time Required:

45 minutes (15 minutes for exercise; 10 minutes to share; 10 minutes for journal or drawing exercise; and 10 minutes for debriefing)

Work
X–X
X, X, X, X

Objectives:

1. To help participants recognize the challenges and efforts involved in relocation
2. To help participants develop appreciation for accomplishments achieved through the relocation process
3. To encourage the sharing of stories and expression of feelings
4. To heighten participants' awareness of personal strengths and attributes
5. To build a sense of community through shared stories

Materials:

- LEGOs or colored building blocks
- Paper
- Pens or colored markers to create their unique timeline
- Sample story (either the one provided here or one from a previous class if permission has been granted to share it)
- Optional: Computer access for Excel printout (see sample story)

Activity:

1. Discuss the various relocations the participants have experienced.
2. Brainstorm a list of challenges and changes encountered during the relocation process.

3. Read a story provided by a previous participant (see sample story) and note how the chart illustrates the student's total expat experience to date by listing all of the places the student has lived, matching the colors to the student's own constructed "transition cube."

4. Ask participants to "construct" the transitions they have experienced by building a "transition cube" using LEGOs or colored building blocks to symbolize their moves and years "in-country."

5. Encourage participants to think of unique situations or experiences they have had during their various transitions.

6. Ask participants to share their LEGO transition cube/time line with another person or in a small group.

7. If stories were shared in pairs, ask the partners to share with the group an interesting thing they learned from hearing their partner's story.

Debriefing Questions:

1. When we look at the cubes of the entire group, what similarities and differences do we see? What are the causes for similarities (e.g., parents were both in military or worked for the same corporation, etc.)?

2. If you found differences between you and a classmate, what was your first reaction?

3. How did you feel during the rounds of introductions about your LEGO transition cube?

4. What cultural misperceptions could happen during the act of explaining our LEGO transition cubes?

Debriefing Conclusions:

1. Expatriates develop personal strengths and attributes by navigating the challenges and solving the problems involved in relocation.

2. It is important to reflect on the transition experience to develop an appreciation for accomplishments achieved.

3. There are many cultural ways of introducing ourselves, and they have implications for how we perceive each other and communicate thereafter. Even when speaking the same language and using the same situations, individuals can interpret the meaning of a situation very differently.

4. Sharing stories and expressing feelings about transition can normalize the feelings and build a sense of community through shared stories.

Additional Information:

- This activity is great for starting discussions with any age group.
- This is a fun activity to do with adults since they seldom get to play.
- This activity is especially effective when used with international students of any age for introductions and building a sense of community.
- Boys can sometimes be reluctant to talk about their experience. This activity, with a building component, can engage them and encourage them to talk and/or write about their transitions.

Optional Processes:

- Participants can do this activity alone or families can do it together, comparing the relative transitions each member of the family has made and sharing what they have learned from each transitional move.
- Include written creativity by having participants write about their total transition experience or an especially interesting, challenging, funny, meaningful, etc. aspect of a particular transition. Poems or drawings can be included as part of this process.
- Create the list of participant's countries of residence in Excel and generate a colored chart to illustrate the total of transitional experiences. This printed chart (see sample) can then be framed as an integrated representation of the individual's transition experience.

This exercise was developed by Julia Simens, M.A. Clinical Psychology, author of *Emotional Resilience and the Expat Child* (2011), at www.jsimens.com.

Sample Story: *Who I Am Story*

I was born in Australia and lived there three years.

I spent a very short time in the U.S. prior to going back abroad.

Then I spent five years in Jakarta and moved up to Duri, Indonesia, for two more years.

I lived in Lagos, Nigeria, for three years and then moved to a boarding school in Switzerland when the school at Lagos didn't have my age group.

I graduated from Leysin American School after living three years in Switzerland.

I then moved to Colorado. I have lived four years in Colorado.

I am a cross-cultural kid in college.

My life—Twenty-One years of transitions

Australia 14%

California 5%

Colorado 19%

Switzerland 14%

Lagos 14%

Duri 10%

Jakarta 24%

Developed by Julia Simens, M.A. Clinical Psychology, author of *Emotional Resilience and the Expat Child* (2011), at www.jsimens.com.

Becoming a Global Citizen

Time Required:

60–75 minutes (5 minutes for introduction; 15–20 minutes for scenarios; 10 minutes for journaling intro; 20–25 minutes for personalizing journals; 10–15 minutes for debriefing)

```
Work
X–X
X, X, X, X
```

Objectives:

1. To enrich the travelers' understanding of self in a global context.
2. To help them experience the possibility of alternative responses/choices.
3. To offer insight into developing and practicing cultural competencies.
4. To engage expatriates in a reflective journaling process.

Materials:

- Chart paper and markers (or ability to project key points)
- Individual personal journals
- Magazines, newspapers, photographs
- Stamps, yarn, glitter
- Scissors and glue
- Markers, pens, and pencils

Process:

1. Define global citizen:

   According to Ron Israel, Executive Director of The Global Citizens Initiative, "A global citizen is someone who identifies with being a part of an emerging world community and whose actions contribute to building this community's values and practices."

We are living in a highly interconnected world. The ease of travel, the immediacy of personal and electronic communication, and the increased opportunity to meet individuals from "foreign" countries has heightened our awareness to a global perspective. Yet, an immersion into a new and unfamiliar culture can totally disrupt our life.

2. Share the following scenarios (or use scenarios specific to the host culture). Ask students to reflect on this question as they read or listen: What is really happening here?

   • While Susan is shopping for fruits and vegetables at the local market of a small town in Mexico, her conversation with the grocer is interrupted several times as local shoppers engage the owner in greetings and various other conversations. Also, the children from the neighborhood run in and out, interrupting everything. Susan had hoped this trip to the market would take fifteen to twenty minutes, but it has now been an hour and she still does not have everything on her list.

     What might Susan be feeling? Thinking?

     How might the market owner's behavior be explained?

     How might he experience Susan's desire for speedy service?

     Describe any cultural differences that might be at play in this scenario. How could these differences influence future interactions? (*Polychronic vs. Monochronic Time, Task vs. Relationship, etc.*)

   • While living in Indonesia, Robert feels he is losing contact with what is happening in the rest of the world. He makes a weekly visit to the local newspaper stand where he usually buys a monthly news magazine and any newspapers available in English. Robert has developed a friendly relationship with the owner, and after several weeks he asks if it is possible for the owner to stock his favorite magazine from "back home." The owner assures Robert he would be happy to stock this magazine. Robert heads home feeling proud that he was able to express his need and is excitedly anticipating the arrival of his favorite magazine. After a month, the magazine has not arrived. When Robert asks the owner about it, he is told, "Do not worry; it will come." After repeating this conversation several times over the next several months, the magazine did not arrive.

     What might Robert be feeling? Thinking?

     How might the owner be feeling? Thinking?

Describe any cultural differences that might be at play in this scenario. *(Direct vs. Indirect Communication, cultural obligation to provide a positive response, relationship orientation, etc.)*

- While working as a manager in the Middle East, Sam asked Hussain to help him by speaking to the local custom's officer and negotiating the release of important materials needed for production. Hussain assures Sam he will try to do as requested. After several weeks, Sam finds out Hussain has not spoken to anyone and the material has not been released.

    What might Sam be thinking or feeling?

    How might Hussain's behavior be explained?

    What cultural differences might be at play in this scenario? How might this situation unfold? Positive outcome? Negative outcome? *(Cultural obligation to provide a positive response, Direct vs. Indirect Communication, Hierarchy, etc.)*

3. Explain to participants that the abstraction of difference in cultural values and beliefs, when explored in a scholarly manner, can be understood intellectually. The actual cultural adjustment comes when we encounter these differences in day-to-day behavior. Although in each of these scenarios, both parties have positive intentions, the misunderstanding resulting from differences in cultural behavior can have a negative impact. Each of these situations could easily become a source of confusion, anger, and deep misunderstanding.

    Emphasize that the actual process of intercultural learning requires reflection, a look inward, to become more culturally self-aware, while gathering information from the other culture's point of view. The desired end result, from a global perspective, is to develop an understanding and the ability to function more effectively and comfortably within both cultures.

4. Tell students that intentionally creating a time and place to record cultural encounters can add to the richness of developing a global life. (Share the following on a screen or chart.)

    The benefits a journal can provide include the following:

    - A record and a reference of your cultural learning and development.
    - An outlet for your emotions as you go through cultural adjustments; benefits can include reduced stress and potential health impacts.

- An opportunity to reflect on your choices/behaviors in relation to specific situations.
- A location to store questions about your observations and/or cultural misunderstandings.
- A resource for developing cultural insight.

5. Ask participants:
   - What has been your prior experience with journaling? Benefits of journaling? Some challenges of journaling?
   - What can interfere with keeping an ongoing journal (e.g., lack of time, boredom with content or structure, uncertainty about what to write, concern about confidentiality, etc.)?
   - What are some suggestions for keeping the journaling experience meaningful, relevant, and interesting?

   Chart response from the group. These may include:
   - Writing about specific events observed during the day
   - Describing a situation that caused conflict or confusion
   - Asking specific cultural questions about practices and values
   - Expressing emotions in a private place
   - Exploring alternative choices for a situation or challenge
   - Writing for a specified amount of time (e.g., five minutes) in a free-flowing, stream-of-consciousness, no-edit format and seeing what emerges

6. Distribute journals. Encourage participants to use art materials to personalize their journals and then to write an initial entry relating their expatriate experience to their vision of becoming a "global citizen."

Debriefing Questions:

1. How do you feel about this definition of a global citizen? About the importance or possibility of such a concept? About your process in becoming a global citizen?

2. What did you observe when we began discussing the different scenarios? Hearing about the possible meanings and alternate interpretations of behaviors? The concept of day-to-day impact of difference?

3. What did you think when the topic of journaling was introduced? How might your past journaling experience influence your perspective (pros and cons)?

4. What are some ways this journaling activity could be useful to you during your time abroad? In your future?

Debriefing Conclusions:

1. Having a concept of a global citizen can enhance the development of a global self.
2. It is important to generate alternative choices and responses to difficult and/or conflicting and confusing experiences.
3. Cultural competencies can be developed and insights gained through reflection on the journaling process.
4. The journaling process promotes reflection on cultural learning and the total expatriate growth experience.

Optional Process:

For coaches, study abroad sponsors, school counselors, and those continuing to work with families in transition, an ongoing involvement can be facilitated by:

*   Generating weekly or monthly journaling topics
*   Building in an evaluative piece attached to ongoing journaling
*   Monitoring all journals on a monthly basis
*   Requiring participants to submit an independent monthly journaling submission such as:
    *   An aha experience
    *   A cultural question
    *   Suggestions for three alternative behaviors to an experience that did not go well

This activity has been adapted from the work of Ray S. Leki, *Travel Wise: How to Be Safe, Savvy and Secure Abroad* (2008).

Picturing Success

Time Required:

90–120 minutes (10 minutes for lecturette; 20–30 minutes for assessment; 10 minutes for introduction of activity; 25–35 minutes for activity; 25–35 minutes for debriefing)

<table>
<tr><td>**Work**</td></tr>
<tr><td>X–X</td></tr>
<tr><td>X, X, X, X</td></tr>
</table>

Objectives:

1. To enrich participants' understanding of the Cultural Orientations Framework (COF)
2. To help participants experience flexibility in deductive and inductive thinking
3. To engage participants in intuitive processing using visual stimulus
4. To offer participants insight into leveraging cultural preferences to enhance change

Materials:

- Appendix C: Cultural Orientations Framework
- Large number of diverse postcards (at least six per participant to allow for choice); if postcards are not available, then a large number of magazines or photographs could also be used
- Paper and pencils or pens

Process:

1. Initiate a general discussion about culture orientation using the lecturette in Appendix C.
2. Ask participants to reflect on their current team or organizational culture:
   - What are the characteristics of your current team/organizational culture?

- What is one aspect of that culture that enables you to accomplish your goals?
- What is one aspect of that culture that interferes with your ability to be fully or easily successful in accomplishing your goals?

3. Display a wide variety of postcards on a table.

4. Advise participants that in a minute they will go to the table and pick up three postcards. They will select one postcard to represent each of the three previous questions. When making their selection, they should allow the postcards to "call out to them," rather than choosing postcards that reinforce their preconceived ideas. Proceed to the table and select cards.

5. Now ask participants to return to the original discussion about culture, look at the image on the postcard, and explore it deeply. Advise participants that they should not be satisfied with just their first insight. Note that this intuitive method invites the heart to speak, not just the head. Remind participants that creativity usually requires time for associations to emerge. Provide access to paper and pen so participants can jot down personal insights.

6. After a few minutes, ask:
- How might card 1 relate to the characteristics of your team/organization culture?
- How could card 2 relate to aspects of the culture that enables you and/or supports your accomplishments?
- Looking at the third card, how might it relate to aspects of the culture that hinder your progress or sense of accomplishment?

Debriefing Questions:

1. What did you think when the concepts of the Cultural Orientations Framework were discussed? Were there any surprises? Aha moments? Was there anything you suddenly remembered or thought about in relation to your team or organizational concerns?

2. Do you generally rely on deductive or inductive thinking? How did you feel when the activity was described? What are your feelings about this inductive (intuitive) activity?

3. What happened when you went to select your postcards? Began to explore the pictures? Completed the exercise?

4. Why might this concept be important when applied to team or organizational change? How could you use this activity or something similar in the future?

Debriefing Conclusions:

1. An understanding of the Cultural Orientations Framework provides insight into personal and cultural bias.
2. Flexibility in between deductive and inductive thinking broadens our range of possibilities.
3. Knowledge of Cultural Orientations paired with an intuitive process opens the door to a broad range of possibilities for team/organizational enhancement.

Optional Process:

Participants can be asked to "pair and share" insights. It is also possible to bring participants together in small groups for discussion of insights. Framing how you will be using the insights prior to the actual activity may help participants decide how deeply they will go into the process. A group activity specific to personal, intuitive insights can be high-risk unless there is a deep level of trust among participants. Asking for volunteers from the large group could allow for shared knowledge while still allowing individuals privacy with their insights.

This activity was adapted from the work of Philippe Rosinski, *Coaching Across Cultures* (2003). Also see www.GlobalCoaching.pro and www.philrosinski.com.

Dialogues: What Just Happened?

Time Required:

40 minutes (5 minutes for introduction; 15 minutes for participants to read and discuss case studies; 20 minutes for debriefing)

Work

X–X

X, X, X, X

Objectives:

1. To illustrate how cultural differences can lead to misunderstandings and/or misinterpretations
2. To illustrate some possible consequences of cultural misunderstandings

Materials:

- Handout: Dialogues: What Just Happened? (one for each participant)
- Place dialogues in a PowerPoint slide presentation if possible.
- The handout used in this exercise is followed by a guide for the facilitator. Be sure to review the guide before starting the exercise.

Process:

1. Explain that the group is going to look at ("overhear") five conversations from the workplace. In each conversation, the speakers are from two different cultures, and because of differences between their two cultures, they misinterpret or fail to understand each other.
2. Give each participant a handout. Place participants in pairs or triads and have them read the five conversations together to try to find the cultural misunderstanding or identify the cultural difference.

Debriefing Questions:

1. How did you feel as you were reading and trying to identify the misunderstandings in the conversations? Was this easy? Difficult?

2. Were there any surprises or aha moments during your discussions?

3. Were the speakers in these conversations aware of these misunderstandings? What implications might that have for the organization? For their relationship?

4. Were any of these misunderstandings deliberate?

5. In each of these examples, who is responsible for the misunderstanding and/or misinterpretation?

6. What might be the result if these misunderstandings happen frequently between two people who work together on a regular basis?

7. How might these misunderstandings be prevented—or at least minimized?

Debriefing Conclusions:

1. Understanding that there are cultural differences (even without knowing exactly what the difference might be) means individuals can step back when confused and say to themselves: *There must be something about that conversation I didn't understand.* Questioning conclusions, rather than rushing to judgment, means there is hope for successful interactions.

2. Many misunderstandings are "innocent" or legitimate misunderstandings—where neither party is aware of or trying to misunderstand or mislead the other. When expats are aware that other people are not trying to mislead them and that they are not trying to misinterpret or mislead others, there are fewer incidents involving blame, recrimination, and hard feelings.

Optional Process:

Use the activity framework with your own culture-specific dialogues related to participants or have participants share their own.

This activity was developed by Craig Storti, Director, Communication Across Cultures, at www.craigstorti.com.

Handout: Dialogues: What Just Happened?

Read the following short conversations and see if you can identify where there was a cultural misunderstanding and/or describe a cultural difference between the two speakers.

1. Completion Date

CARL:	Well, I think that's everything, Indira. Thanks for staying late over there.
INDIRA:	You're welcome. I was just wondering, before you go, about the completion date on that accounting test.
CARL:	Sure. I think that was in an e-mail I sent you. Let me check my sent mail.
INDIRA:	I believe you mentioned the end of May.
CARL:	Here it is. Right: the end of May.
INDIRA:	I see. That's still good for you, I guess?
CARL:	Yes. It's fine.
INDIRA:	Anyway, we'll have updates every week, right?
CARL:	If you'd like.
INDIRA:	That might be a good idea.

2. Resolution

TOM:	How's everything going with the _____ problem?
RODRIGO:	We've tried everything we can think of.
TOM:	So you need a bit more time, then?
RODRIGO:	More time?
TOM:	To resolve the issue.
RODRIGO:	Not really.

3. Mutual Understanding

MS. SMITH:	Mr. Li. I just got your e-mail.
MR. LI:	Great.
MS. SMITH:	But I had a question. In the conference call this morning, you said it would only take your team a week to do those enhancements.,
MR. LI:	Sure. You mentioned, I believe, that it would be great if we could do them in one week.
MS. SMITH:	Right.
MR. LI:	(silence)
MS. SMITH:	But your e-mail says it's going to take two weeks?
MR. LI:	Oh yes. I just wanted to be sure we understood each other.

4. Backlog

MS. LUKACS: Did you hear? We won't be getting a new staff person after all.

MR. JONES: I know; so much for getting rid of our backlog.

MS. LUKACS: Well, we can resubmit the request next summer.

MR. JONES: Actually, I've got a better idea. I've heard about some new accounting software that would make our workload a lot easier.

MS. LUKACS: Has it been tried in organizations like ours?

MR. JONES: In North America. I don't know about here. We could probably get it free if we asked.

MS. LUKACS: And then train everyone in it?

MR. JONES: Right.

5. Writing a Report

MRS. COLSON: How is the evaluation going, Abdallah?

ABDALLAH: It's finished, ma'am. We can start on the report any time now.

MRS. COLSON: Good. How long do you think it will take?

ABDALLAH: Ma'am?

MRS. COLSON: To write the report.

ABDALLAH: I couldn't say, ma'am.

MRS. COLSON: You don't know how long it will take?

ABDALLAH: When would you like it, ma'am?

MRS. COLSON: Well, I want to give you enough time to do a good job.

ABDALLAH: We'll do a good job, ma'am.

Activity developed by Craig Storti, Director, Communication Across Cultures, at www.craigstorti.com.

Debriefing Notes for the Facilitator:

1. Completion Date

This dialogue illustrates how a subordinate (Indira) in an indirect, hierarchy-sensitive culture might tell a manager (Carl) that she is getting behind on something and needs more time. It also shows how the manager from a more direct, less hierarchy-sensitive culture might completely miss the message. Indira "tells" Carl four times that she is not comfortable with the timeline/due date:

- When she says "I was just wondering," she is bringing up for discussion something that was previously decided. This is a nice way in some cultures to say, "We need to discuss this again." But in Carl's culture "I was just wondering" is interpreted as "Indira must have forgotten what we agreed to," so Carl goes looking through his e-mails.
- Then Indira says, "I believe you mentioned the end of May," which is her way of saying, "I know *what* the date is (so you can stop looking through your e-mails). I'm just going to have trouble meeting that date." And it's Carl's move now to offer her more time.
- Then Indira asks Carl a rhetorical question: "That's still good for you, I guess?" This *could* be a question—it certainly would be in Carl's culture—but it could also be Indira's polite way of saying that the date is not good for her. (Of course it's good for Carl; it's *his* date!)
- Finally when Indira says, "We'll have updates every week, right?" she's indicating she'll remind Carl every week that she needs more time, and one of these weeks he'll get it!

In debriefing this dialogue, be sure to point out that neither Carl nor Indira realized this misunderstanding was taking place, and of course neither of them wanted this misunderstanding to happen. And then point out that you can't blame either of them for this; Carl was not trying to misinterpret Indira, and Indira was not trying to mislead Carl.

2. Resolution

The cultural difference here is between the can-do, everything-is-possible U.S. American and the more realistic, some-things-just-aren't-possible Rodrigo. Many U.S. Americans believe that nothing is beyond their control. Some things are harder and take longer to solve, but if people are willing to make the effort, there's nothing that can't be done or can't be changed, which means there is nothing that must just be accepted.

Begin the debriefing by asking what cultural difference the participants see and then get into the discussion as above. Point out that Tom will come across to Rodrigo as very unrealistic, not realizing when he should cut his losses. And Rodrigo will come across to Tom as defeatist, perhaps even lazy, and as someone who gives up too easily. Note that each party would be very surprised to hear how they are characterized by the other. You might also note that even worse is the fact that neither Tom nor Rodrigo will be consciously aware of how they are perceiving the other—but that unconscious negative perception will nevertheless color all their subsequent interactions.

3. Mutual Understanding

Westerners will be pulling their hair out when this sort of thing happens, and much of the rest of the world, certainly folks in the Pacific Rim, will wonder what all the fuss is about. From the point of view of a face-saving culture, Mr. Li had to make a choice in a recent conference call (during a meeting, in other words) to have a public disagreement with Ms. Smith, who really wants these enhancements finished in one week (a serious mistake on her part to say what she wanted and then ask what was possible) or to sidestep the disagreement *for now* and send a clarifying e-mail immediately after the meeting. For the Mr. Lis of the world, this is not a difficult decision; whatever the downside could be from temporarily misleading Ms. Smith, it could never be as serious as the repercussions from a public confrontation during a conference call (where, presumably, members of Ms. Smith's and Mr. Li's staff are all present). If the call was just between the two principals, Mr. Li could have been more "direct."

In a more direct culture where face-saving is not so important, there is nothing wrong with having a disagreement during a meeting—and there is something seriously wrong in saying one thing during a meeting and then saying something quite different afterwards! So Ms. Smith is annoyed, Mr. Li feels he did her a big favor, and things may go downhill from here.

4. Backlog

This dialogue illustrates cultural differences vis-à-vis trying something new, taking risks. U.S. Americans, for instance, are generally greater risk-takers relative to many other cultures, and so the prospect of trying out some new software isn't all that daunting. Even if it doesn't work out, that would not be the end of the world; at the very least, we would have learned something from our unsuccessful experiment.

Ms. Lukacs is evidently from a culture where risk-taking, experimenting, trying out something new has to be carefully considered; it won't be dismissed out of hand, but there is no *automatic* acceptance of something that is new. The approach is this: Let's think about this and let's remember that we don't have much information to go on here, so there's no reason to believe, in short, that this will work out ("Has it been tried in organizations like ours?") and every reason to consider the repercussions of adopting something new (the need to "train everyone in it"). Ms. Lukacs focuses on the potential disadvantages of experimenting; Mr. Jones focuses on the potential advantages. Is one of them more right than the other?

5. Writing a Report

Here we have a boss with a hands-off management style and an employee used to a more hands-on manager. Abdallah is waiting for Mrs. Colson to do her job, which he would define as making decisions, giving detailed guidance, and setting deadlines. It isn't his place to "participate" in these matters, but rather to follow instructions. Meanwhile, Mrs. Colson is likewise waiting for Abdallah to do his job, which she would define as accepting responsibility for this project (which she has apparently delegated), using his own judgment, and generally taking ownership.

Because these two come from cultures with very different definitions of what constitutes a good manager, hence a good subordinate, they are quite disappointed in the behavior of the other. In debriefing this dialogue, the facilitator might take it one step further and ask participants to imagine what would happen six months from now when someone approaches Mrs. Colson and asks whether she thinks Abdallah has management potential. Should he be considered for a supervisory position? She would probably say no, because he doesn't accept responsibility. If Abdallah heard about this, he would be very surprised; he feels he is the perfect candidate for management because he knows his place, respects the hierarchy, and doesn't usurp the authority of those above him!

Activity developed by Craig Storti, Director, Communication Across Cultures, at www.craigstorti.com.

A Different Pair of Glasses

Time Required:

30–50 minutes (5–10 minutes for the introduction; 15–20 minutes for the activity; 10–20 minutes for the debriefing)

Objectives:

1. To help participants identify and challenge cultural assumptions
2. To help participants explore the rationale/value for an opposing point of view
3. To provide participants with insight into cultural/social values, beliefs, and assumptions

Materials:

- Index cards
- Attachment: Sample List of Alternate Behaviors

Preparation:

- Use the Sample List of Alternate Behaviors to prepare a set of index cards, placing a cultural behavior on one side and the alternative behavioral choice on the other.

Process:

1. Introduce this concept of culture:

   When we come in contact with other cultures, we may find our "reality" challenged for the first time. For this exercise, we are defining culture as a set of learned behaviors based on shared values, beliefs, and assumptions about the "right" way to do things, and that are often unconscious (Bennett, 1998; Schein, 1992; Storti, 2007).

2. Fan out the index cards and ask each participant to draw one card.

3. Ask all students to take a card and to (a) choose the statement that most closely matches their own beliefs and behaviors; (b) identify why they selected the statement they did; and (c) consider why someone might select the other statement and why.

4. Have students form groups of four or five and share the information on their cards, including their insight regarding their preferred behavior and the alternate choice.

5. Debrief with the large group.

Debriefing Questions:

1. How did you feel when you read your card? Were you able to identify some cultural assumptions associated with your preference? Was it difficult/easy to identify cultural assumptions motivating the other preference?

2. How do you think the diversity or lack of diversity in your group contributed to the discussion?

3. What behaviors were the most difficult to understand? Did the group discussion generate a broader list of possibilities? Were there any surprises? Challenges? Aha moments?

4. What did you learn?

5. How might you apply this to your daily life? Work life?

Debriefing Conclusions:

1. Our own cultural values influence our interpretation of behavior.

2. Exploring behavior from a cultural perspective can lead to a better understanding of intentions.

3. Discussing differences in perception can generate a wider variety of choices when we interact cross-culturally.

4. Identifying contrasting cultural behaviors can prepare us to be more effective working cross-culturally by adapting our behavior.

5. We can avoid stereotyping by understanding that there are individual differences within every culture.

Exercise developed by Patricia Cassiday, Collaborative Connection, Seattle, Washington (www.collaborativeconnection.org).

Attachment: Sample List of Alternate Behaviors

Susan always makes direct eye contact when speaking.	Sam keeps his eyes down when trying to explain the problem.
After a merger, meetings are scheduled to plan for the new upcoming changes.	After a merger, meetings are scheduled to review the history of the company.
On a team project, Angela says, "Enough discussion; we need to get moving and complete the task."	On a team project, William says, "We need to hear Judy, George, and Ida before we can move forward."
Robert arrives ten minutes before the meeting is scheduled to begin.	Susan frequently arrives ten or fifteen minutes after the meeting is scheduled to begin.
John proudly walks to the podium to get his certificate. He smiles when he is recognized for his contribution.	Tanya hurries to the podium to get her certificate. She forces a weak smile and quickly sits after being recognized.
When I met Margaret, she talked about her children, her husband, and how they spent their money—she was very personal.	When I met Emily, she would only talk about the weather and other "unimportant" things. She never discussed anything personal.
During a fundraising drive, Pat points out how much money he has raised for the cause.	During a fundraising drive, Carla comes around and encourages everyone on the team to contribute!
Before every soccer game, Juan wants to review the official rules.	Anna loves to play soccer, but she seems to have created her own rule book.
Barbara made me so angry! I went over to her desk and told her exactly what she did that was wrong.	I had no idea that I had offended Stan. He never said anything to me. How was I supposed to know?
Mary Beth keeps introducing me as her friend. Why? We just met last week.	The newest member of our team wants to be called Mr. Williams, not John.
Brian keeps talking about where we are headed. Why can't he just focus on what we are doing today?	We always did it this way. We always did it that way. Who cares? Things change!

Whenever I have a question, I go to the boss and ask. There is no sense beating around the bush!	Whenever I have a question, I try to look for clues to the answer. I do not want to bother my boss with my problems.
Kristin comes to work every day, even when she is obviously sick.	Bill has another bad cold and is taking another sick day.
My new boss is a woman who is much younger than me. Can you believe it? I work for a woman.	Peg and Charlie were competing for the promotion. I'm glad Peg was promoted. She is the most skilled.
I am so glad we start each day with the Pledge of Allegiance.	I am confused by everyone standing and pledging their allegiance each day.

Developed by Patricia Cassiday, Collaborative Connection, Seattle, Washington (www.collaborativeconnection.org).

My Cultural Hot Buttons

Time Required:

75 minutes (two 10-minute lecturettes; one 30-minute activity, report out, and discussion; one 15-minute activity, report out, and discussion; 10 minutes for debriefing)

Work
X–X
X, X, X, X

Objectives:

1. To heighten participants' awareness of emotional triggers
2. To help participants discern values under these triggers
3. To help participants understand different cultural values
4. To help participants develop the ability to control emotional reactions by substituting curiosity and new patterns of thought
5. To help participants apply the skills of self-awareness and self-management to interactions with people whose behaviors are likely to provoke judgment
6. To build the participants' capacity to dialogue and develop positive relationships across cultural differences

Materials:

- Survey: My Hot Buttons (one per participant)
- Worksheet: Matching Values (one per participant)
- Display key issues in a PowerPoint Presentation or on charts for lecturettes
- Chart paper

Process:

1. Begin by explaining that we all have "hot buttons" or behaviors that trigger our negative emotions. We then make critical judgments of those who behave in the ways that irritate us. Often these hot buttons involve values particular to our

culture, and they can make adapting to a culture with different values difficult.

2. Make the following key points in the first lecturette (Chart/ PowerPoint):

   - Our emotions are triggered by the meaning we make of behaviors.
   - We make meaning according to values we have learned from our cultural experiences.
   - People from different cultures make different meanings of the same behaviors.
   - We can learn to discern the meanings other cultures may make of behaviors that trigger us.
   - Learning to discern meaning requires curiosity rather than judgment.

3. Ask individuals to use the Hot Button Survey to identify up to three behaviors that provoke negative reactions in them. These do not have to be intensely negative emotions, but at least strong preferences.

4. Have participants break into pairs to sort out the cultural values under individual hot buttons using the Matching Values worksheet. Explain that they may discover that there is more than one value under each hot button.

5. Ask pairs to help each other identify hot buttons on the list that might come from values opposite to their own identified values.

6. Tell participants to mix until they have found another participant who holds a value opposite to one of their own identified values. These people should pair up.

7. Ask pairs to share the story of their hot button related to the value opposite to their partner's. Each individual should share some examples and the feelings she or he has when this behavior occurs, as well as the value(s) identified behind this trigger. Each individual should take four uninterrupted minutes while the partner listens. The listening partner should practice listening to understand and not judge, and then the listening partner should spend one minute demonstrating curiosity, asking deeper questions about the speaker's values and practices. The participants then switch roles.

8. In a large-group discussion, ask participants to consider the following questions: What did you learn? What happened when you became curious? To what extent did this process modify your feelings about a hot button behavior? How difficult was it to talk with someone who holds some opposite

values? How well could you understand and empathize with the other person's values?

9. Make the following key points in the second lecturette (Chart/ PowerPoint):

  - Our values determine the meaning we make of behaviors.

  - We react emotionally to this meaning. In each situation, we have only a moment after recognizing the emotion to choose to exhibit curiosity instead of judgment.

  - When we understand the values behind another person's behaviors, we can evaluate the behavior differently.

  - When we assume a stance of curiosity rather than judgment, we can see the behavior differently.

  - This takes self-awareness and self-management, two key emotional intelligence skills.

  - These skills of self-awareness and self-management are key to successful cross-cultural adaptation and relationships.

10. Ask participants to break into new pairs. Each partner picks a new hot button and shares how she or he can use self-awareness and self-management to discern her or his own emotions and values involved with the hot button, and to be curious about what the values and meaning of the behavior might be for the person behaving in this way. Partners share how this understanding can help them shift their reaction to being positive, open, and curious rather than negative and judgmental.

11. Ask each pair to share some of the ideas they identified in their discussion.

Debriefing Questions:

1. What happened that was different in your two pairing sessions? Which was more difficult? How did you feel in these two pairing sessions?

2. What did you discover about your values?

3. What helps you move from being judgmental to being curious?

4. How difficult was it to recognize that someone else has different, even opposite, values? How difficult was it to understand a behavior that was a trigger for you?

5. What did you learn about being able to share with someone who holds different values from yours? What will you do if you cannot understand the values behind a behavior that bothers you? What emotional intelligence skills will you call on to stay curious instead of judgmental?

6. How will you apply these skills to enhance your experience of living internationally?

Debriefing Conclusions:

1. Although we may not be able to stop initial negative emotions, if we recognize what is causing them, we are more able to shift from judgment to curiosity.
2. When we are curious, we are able to identify the value underlying another person's behavior that bothers us.
3. When we understand different values and meanings, our emotional reactions can change.
4. The emotional intelligence skills of self-awareness and self-management can open the door to the emotional skills of understanding others and creating positive relationships across cultures.

Optional Process:

1. Divide the value pairs on the Matching Values worksheet, placing the top one in each pair on one easel and the second one in each pair on another easel.
   - Have participants identify the underlying cultural values that support the statements on each easel. The facilitator should ensure that the values and reasons identified for each statement are positive.
2. Check those behaviors/attitudes that are normed in the culture in which the participants are living/working and identify coping strategies for how participants can manage the stress they may feel if the culture-specific values are different from their own.

This exercise was developed by Louise C. Wilkinson of Wilkinson Intercultural Consulting.

My Hot Buttons

INSTRUCTIONS: Please circle up to three "hot buttons."

It irritates me when people beat around the bush and can't get to the point.

I feel offended when people call me by my first name before they even know me.

I think it's rude to interrupt people.

At work, I wish people would bring up problems in meetings where we can do something about them.

Work goes much better if people get to know each other and share a little about their lives. It bothers me when people won't take time for that.

It makes me angry when people cut in line.

It makes me crazy when people spend time chatting about personal things when we should be working.

Some people are so insensitive. If people had some respect for other people's feelings, we could have more harmony in the workplace.

It's really annoying when people seem to "manage up," being deferential to those above them in the organization. What about skills and knowledge?

I get irritated when people won't say what they think.

It drives me crazy when people need to have everyone agree before we can make a decision and move on.

I think it's rude and insensitive when people act like a person's position doesn't mean anything, and when they treat people above them just like anyone else.

I get frustrated when people won't join into a brainstorming session and contribute their thoughts. Why should we have to stop and ask them what they think?

I get really annoyed when people rush a decision, just pushing it through without getting everyone's input and buy-in.

I get frustrated when people won't give me the whole picture—and just give the bottom line as if I don't have the ability to weigh all the options and draw conclusions for myself. Maybe there are important considerations they've missed.

I wish people would just say what they want instead of leaving me guessing.

It's pretty disgusting when people talk about their accomplishments and even ask for promotions.

I think it's rude for people to talk over each other and leave no time for listening. It is especially rude to speak before those in authority or those who have more wisdom have spoken.

It is so humiliating for people when others bring up things in a meeting that could look like their fault. If there's a problem, handle it in private!

Developed by Louise C. Wilkinson of Wilkinson Intercultural Consulting.

Worksheet: Matching Values

Who we are is based on our accomplishments; achieving goals and making your mark are measures of success.

Who we are is based on our relationships; our families, work groups, and social relationships give us our meaning.

Honesty is most important; people should speak the truth even if it's hard to hear. It is more respectful to tell the truth than to avoid hurting feelings.

Protecting relationships is most important; people should do whatever they can to avoid hurting others' feelings, disrespecting others, or causing any negative feelings in a relationship.

People should share the key points to make things clear; it is inefficient and confusing to muddy things up with details that don't matter.

People should share the whole context to help others fully understand something; most things are complex, and people should communicate everything that could be relevant.

People should respect others' knowledge, skills, and accomplishments; any hierarchy should depend on merit.

People should respect others' positions; hierarchies enable order and clarity of identity, role, and responsibility.

Decisions should be made efficiently; sometimes some group participation is necessary, but decisions should be made swiftly by whoever has the necessary knowledge and authority.

Decisions should be made by consensus; all considerations from all those involved should be heard. Time taken up front will prevent mistakes later, and when all are involved, everyone will support the decision.

Free-flowing ideas generate creativity; sharing ideas as they form helps others come up with new ideas, and overlapping talk provides added energy and efficiency.

Orderly communication generates the best ideas; those in authority have the most knowledge and should contribute first so time is not wasted on ideas with little knowledge behind them. Contributing well-thought-out ideas and listening to each other carefully demonstrates respect and enables the best ideas to prevail.

People should speak up about what they want, what they know, and what they've done; others can't be responsible for figuring it out.

People should demonstrate humility and honor others; those responsible will see what people need, what they know, and what they've done.

People should take turns in public places; this provides the most orderly and efficient way of being fair.

People are on their own in public; the world is crowded, and when we don't know people, it is not impolite to try to be ahead of others.

Developed by Louise C. Wilkinson of Wilkinson Intercultural Consulting.

29

Differences Do Matter

Time Required:

50 minutes (5 minutes for lecturette; 10 minutes for activity; 20 minutes for dyad discussions; 15 minutes for debriefing/application)

Work
X–X
X, X, X, X

Objectives:

1. To help participants understand how their personal history and experiences influence how they deal with differences
2. To help them gain competency in dealing with differences by using an emotional intelligence tool for analyzing and sharing their experiences with others

Materials:

- Worksheet: Differences Do Matter (one per participant)
- Pens or pencils

Process:

1. Provide the following information in a brief lecturette:

   Emotions are part of all interactions across differences, and Emotional Intelligence (the ability to understand and use emotions effectively) is one critical intercultural skill. One fundamental Emotional Intelligence tool is the Introspective Process, which brings clarity and depth to interactions. It involves understanding and communicating both the facts and the feelings that are part of experiences. The four steps that are involved are:

   1. Describe the importance/relevance of the event or experience.

2. Consider the impact of the event (the ripples in your life).

3. Identify the feelings that are generated.

4. Identify the learnings that resulted.

Let's look at an example of how we can use the Introspective Process to analyze formative experiences that have shaped how we deal with differences.

2. Provide an example by responding to the segments on the worksheet.

3. Allow participants ten minutes to complete the Differences Do Matter worksheet.

4. Place participants in pairs and allow them twenty minutes to share the events they have reflected on, focusing on the feelings generated and the learning that resulted from the experience.

5. Bring the group back together for debriefing.

Debriefing Questions:

1. What was the result of using the Introspective Process in analyzing your experiences with differences?

2. In your experiences, where did you receive validation from others and where were you challenged?

3. As you look at your responses, how has interacting with differences influenced your own growth and development?

4. How have your reactions changed over the years? What has influenced those changes?

5. What did you gain from sharing your responses with your partner?

6. How did sharing these experiences impact your relationship with your partner?

7. How could the learning from these experiences impact your future cross-cultural interactions? What might you do differently next time?

8. What is one action you can take to help you deal more effectively with differences in your cross-cultural experiences?

Debriefing Conclusions:

1. We have emotional reactions to differences.

2. Experiences with differences and the learnings we derive from them influence how we deal with future interactions.

3. Using the Introspective Process to analyze experiences with differences helps deepen our understanding and allows us to focus on intentionally learning from them.

4. Using the Introspective Process in sharing experiences with others brings depth to the interaction, increases trust, and decreases the chances for misinterpretation.

This exercise was developed by Lee Gardenswartz and Anita Rowe, Emotional Intelligence and Diversity Institute, 2013.

Worksheet: Differences Do Matter: Using Emotional Intelligence to Understand and Communicate About Experiences with Differences

Emotions are part of all interactions across differences and Emotional Intelligence. The ability to understand and use emotions effectively is one critical intercultural skill. One fundamental Emotional Intelligence tool is the Introspective Process, which brings clarity and depth to interactions and involves understanding and communicating both the facts and the feelings that are part of experiences. The four steps that are involved are:

1. Describe the importance/relevance of the event or experience.
2. Consider the impact of the event (the ripples in your life).
3. Identify the feelings that are generated.
4. Identify the learning that resulted.

Use the Introspective Process to analyze formative experiences that have shaped how you deal with differences by responding below. Then share your responses with a partner.

You as the Outsider

Event/Experience _____

Importance _____

Impact _____

Feelings _____

Learning _____

Experiences with Differences

You in an Ambiguous Intercultural Situation

Event/Experience _____

Importance _____

Impact _____

Feelings _____

Learning _____

Noticing Yourself as Different

Event/Experience _____

Importance _____

Impact _____

Feelings _____

Learning _____

Developed by Lee Gardenswartz and Anita Rowe, Emotional Intelligence and Diversity Institute, 2013.

30

The Forgotten Role: President and CEO of Your New Expat Home

Time Required:

40–60 minutes (20 minutes for Parts 1–4; 20–40 minutes for Part 5, case studies)

Work
X–X
X, X, X, X

Objectives:

1. To create awareness of expatriate cultural and adjustment challenges in relation to employing domestic/household staff

2. To uncover an individual's perceptions about employing domestic staff

3. To establish awareness of critical tasks performed by the employer to set the groundwork for an effective working relationship

4. To provide an opportunity to discuss how cultural values influence the work relationships within one's home

Materials:

- Attachment A: Introductory Lecturette
- Worksheet: President and CEO of Your New Expat Home Self-Assessment Checklist (one copy per participant)
- Attachment B: Let's Put It All Together: Case Studies (one copy per participant)
- Pens or pencils for use with the Self-Assessment Checklist

Process:

1. Provide the brief introductory lecturette (Attachment A).

2. Distribute the worksheet and ask participants to complete Parts 1 and 2 of the Self-Assessment Checklist.

3. Review Parts 1 and 2 with participants. The debriefing questions and key points follow.

4. Ask participants to complete self-assessment Parts 3 and 4.

5. Review Parts 3 and 4 with participants. The debriefing questions and key points follow.

6. Finally, distribute and discuss applicable case studies (Attachment B). You can share some or all of these case studies with the large group, or depending on group size, divide into smaller groups with each group addressing one case study and then debriefing with the larger group. There are no correct answers or responses to the case studies, as they are intended to spark discussion. Sample debriefing questions and key points are provided. Feel free to create your own scenarios.

Debriefing Conclusions:

1. In summary, when employing people in your home, it important to have an understanding of your own perceptions of the role of domestic staff, a clear idea of tasks required to be an effective employer, and an awareness of the cultural values that may influence the work relationships within your home. Understanding these elements will help ensure you are off to a good start.

2. Much like a traditional work environment, employee-employer relationships that run smoothly are beneficial to all parties. Many expatriate employers stay in contact with people they employed long after they have left the country because the individual was key in improving the quality of their life at the new assignment and became a trusted friend and enduring connection to the host country.

Note: This exercise may be conducted as a self-study, or it may be adapted for use with an individual, a small group, or a large group. Many of the debriefing questions and conclusions, which are called "key points," are embedded throughout the exercise. Encourage participants to contact local expatriate clubs, international women's groups or associations, local employment agencies, their company's local human resources department, trusted colleagues, and web-based resources for more information regarding local employment customs and practices.

This exercise was developed by Christina Cruz-Hubbard, Intercultural Communication and Diversity and Inclusion Consultant.

Attachment A: Introductory Lecturette

No matter where in the world you live, your home is typically thought of as a safe haven for you and your family. Your home is the one place where your values are not questioned—where you can freely express yourself, relax in your surroundings, and simply be who you are.

In an expatriate's world, this notion of home is sometimes difficult to achieve. This may be attributed to a change in the physical environment, such as moving from a sprawling home to a small apartment, or to missing conveniences such as a refrigerator, a dishwasher, or potable water. For some, the challenges may come from different local furnishings (e.g., mats instead of beds) or décor that does not reflect their personality. Recreating a home to one's liking is an exercise in creativity and flexibility. Yet, even when the physical living environment is in place, there are still many adjustments that need to be made and issues presented by the relocation.

While expatriates often receive training and information regarding the new host culture and tips on how to be effective in their new work environment, limited time and attention is focused on issues that may impact life within the walls of your home. The lack of knowledge about potential challenges and misunderstandings may leave expatriates unprepared for transitions and ambiguous cultural interactions in one of the most intimate of spaces. One of these issues, the dynamics created by employing domestic staff, plays a critical role in the day-to-day experience of an expatriate and his or her family. Domestic staff, or household help in this context, refers to roles such as a nanny/caregiver, cook, driver, gardener, security guard, or housekeeper. One individual may serve multiple roles, and he or she may either live in the home with the family or in a separate area on the property, or live out of the house and off of the property in his or her own family home.

Before we continue any further on this topic, let's take a moment to explore your experiences and views about employing domestic staff.

Worksheet: President and CEO of Your New Expat Home

Self-Assessment Checklist

Part 1: What are your experiences and perceptions regarding domestic staff?
Check all that apply.

	I (or a member of my family) have (or has) worked as a domestic staff person in someone's home (e.g., nanny, driver, cook, gardener, guard).
	Employing domestic staff is reserved for royalty and the well-to-do.
	I have employed domestic staff in my home from time to time.
	I have never known anyone personally to employ people in their home.
	I take pride in completing all household activities myself. Therefore, I cannot see myself hiring staff to assist with household activities.
	Most of my social circle and friend groups have employed domestic staff.
	It would be great to have some help in our home, but I/we could never afford it.
	I grew up with domestic staff such as nannies and housekeepers in my home.
	I never thought I would ever employ anyone in my home, but after many expatriate experiences I have grown accustomed to it.
	I can't imagine a stranger living in my home, even if she or he is providing a service.
	Fill in your own if applicable.

Part 2: Reasons why I might employ someone to assist in my home (check all that apply):

	Because it is a luxury I want and can afford.
	I feel it is important to provide jobs in the local economy.
	The roads are not paved; therefore, dust and dirt are an issue in the house.
	I do not speak the local language, and it would be helpful to employ someone who can help me translate or instruct me on cultural norms.
	I work full-time and need someone to oversee the kids' activities and/or household maintenance.
	The safety and security situation necessitates having a guard.
	I'd rather have time to explore the new surroundings than do housework.
	It is an important symbol of status and prestige.

	There are no comprehensive grocery stores in our new location, and it can take an entire day to get the ingredients needed to make one meal.
	There are frequent power outages, and the generator needs daily maintenance.
	In local traffic, it can take up to two hours to travel 4 miles/6.5 kilometers.
	Our company and all of my friends told me it would be a good idea.
	Hiring staff will allow my family and me to explore our new surroundings.
	Add your own:

Part 3: Your role as an employer (check tasks critical to creating a successful work environment):

	Assess needs of the household and determine necessary positions—live in/out.
	Write and/or communicate position duties and necessary qualifications.
	Recruit and interview qualified candidates.
	Create compensation and benefit packages in accordance with local labor laws: overtime pay, health and medical, severance, leave benefits (religious observances, national holidays, bereavement and family), bonuses.
	Assess skill/knowledge gaps and provide necessary training and education.
	Provide orientation and establish ground rules, standards, and expectations.
	Develop employer-employee feedback and communication processes.
	Complete all necessary paperwork in accordance with local laws.
	Conduct pre-employment health and security checks.
	Provide safe work environment, possibly including transportation provisions.
	Measure job satisfaction, manage workplace conflict, determine division of labor.
	Establish disciplinary and termination procedures in accordance with local laws.
	Communicate expectations of workplace dress/uniform.
	Manage and distribute salary and payroll and document accordingly.
	Clarify philosophy and preferred rules, routines, nutrition, and methods of discipline as it relates to care of your children.
	Discuss important family customs, traditions, and unwritten rules.
	If live-in, establish workplace ground rules and norms including: work hours, rules for visitors if allowed, phone and technology use, meal and break times, access to family food and resources.
	Determine local culture unwritten expectations/responsibilities of the employer (e.g., in some cultures, it is not uncommon to approach an employer for a loan; in others, the employer might be asked to find jobs for other family members).

Part 4: Cultural and relocation adjustment considerations (circle any of the cultural factors below that might play a role in your effective management of employees in your home):

Concepts of time and timeliness	Fixed or dynamic gender roles	Importance of teamwork	Importance of the individual vs. importance of group	How recognition, rewards, and feedback are given
Direct or indirect communication styles	Childrearing views and practices	Views of hierarchy and authority	Notions of privacy	Support beyond salary (loans, help in emergencies)
Importance of greetings	View of animals and pets in household	Expression of religious beliefs	Balance between task and relationship	Appropriate manner to deal with conflict

Developed by Christina Cruz-Hubbard, Intercultural Communication and Diversity and Inclusion Consultant.

Part 1: What are your experiences and perceptions regarding domestic staff?

Debriefing Questions—Part 1

Ask participants to share responses. Note common themes and patterns.

1. Did any of the questions/responses generate strong feelings for you?
2. What did you notice as the group began sharing responses? Describe any similarities/conflicting responses.
3. How did perceptions differ for those who have or had previously employed household staff (if applicable)?

Key Points—Part 1

Everyone's views and experiences regarding this topic are different. In some circles, the issue of employing staff to support household activities is a loaded and sensitive topic. It may bring up issues of class, inequality, hierarchy, privilege, race, and culture. There is potential for judgments, misperceptions, and even inner-conflict about employing staff.

Yet others may have grown up with household staff as a typical and important force in their upbringing. The employees may have established long-term relationships with the family, and the employing family may look after the employee's family in times of trouble. In some cultural contexts, it may be a norm for middle- and upper-class families to employ people in their homes long-term and by extension become connected to one another's families. In some cases, they are in fact extended family. In some countries, it is not uncommon for a family with more resources living in a more cosmopolitan area to employ distant relatives from a provincial or rural area. Often the employing family is expected to provide for the needs not just of the employee, but by extension the employee's family who live in the countryside or village.

Others may have themselves worked in a capacity of a nanny, driver, gardener, guard, or cook and have formed their own opinions and approaches to staff based on those experiences.

It is important to have an understanding of your own feelings about employing domestic staff. The perceptions and messages you hold can influence how you deal with ambiguous situations and also influence where you go to seek support or ask questions.

For example, if you come from a culture or mindset where employing domestic staff is a luxury reserved for a privileged few, you may be apt to not discuss challenging issues regarding the staff you employ. Support networks upon which you might typically rely may not fully understand or have patience in understanding your situation. (E.g., Your sister in the U.S., with whom you have shared virtually every trial and tribulation in life, may not receive your concerns about your nanny/housekeeper empathetically as she juggles full-time work, raising three kids, and keeping her own household running smoothly.)

For others, independently completing daily activities such as childrearing, cooking, and cleaning may be a source of pride or means to make up for a loss of income, particularly if they gave up their career to support their partner/spouse's assignment overseas and spend more time with the kids. In these instances, the employer may even feel a sense of guilt if he/she is not 100% doing everything with the kids, etc., or if funds from a now-one-salary household are being used for "luxury" help.

Regardless of your views and experiences, the issues are very real and can deeply impact the adjustment and experience of the entire family.

Part 2: Reasons why I might employ someone to assist in my home

Debriefing Questions—Part 2

1. What were some of the reasons that you checked?
2. Did any of the reasons listed surprise you?
3. Are there any that you'd like to add?

Key Points—Part 2

There are a host of reasons one might employ individuals to support household functions in your home. Many are dependent on your new assignment. Many are reasons that people in your non-expatriate circle may not assume or understand. For the purposes of this activity, we are not tackling the pros and cons, simply the reasons you might elect to hire staff.

- Employing domestic staff from the country in which you are living gives you a window into local culture. They may serve as trusted cultural informants, helping in a broad range of situations—from educating you about local spices, fruits, and vegetables to providing you with insight into ambiguous cultural situations.

- With your or your partner/spouse's new position, there may be increased demands for entertaining or frequent travel, necessitating additional help or expertise in the home.

- Your new location may not have conveniences you may be accustomed to like reliable utility services (water and electric), washers and dryers, large refrigerators (thus necessitating a daily purchase of fresh produce), or delivery services.

- Daily food preparation routines may be more involved if your new home lacks potable water or if you are advised to clean your fruits and vegetables with a special solution. Unpaved roads and/or streets shared with stray or working animals (e.g., horses pulling carts) mean the floors should be cleaned daily as dirt and waste is tracked into your home.

- Perhaps unmarked roads, extreme traffic, and different driving rules warrant hiring a driver in your new country. Maintenance of a household may be entirely different if you live in an area with frequent power outages, either because all work stops or because the generator needs to be filled with gas frequently.

- Perhaps your company or organization recommends or provides additional security because of the local security context. Security might also be warranted because of political instability in the region or perhaps because of the sensitivity of your new position. Frequent maintenance visits or equipment-repair needs may increase the need for security personnel as strangers frequently enter and exit your home for repairs.

- Individuals may choose to employ staff because it is more affordable in the host country and allows them to concentrate on their work and/or experience the world outside the walls of their home. (E.g., while you would have loved to have a nanny or driver prior to being an expatriate, it financially might not have been in your reach because of the local labor costs.)

- Many domestic staff positions provide an important and sought-after source of employment for the local labor force. These positions can provide individuals with formal educations and limited formal education as a means of support for themselves and their families. Furthermore, it may provide room and board as well as access to the higher wages available in metropolitan areas. In developing economies, live-in staff often leave the countryside (and sometimes even their own country) so they can work in the metropolitan areas and send money back to their families in their respective villages or countries.

Part 3: Your Role as an Employer

Debriefing Questions—Part 3

1. How did you feel as you read through this section? What were some of your reactions?
2. Which items did you check? What were your thoughts as you were checking them?
3. What are your main concerns? Questions?

Key Points—Part 3

As someone who employs people in your home, YOU are the president, Chief Executive Officer (CEO), AND your own human resource department. You are in charge of all of the necessary functions the HR department might handle for a company, and these practices should align with the vision you have laid out for you and your family's experience abroad.

Yet it is rare that the head(s) of household create an explicit vision, mission, training and education program, compensation and rewards package, measurable performance standards, and consequences if those standards are not met. Oftentimes, the feeling is that home is a place to relax, not a place to do more work!

However, without clearly defined expectations and roles, the result can be similar to what happens if these steps are not completed in a typical workplace—confusion, dissatisfaction, and disappointment as the expectations are not met on both sides. For expats, these issues are further complicated by the fact that they occur within your home and during times of transition, when stress levels are elevated and the need to have a place to relax are critical. The results can leave you with no escape from the additional workplace misunderstanding and conflicts associated with the new assignment.

An additional phenomenon complicating these matters is that in some instances, the individual who is charged with overseeing these functions (oftentimes a non-working spouse or partner) may not have received training in the local language or had opportunities to attend cultural trainings. Home activities that were once managed independently may require more collaboration based on which individuals have more proficiency with the language.

Part 4: Cultural and Relocation Adjustment Considerations

Debriefing Questions—Part 4

1. What did you think as you read through the chart? Are there any terms or sections you would like defined?

2. Which did you circle and why? How do you feel about those particular challenges?

Key Points—Part 4

Just as in a workplace outside the home, culture influences everything. Your interactions with domestic staff while you are expatriated will be intercultural, even if you speak the local language and are familiar with the local culture (or it is your own). Furthermore, many experienced domestic employees have routinely worked for other expatriates from all over the world who likely had different standards and expectations than yours. In fact, your nanny who is from the local culture may have work norms shaped over the years not only by her country of origin, but by her expatriate employers from Sweden, France, the United States, Singapore, South Africa, Mexico, Brazil . . .

Cultural Norms
It is important to be clear about your expectations, standards, and norms. Even with family members or loved ones, it is hard to be on the same page regarding your preferences of how a household should operate. How many of you have experienced family strife over leaving dirty dishes in the sink or a difference in what is the proper and appropriate way to discipline your children? Many of the norms and standards you have in your household have been created over your lifetime. Additionally, if you are partnered or married and/or have children, these norms have likely been negotiated and shaped via feedback, discussion, and some compromise. These standards have also been shaped by culture and experience.

Just as a company must determine standards and measurable objectives, so must you as the head of your household. "Don't spoil the children" is very different than, "I expect the children to make their own beds and put away their own toys." Indeed, if this is not communicated, the employee may automatically assume it is their role to make the beds and pick up the toys, as it was for others they have worked for, or it can be even more complicated, as they may think you are trying to indirectly communicate that they are not doing their job every time you tell your kids they need to clean their room.

- Being an employer requires clear communication. This can be a particular challenge if you have limited fluency of the local language or if the language you and your employee share is a second or third language of either party (e.g., perhaps you both have limited knowledge of French as your second language, but it is the only language you share). It may be useful to use visual examples or demonstrate what you mean through action. It may also be helpful to enlist a translator.

- You may miss having the house to yourself, or feel as if you need to change your behavior because of having staff in your home. Perhaps you feel the need to change into more formal clothes before breakfast, whereas at home you would have lounged in your sleepwear. You may have limited privacy, and the staff may be witness to family arguments or private family moments. Live-in staff will see you in your best and worst parenting moments, like it or not. It may be assumed that they know not to share with their peers the goings-on in your household, but your expectations should be outlined to ensure this is true.

- An important component of building trust is how one handles conflict. It is important to consider how your own cultural background might differ from the host culture, or the culture of your employee. Do you address conflict directly, or do you address it in a more indirect fashion? For people who come from a culture that values direct communication, solving conflicts indirectly can feel like "talking around in a circle" or avoiding the issue. To an indirect communicator, approaching a conflict directly may feel harsh, shaming, and unkind.

- If you are not used to having people other than your family in your home, having a relative stranger working and possibly living in your house can be an adjustment. Even simple everyday occurrences such as not being able to find your new sunglasses can turn into "Did an employee move them or take them?" Building in routines, particularly when in transition, can decrease these occurrences. For example, establishing a secure place for keys, purses, and wallets so you can readily find them decreases the potential for these incidences.

- As the President and CEO of your household, you may also feel the weight of providing salaries, managing paperwork, and scheduling for more than just your family. This can cause additional stress. If you are co-running a household with a spouse or partner, it is important to jointly determine roles regarding this to prevent misunderstanding.

This exercise was developed by Christina Cruz-Hubbard, Intercultural Communication and Diversity and Inclusion Consultant.

Part 5—Attachment B: Let's Put It All Together: Case Studies

Case Study #1:

Rosalyn has been an excellent and trusted live-in nanny for the past year. Jessica was initially against a live-in nanny because the reason she gave up her career was to be with the kids more. Yet she and Rosalyn have developed a good working balance, and she has come to lean on the "extra hands," especially while Karl is traveling. This is why Karl and Jessica are torn about Rosalyn's recent leave request for two weeks. Her second cousin recently died in a car accident, and she wants to return to her family's house in the provinces to be there for the services. Karl and Jessica want to be understanding, so they approve one week's leave so Rosalyn can return before Karl's next trip. Rosalyn seems disappointed and later somewhat withdrawn, but does not argue for more time. Karl and Jessica feel one week is quite generous. After all, it was only Rosalyn's second cousin (it wasn't her immediate family), and Karl knows that it is just two short flights to get to Rosalyn's province. Truly, Rosalyn could fly down, stay for the service, and fly back the next day. The extra days they've given her are an example of their generosity and thoughtfulness.

After the one week is up, Rosalyn doesn't return.

Case Study #2:

Laura is single and does not have a big need for a housekeeper, but she has hired one because she would like a local friend who can provide insight into the culture. She also feels it is important to provide much-needed jobs to the local economy. Laura is a friendly person and loves all she is learning from her housekeeper, Mimi. She is stumped though, as to why Mimi insists on eating crouched down in a corner in the back room even though Laura has repeatedly asked her to sit down and join her while she eats her own meals. The times Laura is successful in getting Mimi to sit down at the table, she won't eat. She will only politely answer Laura's questions. Mimi insists on calling her "Mademoiselle" even though Laura insists she call her "Laura." They have a good relationship, but showing that they are equal is important to Laura, so she is disturbed by this behavior and wonders why Mimi isn't comfortable with her.

Case Study #3:

Charles and Laura are embarking on a new journey. They both have had fruitful careers, but Laura just received a fantastic opportunity to head a major initiative that will require the family to relocate out of the country. Both have agreed that Laura will need full focus on her new role, so Charles will handle all of the household details, including meals, kids, and all the logistics regarding the home. Charles has always loved cooking and is excited to have the time to perfect this craft. He is also excited to catch up on time with their two kids. They hired an individual, Ellie, to support household activities such as cleaning, some cooking, and helping with the kids. Ellie is pleasant, efficient, thorough, and eager to please. However, if there is a question regarding the kids, what to buy at the market, or an issue with the house, she often waits until Laura is home to ask. This means a whole day passes when Charles likely could have addressed it. This begins to cause strain because Laura, tired after a long day at work, assumes that Charles has been handling all of these things. And Charles has noticed that just as he is ready to put together one of his culinary masterpieces, Ellie tends to jump in the kitchen and insist on helping. Even if he insists he can do it, she continues to insert herself or worse, becomes withdrawn and worrisome.

Case Study #4:

Elliott and Kendall were excited for their move to Country X. They didn't have any children, but when asked, they would say their two children each had four legs and lots of fur. They adored their two dogs and treated them as family members. Prior to arrival at their new assignment, Elliott's colleague said she knew of a great "all-around" staff person who could handle all of the couple's needs. The colleague said the employee would likely get snatched up quickly as she had a great reputation for being efficient and thorough. Elliott and Kendall hired Hana without an interview as they had not yet arrived in-country. They would work that out when they arrived. They were excited to find a good fit as their budget only allowed for hiring one individual to do household upkeep, shop, cook, and care for the dogs. The first week they were in-country they spent exploring while Hana completed her tasks. It was great to arrive home to a nice meal and clean apartment, but they were upset that the dogs were in a closed back room. They wondered how long the dogs had been left there, as one had relieved himself inside the room. Hana was so conscientious with everything that this did not make sense.

Case Study #5:

Louis is employed as a night guard at Leslie's home. Leslie has always felt safe and secure, but everyone seems to have a guard, and it is a convenience when she needs a little extra help carrying things in the house, or opening the gate to the driveway so she doesn't need to climb out of the car. Leslie has gotten to know Louis over time and enjoys hearing about his family. She knows he is trustworthy, as he repaid a loan Leslie had given him because of a family emergency. Louis had even asked Leslie to help find work for his extended family, which she did successfully through her expat network. She knows that Louis' family struggles and that he even works another job to make ends meet. Furthermore, he travels a long distance by bus to get to the house each night. Because of this, Leslie has understood the couple of times when she has found him sleeping in his guard chair. Once even, she had to raise her voice to wake him, and she reminded him to not have keys dangling out of his pocket.

Leslie is torn because there was a string of break-ins in the neighborhood, and her home was one that was targeted. Louis was there and intervened just as the burglars were leaving, but he was unable to catch them. A few things of value were stolen, but thankfully no one was home and everyone was OK. Her colleagues have advised her to let Louis go because they had heard about him dozing off. They have urged her to find someone new. Leslie wants to ensure her home is safe, but she can't stop thinking about Louis' family.

In summary, when employing people in your home, it important to have an understanding of your own perceptions of the role of domestic staff, a clear idea of tasks required to be an effective employer, and an awareness of the cultural values that may influence the work relationships within your home. Understanding these elements will help ensure you are off to a good start.

Much like a traditional work environment, employee-employer relationships that run smoothly are beneficial to all parties. Many expatriate employers stay in contact with people they employed long after they have left the country because the individual was key in improving the quality of their life at the new assignment and became a trusted friend and enduring connection to the host country.

This exercise was developed by Christina Cruz-Hubbard, Intercultural Communication and Diversity and Inclusion Consultant.

Facilitation Notes for Case Study Debriefing:

1. What might be the cultural issues involved?
2. How might what happened have been affected by the expatriate's feelings about the role of domestic staff?
3. Is there anything the expatriate could have done as an employer to either prevent or alleviate this situation? What can be done next to address the situation by the employer?

Case Study #1 Key Points: Understanding employee circumstances, high-context communication, extended family connections, differing cultural and religious traditions

- Cultural and religious practices may involve ceremonies and traditions that take place over multiple days, not simply a service and burial.
- Rosalyn's second cousin may be as close as a sibling because of extended family networks.
- It was not her place to argue about the length of stay, so Rosalyn did not say anything—hierarchy, saving face, and high-context communication.
- Many staff cannot afford air travel, opting for other modes of transport taking several more days (bus, ferry, rail, motor car, shared taxis).
- After a year of employment, Rosalyn may have been entitled to vacation.

Case Study #2 Key Points: Want to provide jobs on local economy, differing orientations toward hierarchy, unclear roles and expectations

- Mimi views herself as employee; Laura views her as friend.
- Mimi may have been taught it is not appropriate for her to sit at the table, or "to make herself at home."
- Mimi may have ingrained beliefs with respect to hierarchies, especially involving titles for use in employment. She may feel it is disrespectful to call Laura by her first name regardless of how many times Laura insists.
- Mimi might want down time for meals; it is tiring to be "on" all the time.

Case Study #3 Key Points: Gender roles and unclear employee roles and expectations

- Ellie may have fixed notions of roles of each gender, whereas Charles and Laura's views are more flexible.
- Ellie may believe it is not appropriate to speak with the male of the household directly or regarding household activities. Charles and Laura may expect that she speak with whomever they have deemed responsible for overseeing the activities.
- Ellie may believe that she was hired to cook and that if anyone else does, it is a threat to her job or she is being sent an indirect message that she is not doing her job. Charles may view

it as interfering, questioning his own abilities, or not allowing him his space to create in his own home.

Case Study #4 Key Points: Appropriateness of animals in the home, insufficient screening, and unclear job responsibilities

- Many cultures do not see indoor pets as the norm, especially dogs as they may be considered dirty.
- Outlining job duties beforehand may have prevented this situation. An interview may have flagged any concern regarding pets.
- Clarifying expectations about how the dogs are to be treated may be helpful. Perhaps Hana's last employer insisted dogs remain in a closed room.

Case Study #5 Key Points: Expectations of employer, adherence and consequences to key duties not being met

- It is important to have clear expectations of appropriate behavior and consequences if these expectations are not met.
- Local customs/norms may vary regarding an employer's role in relation to the employee and his or her family. Cultural informants may be helpful in understanding what these expectations are. Many times these are not set rules or laws, so there is no legal requirement.
- If she does let him go, it is important that she understands the local laws regarding this.

This exercise was developed by Christina Cruz-Hubbard, Intercultural Communication and Diversity and Inclusion Consultant.

A Values-Based Approach to Understanding Self

31

<table>
<tr><td>Work</td></tr>
<tr><td>X–X</td></tr>
<tr><td>X, X, X, X</td></tr>
</table>

Time Required:

3–5 hours, depending on the depth of discussion; 2 hours if you skip either section C or D

Objectives:

To enable learners to:

1. Understand themselves better, as individuals, and if appropriate, as a couple or family. Thus, they will be better able to:

   a. Learn and grow during the expatriate experience, while also remaining true to themselves.

   b. Anticipate and understand their responses to new experiences.

   c. Explain themselves better to new colleagues and friends.

   d. Deal more constructively with culture shock.

   e. Be better positioned for collaboration and friendship.

   f. Be better able to support their own and their family members' adjustment (effectiveness abroad, personal growth, while holding onto their own authenticity).

2. Improve their abilities to bridge cultures, adapting their behavior and broadening their values repertoire for success in their new home (target culture), while remaining true to their core selves.

Materials:

- Worksheet: Core Values
- Values information on "home" culture and "target" culture
- Computer with Internet connection
- Projector if face-to-face; screen-share ability if conducting virtually

Process:

Section A

Guide learners to clarify their individual core values, and record them on the Core Values worksheet. (Plan on 60–120 minutes, depending on the group and selection of activities.)

1. Introduce the objectives of the activity, and tell a story from your own experience about why self-understanding is important to success abroad.

2. Show the popular YouTube video "The Mom Song," or something similar, in which a singer humorously repeats many of the messages mothers (in this case in the United States) tell their children as they are growing up. This one is sung to the music of the *William Tell Overture* (www.youtube.com/watch?v=CXgoJ0f5EsQ). Discuss how childhood messages can stick with us and guide us, even decades later, and how such innocent messages may end up forming some of our core values. Or, in contrast, they may sometimes form a few of our core "allergies" and, by default, influence the adoption of core values that are opposite the childhood message.

3. Use two or three values exploration activities. (See Stringer & Cassiday, 2003.)

4. Provide time for participants to complete the Core Values worksheet.

5. If working with a couple or family, allow time for each person to share his or her Core Values with the others. Other participants should listen actively, clarifying to understand.

6. Ask participants how they felt while doing the exercise. What was easy, and what was difficult? Once participants have completed their Core Values worksheet, they are generally glowing—quite happy and proud of whom they are. Remind them that this is a terrific attitude to take into a new culture.

    a. Explain that self-esteem can help us to be more flexible, to more readily attempt new experiences and adapt our behavior. It also helps us to remain true to ourselves while we learn and grow, and to deal constructively with culture shock.

    b. Note that learners often mention that they didn't like thinking about how others might see them negatively. Explore the idea that it seems to be human nature to judge what we don't empathize with or understand, and it is no reason to take offense while living abroad. Rather, we can learn from and clarify who we are, and who we want to be, from both the judgments we catch ourselves making, and those that others might make about us.

Section B

Introduce the definition of culture. (Plan on 10–20 minutes.)

Explain that culture is not just about nationality; rather, we are all influenced by multiple cultures: gender, generational, spiritual tradition, sexual orientation, etc.

1. Explain that when learning about a new place, we talk about central tendencies, norms of a society, the mainstream tendencies. There will always be exceptions to the norm, and no individual is "representative" of all people they will meet.

2. Explain that next they will look at a set of values for one of their "home" countries, and that these values represent the central tendency of millions of people. Because it is a culture with which they are intimately familiar, they will understand that not ALL people from that culture hold those values, and that there is huge diversity within the culture. They may also feel that one or more values they consider to be "core" to their home culture is missing from the set. This is normal; because we know our "home" culture so well, we are able to see these nuances and complexities.

Section C

Contrast learners' core personal values with the core values of their birth or "home" country. (Plan on 30–60 minutes.)

Note: Facilitators may also choose to contrast personal values with those of other pertinent Values Lenses (gender, generation, sexual orientation, religious tradition).

1. Show a birth or "home" culture values set.

2. Give learners 10–15 minutes to individually compare their personal values with the "home" culture values. Ask them to consider the following questions:

   a. What similarities do you see, if any?

   b. What differences do you note, if any?

   c. In what ways do you feel that who you are has been influenced by this "home" culture?

3. Discuss learners' findings as a couple or family, if appropriate, or have the individual learner share his or her findings with the facilitator.

4. If time allows (or as homework), urge participants to contrast their personal values with values from another culture to which they "belong" (gender, generation, sexual orientation, religious tradition) and to ask themselves the same questions as above.

Section D

Contrast participants' core personal values with the core values of the target culture to which they are relocating (or have relocated). (Plan on 70–120 minutes.)

1. Review with participants a values set for their "home" culture. Remind them about the variations and exceptions they noted in their "home" values perspective, and remind them never to use a values perspective to "box" anyone in. The values set for a country shows the core values for a huge group of people; there will always be regional, generational, socio-economic, and personal variations among individuals.

2. Show learners a value set for the target culture. Take some time to explain each of the values in the set, using stories from your own experience. (Plan on 30–60 minutes.)

3. Give learners 10–15 minutes to individually compare their personal values with the target culture values set. Ask them to consider the following questions:
   a. What similarities do you see, if any?
   b. What differences do you note, if any?
   c. What values in the target culture might you enjoy or find easy to adapt to?
   d. Which values in your new home might you find challenging? How might you link that "challenging" value to one of your own—to complement or supplement your normal nature? How might you adapt to, or at least constructively work with, someone who demonstrates a value that is personally challenging for you?

4. Discuss participant findings as a couple or family, if appropriate, or have the individual learner share his or her findings with you. Guide their understanding of the target culture.

Debriefing Questions:

1. What have you learned about yourself, and your family, through these exercises?
2. How can you remain healthy and centered while overseas?

3. How can each of you support one another while abroad—encouraging growth and learning while offering each other comfort and security?

4. What does it mean to adapt, learn, and grow while overseas, while also being "true to yourself"? Where is the balance between the two? How will you know when you are stretching and trying "enough" vs. "too much" or "not enough"?

Debriefing Conclusions:

1. Just as each of us are distinct individuals, and also influenced by the cultures to which we belong, the colleagues and friends we meet in different cultures have individuality and complexity as well. They will be influenced by their national cultural values, but also by many other experiences. Never stereotype; rather, use cultural information as clues for discovery.

2. Urge learners to make notes of activities that help them feel good (i.e., to feel capable and calm), and to try to do those activities regularly while abroad.

3. Encourage the family to do family activities to feel connected, supported, and loved, while also pushed to be their best, to learn, and to grow.

4. Finally, urge participants to keep and revisit their Core Values worksheet throughout their assignment. They may be surprised how much their values change or deepen through the experience abroad.

Optional Process:

Another option is to have participants create their Core Values worksheet and stop there. That will take 60–90 minutes. Then proceed with your normal orientation to living abroad, using their Core Values worksheet as a resource for discussion.

> *Note: Easy access to in-depth Cultural Values Lenses and materials are available from Cultural Detective: www.culturaldetective.com.*

This exercise was created by Dianne Hofner Saphiere, Principal, Nipporica Associates LLC (www.culturaldetective.com).

Worksheet: Core Values

1. What are some of the sayings from your childhood that still sometimes echo through your mind or heart, motivating and driving your behavior? Record them below, along with the key value those words have for you.

Childhood Sayings	Personal Core Values

2. Reflect on a very difficult decision you have had to make. What were the key factors you considered in that decision? Between what values were you torn? Which values "won"? List them here.

_____

_____

_____

3. People may misperceive or negatively judge nearly any positive intention, and most values can be taken to such an extreme as to become a liability. For example, we may think ourselves generous, but a more frugal person finds us wasteful. We may find ourselves tolerant, but someone else judges us as lacking conviction.

   For each of the personal core values you have noted above, please also record one to three possible ways in which people who don't share your values might judge you poorly.

Personal Core Values	How You Could Be Judged Poorly

Created by Dianne Hofner Saphiere, Principal, Nipporica Associates LLC (www.culturaldetective.com).

32

Reflective Silence in Global Leadership Practice

Time Required:

15–30 minutes

Reflective silence is a leadership practice that should be introduced at the beginning of a training session and then repeated throughout the training, at times of transition, conflict, decision-making, etc.

Work
X–X
X, X, X, X

Objectives:

1. To introduce the concept of guarding time for daily reflection
2. To help learners explore the relationship between reflection and extraordinary leadership
3. To encourage participants to develop rituals for quiet, reflection, and contemplation

Materials:

- Stopwatch or timing device
- *Leadership Insight* journal by Nancy Adler (Routledge) (optional)
  - View: www.mcgill.ca/desautels/integrated-management/ beyond-business/teaching-and-research/art-leadership/ journal
  - Order: www.routledge.com/books/details/9780415877626/
- Quotes to be used for reflective silence (optional)
- A chime or bell (optional)

Process:

1. Introduce the concept of leadership reflection using the following narration:

   "Management and leadership, both as they are taught and as they are practiced, focus primarily (and in some cases, exclusively) on action, rather than reflection. This activity is designed to bring back the possibility of extraordinary global leadership through reintroducing daily rituals of quiet, reflection, and contemplation" (Adler, 2004, 201).

2. Ask participants to brainstorm ways they currently, or could possibly, guard time for reflection (e.g., writing in a journal, meditating, closing the door to contemplate in quiet, taking a walk alone, practicing tai chi).

3. Remind learners that many of us guard little or no time for reflective silence. Reflective silence doesn't "just happen"; it is a choice—a practice.

   With participants, brainstorm to identify various forces in our organizational culture that support reflective silence. Then brainstorm to identify the forces that tend to undermine reflective silence. From this multicultural perspective, help participants explore the ways various cultures support the daily practice of reflective silence and how cultures can undermine reflective silence.

4. Tell participants, We have an opportunity to build "systemic" reflective silence into this training session and our own daily practice of leadership. Start with very brief periods of reflective silence at the beginning of each session or new activity. (Plan on two to three minutes.) As the training progresses, participants will begin to look forward to the periods of reflective silence. Then you can gradually increase the amount of time to approximately ten minutes with progressively less structure needed. Some suggested ways to introduce the reflective silence include:

   • Read a brief inspirational or reflective quote.

   • Ask a deep, personal question about the implications of the material participants are discussing in the training.

   • Invite silence. Simply suggest that each person become quiet.

   • Ring a chime or bell to signal the beginning and end of the period of reflective silence.

Debriefing Questions (to be used at the end of the first day of multiday sessions):

1. How did you feel when the concept of reflective silence was introduced?

2. Which points did you find the most interesting in the initial discussion? Why?

3. Did you notice any changes in yourself as the day unfolded? In the group?

4. What insights raised by the reflection are the most meaningful and/or of the biggest concern for you? Why?

5. How might you apply what you learned today about leadership reflection to your professional life? Personal life?

Debriefing Conclusions:

Harvard professor Howard Gardner identifies reflection as one of three competencies (along with leveraging and framing) that distinguish extraordinary leaders from ordinary leaders and managers. According to Gardner (Adler 2004, 201):

> Reflection means spending a lot of time thinking about what it is that you are trying to achieve, seeing how you are doing, continuing if things are going well, correcting course if not; that is, being in a constant dialectic with your work, your project or your set of projects and not just going on blind faith (for extended periods) without stepping back and reflecting (Gardner 1998, 20).

1. Reflective silence allows leaders time to tap into their personal perspective, imagination, and wisdom.

2. Envisioning extraordinary possibilities requires reflective time to draw from the depths of one's hopes, aspirations, and creativity.

3. Wisdom is found in reflective silence.

4. A daily reflective practice facilitates leaders' access to their personal wisdom.

Additional Resources to Support Facilitation:

Adler, N. J. 2010a. *Leadership insight*. London: Routledge.

Adler, Nancy J. 2010b. "Going beyond the dehydrated language of management: leadership insight," *Journal of Business Strategy, 31*, no. 4: 90–99.

Frank, F., Roze, J., & Connolly, R., Eds. 2000. *What Does it Mean to Be Human?* New York: St. Martin's Press.

Roberts, E., & Amindon, E. 1991. *Earth Prayers*. San Francisco: Harper.

Whyte, D. 1994. *The Heart Aroused: Poetry and the Preservation of the Soul in Corporate America*. New York: Currency Doubleday.

Exercise was excerpted and adapted from:
Adler, Nancy J. 2004. "Reflective Silence: Developing the Capacity for Meaningful Global Leadership." In *Crossing Cultures: Insights from Master Teacher*, edited by Nakiye Avdan Boyacigiller, Richard Alan Goodman, and Margaret E. Phillips. London, England: Routledge: pp. 201–218.

This exercise was contributed by Nancy J. Adler, S. Bronfman Chair in Management at McGill University, Montreal, Canada.

33

Exchanging Feedback

Time Required:

95–120 minutes (15–20 minutes for lecturette, including constructive feedback worksheet; 10 minutes for setup of activity; 40–45 minutes for group discussion/videotaping; 30–45 minutes for follow-up video observation, discussion, and debriefing)

Work

X–X

X, X, X, X

Objectives:

1. To enrich participants' understanding of the Cultural Orientations Framework (COF)
2. To help learners leverage protective and sharing orientations
3. To enhance participants' awareness through feedback and self-disclosure
4. To provide learners with practice in giving cross-cultural feedback in a safe and constructive manner

Materials:

- Video camera
- Setting for six to eight participants to be fully visible when recording
- PowerPoint or chart with "Tips for Exchanging Constructive Feedback" (see handout)
- Copies of the handout: "Tips for Exchanging Constructive Feedback" (one per person)
- Appendix C: Cultural Orientations Framework (optional)

Process:

1. Using the Cultural Orientations Framework, discuss the territory/boundaries continuum as it relates to giving and receiving feedback. If time allows, also discuss the other COF continuums.

2. Discuss the importance of giving and receiving constructive feedback and share the "Tips for Exchanging Constructive Feedback" handout.

3. To introduce the activity, use language such as the following: "The purpose of today's activity is to enhance your awareness through feedback and self-disclosure. We will videotape a group discussion and then review the interaction (including nonverbal behavior) on the tape. This will give you an opportunity to explore the virtues both of a sharing orientation and acknowledge the protective orientation as well. You will choose what you are prepared to share, and you will decide if you want to receive feedback."

4. Arrange for the group to have an uninterrupted discussion, which you will record on video for at least thirty minutes. The topic should be somewhat controversial for the group. The goal is to observe team dynamics in a challenging situation where some disagreement and confrontation is expected.

5. Once you have a solid thirty-minute video segment (the first few minutes may not be as rich as later when the discussion evolves), invite the participants to watch the video and share comments. Stress that this "safe experience" is designed as a laboratory, not an assessment center. Specifically:

- Review how to give and receive feedback.
- Invite the group to observe the nonverbal behaviors (changes in position, gestures, tone of voice) as well as verbal communication.
- Pause the video frequently to let people ask for feedback or self-disclose how they were feeling or what they were thinking at that moment.
- Challenge participants to only exchange feedback and self-disclosure, not to re-discuss the content itself.
- Caution against the tendency to passively watch the tape without taking the risk of speaking up.
- Give people permission to try new behaviors and make mistakes (in this safe environment). The purpose of the activity is not an evaluation but a chance to explore new behaviors and observe current styles.

Debriefing Questions:

1. How did you feel when the activity was introduced? How are you feeling now about this "experiential activity"?

2. How do you think an understanding of difference in feedback style might affect performance when crossing cultures?

3. What did you think when you were watching yourself in the video? Were you surprised by your tone of voice? Body language? What did you think about your impact during the discussion?

4. Explain what happened during the group discussion. What did you observe during the feedback and self-disclosure session? Were there cultural differences evident during the discussion?

5. How could you use this activity or something similar in the future? What is most helpful about what you have learned?

Debriefing Conclusions:

1. An understanding of the Cultural Orientations Framework provides insight into personal boundaries and the ability to "hear" what is being said.

2. When working across cultures, people find that respecting both the protective and sharing orientation provides flexibility in behavior and can enhance productivity.

3. Effective use of feedback and self-disclosure strategies promotes team cohesiveness when they are culturally appropriate.

4. Flexibility when providing feedback and asking for self-disclosure can enhance cross-cultural evaluation and performance.

This activity was adapted from the work of Philippe Rosinski, *Coaching Across Cultures* (2003). Also see www.GlobalCoaching.pro and www.philrosinski.com.

Handout: Tips for Exchanging Constructive Feedback

Here are some tips for exchanging feedback in a safe and constructive manner, together with remarks about cultural dimensions to be considered.

When *giving* feedback, remember the following suggestions:

1. Describe the context, the behavior, and its impact.*

   Be precise when you describe the behavior, referring to "low-context" information (the words said) as well as "high-context" content (how the words were said: posture, gestures, tone of voice, etc.).

2. Focus on what is changeable. For example, do not say, "You are too tall or too short." There is not much that can be done about height except to choose different heels and shoes.

3. Refrain from giving advice, proffering judgments, or proposing a psychological interpretation. These things can be valuable in a different context, but they are not feedback and tend to put people on the defensive rather than inviting them to take ownership and responsibility.

4. Be honest. Building confidence and ensuring mutual respect and appreciation are prerequisites before sharing difficult feedback. Admittedly, the injunction to give candid and honest feedback reflects a bias toward directness. If the person giving or receiving feedback prefers indirectness, someone must go outside his or her comfort zone. This sort of a situation has to be handled much more sensitively.

5. Attend to cultural differences, including:
   - Hierarchy/Equality (e.g., giving feedback to a "superior" may feel/be inappropriate)
   - Being/Doing (e.g., feedback should refer to what a person does [doing] and not to who the person is [being]; however, constructive feedback can have the effect of helping a person grow [being])
   - Individualistic/Collectivistic (e.g., singling out an individual for feedback, even positive, may feel awkward and embarrassing in a collectivistic culture)

6. Conduct delicate conversations privately to maintain harmony and avoid loss of face.

7. Balance negative feedback with positive feedback over time. People tend to remember negative feedback more than positive. One rule of thumb says that 80 percent positive, 20 percent negative will be remembered as 50 percent positive and 50 percent negative! So be sure to catch people doing the right thing.

---

* This is an adaptation of the Center for Creative Leadership's S-B-I Model (Situation-Behavior-Impact).

When *receiving* feedback, bear in mind these tips:

1. Consider the feedback a gift. Remember that the person giving you feedback is taking a risk. His or her goal is to help you. Even if you do not believe that his or her intention is positive, you are better off assuming it is, because such a belief is conducive to a constructive exchange. Encourage more feedback by thanking your feedback-giver.

2. Seek to understand, not to agree, justify, or defend. You have good reason to behave the way you do. The purpose of the feedback exchange is not to discuss those reasons but to understand the impact of your behavior. You can debate an opinion, but when it comes to appreciating the impact of your behavior, all you can do is understand how the other person perceives it.

3. Listen, ask probing questions, and reformulate. To understand, the best tactic is to actively listen. You may also ask probing questions and reformulate what has been said. Reformulation allows you to think, digest a possible emotional blow, ensure you have understood what was said, and reinforce a sense of connection with your feedback-giver.

Adapted from the work of Philippe Rosinski, *Coaching Across Cultures* (2003). Also see www.GlobalCoaching.pro and www.philrosinski.com.

34

Growing Up Mobile

Time Required:

55–80 minutes (reflection activity 10–15 minutes; individual reading 10–15 minutes; group discussion 20–30 minutes; group reading of poetry 15–20 minutes)

<table>
<tr><td>**Work**</td></tr>
<tr><td>X–X</td></tr>
<tr><td>X, X, X, X</td></tr>
</table>

Objectives:

For participants to:

1. Consider the process of transition and of growing up mobile, and identify some common themes.
2. Reflect upon their own transition experiences and how those transitions have impacted their sense of identity.
3. Become able to more intentionally and successfully engage in their current and future transition experiences.

Materials:

Handouts of selected poetry (or short pieces of prose) written by peers of the participant group (See attached samples, which were written by globally mobile youth between the ages of twelve and eighteen)

Process:

1. Lead the self-reflection activity:
   - Ask participants why people write poems.
   - Summarize their answers: typically it's to creatively express feelings: happiness, sadness, fear, amazement, and so forth.
   - Tell participants you have a selection of poems written by people like them (in the case of the attached samples, expatriate teenagers who have moved and lived around the world).

2. Encourage reading and reflecting:
   - Distribute several copies of several poems, so that each person has a poem and so that three or four people all have the same poem.
   - Give participants time to read the poems and to reflect on the transition themes the poets are writing about. Encourage participants to take a few notes about those themes, and how those themes reflect (or vary from) their own experience of moving globally.
3. Set up the small-group discussion:
   - Break participants into small groups by poem.
   - Ask participants to discuss some selection of the following questions:
     a. What do you think this writer is saying about transitions?
     b. How does his or her experience compare with your own?
     c. What life skills do you think this person is learning by growing up mobile?
     d. What life skills have you learned/are you learning from growing up mobile?
     e. How has growing up mobile impacted your sense of identity?
4. Ask each group in turn to read their poem and to report out on the key points of their discussion.

Debriefing Questions:

1. What did you discover by reading and discussing these poems?
2. What are some of the ways you think experiencing transitions and growing up global can impact a person's sense of identity?
3. Calling something a "life skill" implies it has value beyond the specific situation, in this case beyond transitions alone. What made you call the life skills you found in the poem "life skills"? What makes them so useful?
4. What do you think these poems can teach us about the transition experience, and about being successful growing up mobile?

Debriefing Conclusions:

1. Poetry and prose and other forms of creative expression can be very powerful ways to work with experiences like transitions, which are, by their very nature, emotional experiences.

2. We can learn to engage intentionally with our transition experiences, and can pull from them life skills that will serve us in future transitions and in other realms of our lives.

Optional Process:

Give participants the opportunity to write their own poems or short pieces of prose, expressing some aspect of their own transition experience.

Note: Facilitators should only share participant writing with prior permission.

This activity was created by Barbara F. Schaetti, Ph.D., Owner/Consultant, Transition Dynamics (www.transition-dynamics.com).

Moving

We're going to move?
When?
Where?
I don't want to.
Yes . . . I do?   When we arrive,
                                   I am curious

Cleaning,   And excited
Rummaging,   And scared.
Finding,   Will this place ever be home?
Remembering,   It is so very new.
Packing,
Memories,   Sometimes homesickness blows in,
Empty boxes,   Like a summer storm.
Full boxes,   But luckily,
Memories,   With each passing cloud,
Last day: It ebbs further and further away.
Tired,   Until,
Empty,   Finally,
Memories,   I am at home again.
A lump,
In my throat,
Goodbye.

Naomi Gross
U.S. American global nomad, age fifteen
Talking Leaves: A Literary Magazine
    International School of Geneva (LGB), 1993

Barbara F. Schaetti, Ph.D., Owner/Consultant, Transition Dynamics

Corridors

In corridors which wind in me,
I sometimes sense but never see
The pulse so faint of shattered mind
The throbs for what I left behind
The echoes of my lurking fears
The distant dripping of my tears
The far off rumble of my laugh
The striking of my honor's staff—
They sound inside me quietly
In corridors I never see

Farhan Haq
Pakistani global nomad, seventeen years old
Video Cassette Reading—The Fine Arts Magazine
of The International School of Islamabad, 1984–1985

Barbara F. Schaetti, Ph.D., Owner/Consultant, Transition Dynamics

Want to Go Back

Never wanted to come here
want to go back
Hate speaking English here
want to go back
Hate all the homework
want to go back
Miss all my friends there
want to go back
Don't like the people here
want to go back
I hate Holland
want to go back

Alexandra Johansson
Norwegian global nomad, twelve years old

Barbara F. Schaetti, Ph.D., Owner/Consultant, Transition Dynamics

To Jo

A subtle touch of sad goodbyes
Is echoed from the walls.
The roar of revving engines blends
With flight computer calls.
Those who leave bear anxious smiles
For those who smile and stay
But after flight departures
All smiles have blown away,

Sandshoes and stiletto heels
Make for exit doors;
Grey uniformed attendants stay
To polish sterile floors.
The airport bears no sympathy
For those who do not fly.
But I'd rather be the one that stays
Than have to say goodbye.

Fiona Lowery
Australian global nomad, sixteen years old
Video Cassette Reading—The Fine Arts Magazine
of The International School of Islamabad, 1984–1985

Barbara F. Schaetti, Ph.D., Owner/Consultant, Transition Dynamics

How Do You Fill This Out?

When I was six, I was sure that I was an Australian. When I was ten, I thought I was a Japanese. When I was eighteen, I thought I was a U.S. American. . . . Until recently, I thought I had to tell everyone my life story to explain where I am from. But now I have learned not to equate the countries *I* am from with the countries my *cultural identity* is from.

I love peanut butter and jelly sandwiches, riceballs, and Vegemite sandwiches. What's wrong with that? I love singing "Waltzing Matilda," "Brady Bunch," and "Sukiyaki Song." These are all part of me! We don't have to come from somewhere. We can be, for instance, Australian, Japanese, and U.S. American at the same time. I don't feel that *I* am from any of those countries, but my *cultural identity* does come from all of them.

S. Michael Nagasaka
Japanese global nomad
Perspectives, Global Nomads International
Vol. 4, No. 1, Spring/Summer 1996

Barbara F. Schaetti, Ph.D., Owner/Consultant, Transition Dynamics.

35

Working Together/Teamwork

Time Required:

65–95 minutes (5 minutes for introduction; 10–20 for Worksheet A; 20–30 minutes for Worksheet B; 15–20 minutes for sharing action plans; 15–20 minutes for debriefing)

Work

X–X

X, X, X, X

Objectives:

1. To heighten participants' understanding of differences between individualistic and collectivist team members
2. To heighten participants' understanding of differences in risk-taking tolerance
3. To help participants explore the preferences and perspectives of each style
4. To encourage understanding and promote an effective team environment

Materials:

- Worksheet A: Working Together (one copy per participant)
- Worksheet B: Working Together (one copy per participant)
- Pens or pencils
- Chart paper and markers

Process:

1. As an introduction to the activity, explain that people coming from different cultural backgrounds can have very different perspectives on what it means to be a "good team player." Multicultural teams can run into trouble when the team members assume they are all operating with the same basic assumptions about teamwork. This exercise is designed to promote insight into two key value differences that impact teamwork: individualism/collectivism and risk-taking orientation. Having a better understanding of these differing views can encourage team

members to ask questions, it can also improve acceptance, and as a result, it can help teams work together more effectively.

2. Distribute Worksheet A. Ask participants to read the information on Individualism and Collectivism and place an X on the values continuum, based on where they feel their personal value lies. Stress that this is a continuum and they can be anywhere along the line, not just on either end.

3. Discuss with the group the possible impact of this difference in perspective on individuals on the team and on overall team performance:

   a. Why might this be important information for members of a multicultural team to consider?

   b. How might this impact an individual from either one end of the continuum or the other?

   c. Does this information clarify any behavior you may have observed on your team or another team?

4. Return to Worksheet A. Ask participants to read the information regarding high risk-taking tolerance and low risk-taking tolerance and again score themselves on the continuum provided.

5. Again, raise the discussion in the large group about the possible impact of this difference on the individual and on the team performance:

   a. How might risk tolerance impact team performance?

   b. What are some strengths to each perspective?

   c. What could be problematic with each perspective?

6. Distribute Worksheet B. Explain that participants are now going to look deeper into the possible impact of these implicit belief systems. The information on Worksheet B should not be used as an absolute, but as more of a tendency or generalization of preferences related to the cultural values.

7. Ask participants to form groups of four to six people to discuss this additional information. Participants should begin by sharing within the small group their score on the two continuums. Are there similarities? Differences? How might this impact their team performance?

8. Encourage groups to read over the additional information and discuss these differences as they might impact: problem-solving and disagreements, meeting styles, negotiations, policy and regulation development, "ethical" behavior, etc. In what way might these differences in cultural beliefs affect perception and performance? Then ask participants to generate several action steps that could be taken to encourage

understanding and stimulate their team's performance. (Provide chart paper and markers.)

9. Ask each small group to then share with the large group one or two action steps that could be taken toward more effective teaming.

Debriefing Questions:

1. What were your thoughts when you read the information on Worksheet A? When we discussed the differences in the large group? When you compared your preference with others in your small group?

2. What were your thoughts when you read the information on Worksheet B? What were your feelings and observations? Was your discussion in the smaller group different than the discussion with the larger group?

3. What did you observe during the exercise? Differences? Similarities? Were you surprised by anything you saw? By what you experienced?

4. How do you feel now that the activity is complete? How do you feel about the possible actions to be taken? What did you learn about this group?

Debriefing Conclusions:

1. Team performance can be impacted by implicitly held values, beliefs, and assumptions.

2. Understanding the cultural perspectives of team members related to individualism and collectivism and their tolerance for risk-taking can help to build team effectiveness.

3. Team performance can be enhanced by taking action steps based on acceptance and accommodation of diverse perspectives.

Exercise adapted from the work of Don Rutherford at www.culture-connect.com.

Worksheet A: Working Together

Read the descriptions and place an X on the continuum for your preferred style.

Individualism:

An underlying belief of this system is that individuals should take care of themselves. People ideally take the initiative, assume personal responsibility, and achieve on their own. Their actions are frequently based on their own personal interest. They believe the organization and/or the larger group will be successful based on individual contributions.

Collectivism:

The underlying belief in this system is that a person's identity is tied to his or her group membership (organization, family, etc.). If the group is successful, it reflects on the collective effort of all of the members. The needs of the group take precedence over the needs of the individual. Group loyalty is strong and the individual contributes to the group (practically, psychologically, and even monetarily), and in return the group protects, supports, and advises the individual.

INDV   COLL

└─────────────────────────────────┴─────────────────────────────────┘

High Risk Tolerance:

With this orientation, people can cope well with risky situations, where it is difficult to predict the outcome. People in these cultures are encouraged to take the initiative, and within organizations employees are encouraged to take risks. Individuals are encouraged to "do their own thing," and if things go wrong, they may take individual responsibility for the problem. Action may be taken quickly and may be based on limited information.

Low Risk Tolerance:

People from cultures with a low risk tolerance are comfortable following rules and regulations. Organizations in these cultures usually follow a standardized management practice with clear structures, expectations, and codes of behavior. The group tends to gather and review information prior to decision-making. Action can take time while information is being gathered.

HRT   LRT

└─────────────────────────────────┴─────────────────────────────────┘

Adapted from the work of Don Rutherford at (www.culture-connect.com).

Worksheet B: Working Together

Individualism

- Use the word "I" extensively
- Describe personal accomplishments
- Make it clear it was my idea
- Have a strong sense of privacy
- Prefer an individual work space and their own materials, etc.
- Are less likely to share a network of contacts
- Provide help only on request
- Focus on their own role and responsibilities
- Make decisions based on their own area of responsibility
- Expect people responsible for other areas to speak up if the decision will adversely affect them
- Speak up at meetings if they have a point to make, and fight for their position

Collectivism

- Use the word "we" extensively
- Describe group (department/organization) accomplishments
- Present ideas as a collective process
- Have less expectation or need for privacy
- Focus on sharing space and materials
- Share their network of contacts with the group
- Provide help when they consider it is needed (even without a request for help)
- Keep track of what every team member is doing
- Make decisions based on the impact on the whole group
- Expect everyone to consider the impact of his or her decision on everyone else
- In meetings, wait to be asked for their opinion if the decision at hand relates to their work group

High Risk Tolerance

- Plan over a short period of time
- Plan with detail the first few steps and examine only the most likely contingency scenarios
- Have a "We'll cross that bridge when we come to it" attitude.
- Want to "keep things moving"
- Focus more on practice, rule of thumb, and empirical formulas

- Are willing to take a greater risk to get larger financial rewards
- Welcome compensation and incentives based on performance
- Focus on short-term rewards
- Are most comfortable with few rules and regulations
- Create rules that describe "the spirit of the law" vs. "the letter of the law"
- Prefer spur-of-the-moment vacation plans (are usually flexible)

Low Risk Tolerance
- Planning is over a long period of time
- Plan over the entire life of the projects for all possible "What ifs"
- Have a "We can avoid rework with detail planning" attitude
- Ask for additional information in order to have a "good grasp" of the situation before moving forward
- Focus more on theory and differential equations derived analytically
- Are willing to accept a lower but stable income
- Avoid performance-based compensation plans
- Plan for the long term
- Are comfortable with many rules and regulations to be followed
- Create rules in a logical step-by-step manner
- Plan vacations well in advance (tend to have little flexibility, as others are usually involved, including family, friends)

Adapted from the work of Don Rutherford at www.culture-connect.com.

36

It Is All About the Team

Time Required:

30–55 minutes (individual selections of squares 5–10 minutes; discussion of selections 20–30 minutes; debriefing 5–15 minutes)

```
Work
X–X
X, X, X, X
```

Objectives:

1. To explore different cultural influences on day-to-day team activities
2. To gain insight into cultural differences toward risk-taking, decision-making, consensus-building
3. To normalize the feelings associated with style differences
4. To strengthen cooperation for successfully achieving common goals

Materials:

- Handout: "It Is All About The Team" (one per participant; alter content as needed)
- Large chart paper and markers for each group of ten

Process:

1. Review the objectives for this activity.
2. Provide each participant with a handout similar to Attachment A. (The facilitator should change the information on the handout to most closely match the cultural groups participating in the training.)
   - If you are working with a team of ten or fewer people, you can facilitate the group with one chart. If you are working with a larger group, be sure each breakout group has a chart with a list of questions.

- Ask each team member to individually select a square from the handout that represents what he or she believes is most important for effective team performance.
- Give each participant an opportunity to share. Why is it important? Ask for examples. What happens if this is not present?
- List similarities and differences. Compare and contrast responses: How might these similarities/differences influence team members' perceptions of each other and/or team performance?

3. Summarize the key points of the group discussion. Refer to the sample quotes at the bottom of the handout. Ask if there is a quote the team members would like to choose for their team. Would they prefer to develop their own statement? How might their "team quote" influence team performance? Customer satisfaction?

Debriefing Questions:

1. What happened as your group began to discuss the squares? Were you surprised by some of the opinions expressed? How might cultural preference account for similarities/differences in team behavior/contributions?
2. How did you feel identifying the square you thought most important? When others disagreed or agreed with you? As other squares were identified?
3. How might this discussion influence your future actions? Attitudes? The team's overall performance?
4. How easy was it for your group to select a quote for future team identification? How might that quote change/enhance/ encumber future team activities?
5. What is something new you learned from this activity?
6. How might you use this if you are on/leading a different multicultural team in the future?

Debriefing Conclusions:

1. Members of multicultural teams have personal expectations and preferences about team behavior/interaction.
2. Feelings about culturally influenced style preference can enhance or interfere with the team's ability to solve problems or make decisions.

3. Understanding style preferences can enhance team cooperation, consensus-building, and performance.

4. There is no one right or wrong road leading to team effectiveness. Learning from cultural differences can enhance the team.

Optional Process:

Ask each participant to rank his or her top five squares as they apply to successful team performance. Then ask the group to share and list the most important, using team consensus to develop the ranking. Depending on the results, obvious cultural preference can be examined and debriefed.

This exercise was developed by Patricia Cassiday, Collaborative Connection, Seattle, Washington (www.collaborativeconnection.org).

Handout: It Is All About the Team

To be most effective:

Personal initiatives and contributions need to be recognized.	Having a well-organized plan ensures the success of the team's efforts.	Staying on schedule is essential to meeting the demands for product completion.
A team without a leader is a team that is heading nowhere.	It is most important to stay focused on the task assigned to our team.	Trust is built when team members speak openly and honestly.
Flexible scheduling is important. It allows for fresh opportunities.	Opposing a team member's point of view can cause stress and break trust within the group.	No one person on a team is as effective as the whole team pulling together.
If we want to have the best product, we need time for each person to share his or her ideas.	Teaming is all about shared and fluid leadership opportunities.	Imagination, creative spontaneity, and a bit of synchronicity will lead to the best result.

Sample Quotes

- "Individual commitment to a group effort—that is what makes a team work, a company work, a society work, a civilization work."
  —**Vince Lombardi**

- "Rise above sectional interests and private ambitions. . . . Pass from matter to spirit. Matter is diversity; spirit is light, life, and unity."
  —**Muhammad Iqbal**

- "Vision without action is a daydream. Action without vision is a nightmare."
  —**Japanese Proverb**

- "It is not necessary to change. Survival is not mandatory."
  —**W. Edwards Deming**

- "Diversity: the art of thinking independently together."
  —**Malcolm Forbes**

Developed by Patricia Cassiday, Collaborative Connection, Seattle, Washington (www.collaborativeconnection.org).

Reentry

The Importance of Reentry Preparation

Bruce La Brack, Professor Emeritus and Former Director of
University of the Pacific's Institute for Cross-Cultural Training

Of all the phases of adjustment involved in an international sojourn cycle, the "coming home" (reentry) can prove among the most difficult and challenging part of the process. The basic definition of "reentry" as the process or act of returning to one's native (passport) country after living, studying, or working internationally is deceptively simple, masking the potential complexity, emotional impact, and psychological importance that may underlie the actual event.

Reentry has become recognized as perhaps *the* most crucial component involved in whether returnees (and their families, teachers, employers, and communities) consider their time abroad as successful or not. Increasingly, the overall success of international sojourns are being measured and linked not only to how well individuals adapted or performed overseas, but also to how well the individual manages the reintegration back home. A smooth return home can help support an individual's intercultural competence and career goals by enhancing the ability to apply past lessons and skills gained abroad to new circumstances at home. Conversely, an unsuccessful or stressful reentry can be destructive and unsettling, personally and professionally.

There are many dimensions that contribute to returnees' self-evaluations, but three core circumstances seem to be universal. First, residing in another culture frequently results in alterations of an individual's behavior and attitudes that, over time, become "normal." Travelers are often not fully aware of the ways in which they may have changed, until they return home. Second, upon reentering their home societies, travelers are frequently dismayed to find that "home" is no longer exactly as they remembered it. Third, these situations, taken together, may result in cognitive dissonance that can trigger "reverse culture shock"—a common reaction that is rarely anticipated, but frequently experienced, by returnees. Unlike initial culture shock, which occurs upon entering an unfamiliar context, and which is frequently anticipated by travelers, reverse culture shock often comes as an unpleasant and unwelcome surprise.

Reentry has proven to be, at the very least, a problematical time for the majority of returnees at some point. When issues arise, as they inevitably do, they are likely to be both disconcerting and perplexing, especially if the local community, workplace, or educational institutions seem uninterested or unreceptive to the returnee. This becomes intensified if returnees are unprepared for the transition.

Long lists of common "triggers" that intensify reverse culture shock have been identified. A few examples include:

- Idealized or unrealistic expectations about what home will be like.

- Surprise and dismay at the degree to which relationships at home may have changed, and the difficulty in reconnecting, especially if the returnee is expected to have remained essentially the same.

- Frustration because few people at home want to hear about a returnee's international experiences, at least to the extent the returnee would prefer, and even when they are willing to listen, it can be very difficult for the returnee to explain.

- Some degree of "Reverse 'Home' Sickness" and sense of loss related to leaving former friends, colleagues, and important places behind.

- Major changes involving a returnee's professional/social status and home lifestyle may be involved.

- Returnees frequently view their nation and culture from a more critical, comparative perspective, and discover that few people at home are receptive to such opinions.

Conflicts surrounding reentry can be significantly lessened—and reverse culture shock somewhat mitigated—by making people aware of the potential pitfalls involved. Unfortunately, if such information and advice is not provided (either before, during, and/or after the sojourn), it is extremely unlikely that this will happen automatically. Returnees need to be provided information about what they might face and what the process entails. Without this awareness, when returnees encounter the symptoms of reverse culture shock, they may be both bewildered and lack the tools to deal with it effectively. Both the returnees—and those at home—need to understand that the returnee may have changed in fundamental ways: some obvious, some invisible.

The reentry exercises in this section can be used by individuals independently or integrated into existing cross-cultural pre-departure training courses/orientations, as well as being introduced in pre-return, in-country discussions. Ideally, such briefings should begin approximately three months prior to departure from the host location. Suggestions for suitably bringing closure and saying culturally appropriate goodbyes, as well as providing basic information designed to prepare the individual for the possibility of "reverse" culture shock, should be included at this time. Providing reentry support to returnees demonstrates a commitment from the organization or institution to the individuals, which can facilitate successful reentry as well as show appreciation for their accomplishments—all factors that build loyalty and help welcome them home.

Offering post-return debriefing opportunities are also very important, both to assess a sojourner's progress toward reintegration and readjustment and to offer them opportunities to explore ways to apply their new skills and knowledge. Such meetings are typically scheduled one month to six months after return. If an assessment instrument (e.g., Intercultural Development Inventory) was administered pre-departure, a post-assessment comparison using the same instrument can provide insights into personal growth. Specific data relevant to training and teaching design may be generated, and if an individual debriefing or feedback session is possible, this may be part of creating a contemplative space for guided discussions during reentry.

Such activities have high potential to generate additional insights and add richness to conversations related to a person's international experience. It is important to facilitate individual and group conversations and reflections whenever possible about both their time overseas and how it influences and impacts their ongoing adjustment at home. Thoughtful interventions can also be extremely effective, particularly when those involved (friends, colleagues, and trainers) have their own personal reentry experiences and can offer practical and authoritative guidance. Professional and personal peers have automatic credibility, and often prove to be the most effective channels to convey necessary perspectives and advice to returnees.

Organizations hoping to retain expatriates need a strategic plan for their placement upon return. While the employee has been working abroad, organizational leadership may have changed, and the way to get things done may now need to be restructured to meet new leadership styles and expectations. Expatriate reintegration and retention are ongoing challenges for corporate organizations, as well as academic groups involved in international educational exchange programs. Those returnees who have survived and thrived in overseas settings have learned to face complex problems and meet day-to-day challenges effectively. Returning to a situation that builds upon "lessons learned"—while offering new challenges and a degree of autonomy—will enhance the possibility of maximizing an expatriate's intercultural insights and talent. Providing an avenue for processing the international experience can provide the organization with novel perspectives and the chance to utilize the wisdom resulting from the individual's cross-cultural experience.

University study abroad programs face similar integration issues. They need to provide similar opportunities to their returnees, as well as provide occasions for them to apply their new knowledge and abilities within the home educational context. Like all learners, returnees need both challenge and support.

Finally, while a pre-departure orientation might last only several hours or days (or in rare cases a few weeks or months), reentry is, theoretically and psychologically, an ongoing process that only *begins* upon arrival home. It has the potential to impact travelers for the rest of their lives. Properly designed and delivered, post-sojourn training can help ensure a much more productive, positive, and satisfying experience for returnees, and pay multiple dividends for the sponsoring organizations.

Expatriate Transformation: Reflections and Understanding

37

Time Required:

240–480 minutes, depending on the number of video clips used and time for sharing and framing experiences

Work
X–X
X, X, X, X

Objectives:

1. To furnish current and returning expatriates with a framework for making sense of their experience

2. To provide participants with a better understanding of the complex, transformational nature of the expatriate experience

3. To assist participants in reflecting on their personal experience and evoke a deeper understanding of the value of "lessons learned"

Materials:

- Appendix F: The Myth of the Hero's Adventure and the Expatriate Experience

- Mythical stories about heroes, Joseph Campbell material to frame concept, and/or video clips from the first *Star Wars* movie (or *Dances with Wolves* or *Braveheart*)

- Paper and pens

- Hero Quote on a chart or PowerPoint:

    A hero ventures forth from the world of common day into a region of supernatural wonder: fabulous forces are there encountered and a decisive victory is won: the hero comes back from this mysterious adventure with the power to bestow boons on his fellow man. —Joseph Campbell, *The Hero With a Thousand Faces*

Process:

1. To introduce the activity, explain that the mythology of the hero's journey is one of the most common mythical themes and is formulated on a basic plot:

   - A separation from the familiar
   - An initiation (learning) that results from "going out on the adventure" and provides a new source of power
   - A return (with benefits to share with others) from the adventure

   Note that many expatriates consider their "journey abroad" to be one of the most significant experiences of their lives. When expats come together, they are likely to swap stories about what happened to them and to other expatriates.

2. Tell one of your favorite stories, and ask participants to listen carefully for underlying themes. (Try to use a story that has many of the stages of the hero's journey in it.) Then ask the following questions:

   a. What can we learn from a story like this?

   b. What themes did you hear in the story?

3. Ask the participants to briefly tell one of their own expatriate stories.

4. Have participants identify any common themes they begin to hear. Here are some sample themes they may identify:

   - A sense of mastery from learning to work effectively after grappling with a foreign language, and learning to crack the "cultural code."
   - A sense of heroic accomplishment from rising above difficult occasions and accomplishing what had previously seemed impossible.
   - A sense of accomplishment from recognizing, processing, and handling paradoxical information and situations they encountered.
   - A sense of personal transformation as a result of opening themselves up to another culture.

5. Presentation of the Framework (Appendix F).

   - Provide Campbell's description. (See Appendix F.)
   - Ask for what stage this would be in the *Star Wars* film (if using the film).
   - Explain the stage's significance for the expatriate.
   - Share the relationship of that stage to expatriate issues in general.

6. Ask participants to keep The Hero's Journey stages in mind and take the next thirty minutes to write their own "Personal Hero's Journey."

7. Ask participants to pair and share stories (ten minutes each).

8. Ask for a few participants to share with the whole group once their paired discussions end. "Who just heard an interesting story about _____(e.g., a magical friend)?" This will give you a chance to tie their stories to the model in a different way and add more information about the expatriate experience.

Debriefing Questions:

1. What did you think as you learned about the Hero's Journey Framework? When various stages were described in more detail? When examples of video clips or stories were tied to the framework? Did the framework seem valid to you?

2. How did you feel about writing your story? Sharing your story with someone else? Hearing the stories of others?

3. Describe some observations you made during this exercise. Were there any surprises? Aha moments?

4. How can you use some of the lessons you learned abroad in your future? How might your organization benefit from your learning?

Debriefing Conclusions:

1. "The Hero's Journey" framework is a tool that can assist expatriates in making sense of their experience.

2. The expatriate experience is complex and transformational in nature. Reflecting on the experience can deepen personal understanding.

3. Reflecting on personal expatriate experiences can evoke a deeper understanding of valuable "lessons learned."

Note to Trainers: How This Framework Fits into the Expatriate Literature

Although some hybrid models exist, most expatriate adjustment theories can be classified in four categories: (1) learning models; (2) stress-coping models; (3) personality-based models; and (4) developmental models.

The learning-based models imply that the key to adjustment is for expatriates to learn the ways of the new culture to which they are assigned. Oberg's (1960) culture shock model is quite well-known and views adjustment as an illness. In contrast, more recent research has focused on adjustment as a normal stress reaction to uncertainty, information overload, and loss of control. Personality-based models focus on identifying expatriate competencies and looking at relationships with the Big Five personality dimensions.

Some of the development models assume that contact with another culture causes individuals to psychologically disintegrate, regroup, and then attain a higher level of development and maturation. This is reminiscent of Lewin's (1947) unfreezing, moving, and refreezing process of change. The hero's journey framework is a developmental model involving grounded theory and qualitative research. This metaphor makes no pretense of assigning time markers to each stage, because personal transformation is an unpredictable and non-linear process (Mendenhall, 1999). The hero's journey model goes beyond adjustment, a more frequent focus in expatriate research, to underscore the importance of the broader concept of personal transformation.

This activity was adapted from the work of Joyce Osland, professor at the Global Leadership Advancement Center, San Jose State University.

38

Simon Says: Let's Reenter

Time Required:

15–20 minutes (This activity is often used as an icebreaker.)

Objectives:

1. To get participants physically energized and interacting early in the training
2. To frame various aspects of expatriate experiences
3. To illustrate the wide range of cross-cultural experience in the room

Materials:

- Area for participants to play
- Rewards for "winner" in each category (e.g., small candy, pen, coupon)

Process:

Ask participants to form a straight line (shoulder to shoulder) in the back of the room. Then use language such as the following.

1. We are going to play the game Simon Says, which may be familiar to some of you. The goal of the game is to be the person who can take the most steps forward.
2. Simon says:
   - Take one step forward if you speak one language. [Command a step for a second language, another step for a third language, etc., until the person with the greatest language proficiency is discovered. Present a small token.]
   - Everyone returns to "start."
   - Take one step forward if you have moved more than three times; a step if you have moved more than six times; a step if you have moved more than . . . [You can go by single

numbers as the group begins to thin. The person with the greatest number of moves receives a prize.]

- Everyone returns to start.
- [Repeat the process for the "number of countries lived in."]
- [Repeat the process for the "number of reentries to your country of passport."]

Debriefing Questions:

1. What did you think when you heard the directions for this activity? When you realized you were going to play a game? Move around the room?

2. What did you observe during the exercise? Differences in categories? Were you surprised by anything you saw? Experienced?

3. How might you use the information you gained from this experience?

Debriefing Conclusions:

1. There is a wide range of cross-cultural experience in the room.

2. Language, country of residence, frequency of moves, and frequency of reentry experiences are all factors that help to form an expatriate's frame of reference.

Optional Process:

Simon Says can also have "gotchas," just like in the original game. For instance, instead of beginning with the phrase "Simon Says," you simply say, "Move three steps forward if you have moved in the last month." Participants should move only when you include the phrase "Simon Says," so if your direction is not preceded by this phrase, there is a penalty. Using this option, you can begin the activity by giving each person a handful of wrapped candies, and they will need to give one back for each time they move when "Simon Says" wasn't in the instruction.

This exercise was developed by Patricia Cassiday, Collaborative Connection, Seattle, Washington (www.collaborativeconnection.org).

Repatriation Quiz: So You're Getting Ready to Go Home

Time Required:

10–15 minutes

Note: This is a brief introductory activity that should be among the very first things done in a workshop, mainly to set a lighter tone.

Work
X–X
X, X, X, X

Objectives:

1. To introduce some key themes of a repatriation workshop
2. To set a light tone for what can be "heavy" issues
3. To encourage repatriates to laugh at themselves

Materials:

- Worksheet: Repatriation Quiz (one copy for each participant)
- A PowerPoint slide version of the quiz
- Quiz "answers":
  (1) True; (2) E; (3) A; (4) E; (5) B; (6) B; (7) B; (8) False; (9) B; (10) E

Process:

1. Distribute the quiz.
2. Ask participants to answer the questions.
3. Go over the quiz, soliciting participant responses.

Debriefing Questions:

1. How did you feel as you were completing the quiz?
2. Which questions did you find the most interesting? Why?
3. Did you find any of these questions amusing? Why?

4. Which issue raised by this quiz is the most meaningful and/or the biggest concern for you? Why?
5. How might you apply what you learned here to your reentry process?

Debriefing Conclusions:

1. Reentry can present unexpected challenges.
2. Keeping a good sense of humor helps facilitate a smooth return.

This activity was developed by Craig Storti, Director, Communication Across Cultures, at www.craigstorti.com.

Worksheet: Repatriation Quiz: So You're Getting Ready to Go Home

1. True or False: Most returnees find repatriation as hard or harder than their adjustment to the foreign culture when they went abroad.

2. For most people, the essence of "home" is which of the following:
   a. A place where they know most people (they interact with every day) and most people know them.
   b. A place where they can relax and be themselves.
   c. A place where they have developed numerous daily routines and a set of unconscious habits.
   d. A place where there are few surprises, few unexpected events or situations that they are not used to.
   e. All of the above.

3. For most returnees, the place that best fits the description in #2, above is:
   a. The foreign country they are about to leave.
   b. The original home country that they are returning to.

4. Most repatriates will face adjustments in which of the following areas?
   a. Personal
   b. Professional
   c. Family
   d. Financial
   e. All of the above

5. The principal reason most people find reentry so challenging is:
   a. They get no briefing or preparation for reentry.
   b. They assume it's going to be easy. ("How hard can it be to adjust to your home?")
   c. Friends have told them it's not so difficult.

6. If there are things you find you do not like about your home country when you come back, the best thing you can do is:
   a. Criticize home to your family and friends.
   b. Grin and bear it.

7. If you complain about how hard reentry is, most people back home will:
   a. Understand and be sympathetic.
   b. Have no idea what you're talking about.

8. True or False: While I was away, nothing significant happened to my family and close friends; they have not changed.

9. When people ask you, "How was it in [name of country]?" the best thing to do is:

   a. Tell them as much as you can about what happened to you when you were overseas.

   b. Say "Very nice" and then ask them to please pass the potatoes.

10. Which of the following suggests that you have not successfully readjusted to your home country?

    a. You refuse to admit there are some nice things about being home.

    b. At the grocery store, you only buy enough food for one day.

    c. You get very upset when people say, "It must feel great to be back home."

    d. You always seal the garbage can lid tight for fear of attracting hyenas.

    e. All of the above.

Developed by Craig Storti, Director, Communication Across Cultures, at www.craigstorti.com.

Envisioning Your Future

Time Required:

75–100 minutes (5 minutes for introduction; 15–20 minutes for worksheet; 35–45 minutes for activity; 20–30 minutes for sharing and debriefing)

Objectives:

1. To help participants frame reentry as an ongoing, lifelong experience
2. To help participants identify the rewards of an international experience
3. To introduce the concept of a "vision board"
4. To help participants envision possibilities for "what is next"

Materials:

- Worksheet: Envisioning (one copy for each participant)
- Pens or pencils
- A variety of colorful magazines (travel magazines, copies of *National Geographic*, etc.)
- A few sample vision boards (you will display these or project them as PowerPoint slides)
- Scissors
- Poster board
- Glue sticks

Process:

1. Begin the introduction with the following narration:

   Living abroad is not for everyone. It can be challenging mentally, physically, and emotionally. Yet many returning sojourners report their time abroad was "life-enhancing" and even "life-changing."

Life in one's home culture may then seem like a black-and-white photograph when compared to the colorful sights, sounds, smells, and so forth found in the host culture. Return-ees sometimes feel "on-hold," not being able to fully engage, just waiting for another opportunity to return to an overseas assignment. One of the challenges in reentry is to once again find a spark of uniqueness in day-to-day life.

Our activity today is designed to help each person identify the rewards stemming from his or her international experience. With an understanding of these rewards, we will then use a creative process with the intention of filling our "what's next" with meaningful experiences.

2. Distribute the Envisioning worksheet and ask participants to find a comfortable space to complete it. Assure them this information is only for personal use.

3. When participants return to the full group, briefly discuss the importance of reflecting on one's international transition to deepen understanding of the experience.

4. Introduce the concept of the "vision board" as a tool to help bring clarity, and to help maintain focus on a specific life goal. Use language such as the following:

The board will literally display pictures and words of your "what next" desires for your personal and/or professional life. This is a creative process. You have just brought to mind many of the things that are important to you and that you desire for your future. Use any of the pictures and words that you feel drawn toward; do not try to analyze the "why." Just enjoy the process and trust that your completed board will be a reflection of your highest intentions for "what's next."

5. Offer a few sample vision boards for display, or project a few samples on PowerPoint slides.

6. Allow approximately 30–45 minutes for participants to create the boards.

7. Ask willing participants to display their boards.

8. Provide a silent time for participants to walk around the room and observe others' boards.

Debriefing Questions:

1. How did you feel completing the worksheet? How easy or hard was it to remember?

2. What did you think when you heard about the vision board? Describe your experience in selecting the pictures and words for use on your board.

3. What did you learn about this group by observing the various vision boards?

4. How might this process be useful in the future? Personally? Professionally?

Debriefing Conclusions:

1. Reentry is the one stage of international transition that can be lifelong, full of ongoing and often unexpected moments of insight.

2. An international living experience offers many challenges but is also full of rewards.

3. Identifying the most rewarding aspects of an international experience awakens possibilities for the future.

4. A vision board creates a clear, tangible picture of specific intentions for "what's next."

Alternative Process:

Participants might instead create a "digital vision board," which can then be displayed as a computer screen saver or easily displayed on a personal mobile device. Sites offering digital vision board possibilities can also be a resource for pictures that can be printed for use with this activity.

This exercise was developed by Patricia Cassiday, Collaborative Connection, Seattle, Washington (www.collaborativeconnection.org).

Worksheet: Envisioning

Please take a few minutes to write down any special thoughts or feelings from your international experience. We will then explore how this information can be of value to you as you envision your future. It is important to give your most candid answers. You will not be asked to share this information with anyone.

Think back to the time you first thought about the possibility of living abroad:

1. What motivated you to contemplate the possibility?
2. Did you discuss the idea with family members? Friends? How did they react?
3. What steps did you have to take to make your idea a reality?
4. If the move was NOT your idea, think back to how you felt. What were your thoughts? Motivation for accepting the position?

Now think back to your time in-country. You had many new experiences, met many new people, and created many new memories. As a result of your international experience, you may see the world differently (history, political structures, value systems, etc.). Life itself may be viewed through a different cultural lens.

1. Think of the unique people you met while abroad. Did they share their stories? How did those stories affect you?
2. Think back to challenging situations and/or unfavorable circumstances you overcame. What did you learn about yourself? How does that make you feel?
3. How did you find balance? Adventure? Joy?
4. Have your priorities changed regarding what is a necessity? A "must-have"? What is of primary importance?
5. What new attitudes or perspectives have you gained?
6. How is your return going?
7. What are some things you love about being back "home"?
8. What are some things you really miss about your life since returning from your international assignment? Are there any opportunities to bring these things into your current life?

Thoughts about your future:

Developed by Patricia Cassiday, Collaborative Connection, Seattle, Washington (www.collaborativeconnection. org).

41

Shoes for Reflection

Time Required:

20–30 minutes (This activity is usually done as an icebreaker.)

Objectives:

1. To initiate reflection on the individual's overseas experience
2. To facilitate articulation about the meaning of the international experience to the individual

Materials:

Pictures of various types of shoes, such as hiking boots, running shoes, ballet slippers, men's dress shoes, women's high heels, bedroom slippers, loafers, work boots, flip-flops, etc. (Only three to four types of shoes will be needed for a small group. Larger groups require more choices.) These pictures should be posted on the walls of the meeting room prior to the training.

Process:

1. For the introduction, note that participants are reaching the end of their international assignment and this is an excellent time to reflect back over their experience. Most people find it useful to think about this overseas experience as they prepare to return home. They have "walked in the moccasins" of another culture and learned many new things.

2. Ask participants to take a moment to reflect on their time in [country]. Then ask them to walk around the room and stand next to the picture of the type of "shoe" that best represents their international experience.

3. Ask participants to share answers to the following questions with the others gathered at this "shoe": Why did you select this shoe? How does this shoe represent your experience? (If there is a very large group at any one shoe, you can split them into

Work	
X–X	
X, X, X, X	

two or three sub-groups. This will give everyone an opportunity to share.)

4. Allow an appropriate amount of time (five to eight minutes depending on the size of the group) for discussion. Then ask each group to report on the core of their conversation (while still standing by their shoe).

Debriefing Questions:

1. What did you think when you were asked to select a shoe to represent your experience?
2. How did you feel when you heard the stories of others? How did you feel when you shared your own story?
3. What did you learn?
4. How might reflection on your experience abroad be applied to your personal/professional life?

Debriefing Conclusions:

1. Reflecting on your international experiences can be helpful in planning for the return home.
2. Strengths and skills acquired during the time abroad can enhance your ability to perform in new personal and professional settings.
3. Talking with others who have lived abroad and reentered your home culture can help to normalize your reentry experience.

This exercise was developed by Sandra M. Fowler, Intercultural Consultant and Trainer.

42

Planning & Building Your Reentry Network

Time Required:

75 minutes (5 minutes for introduction; 30 minutes for discussion and Network Planning Sheet; 10 minutes for planning; 15 minutes for practice; 15 minutes for debriefing)

Work
X–X
X, X, X, X

Objectives:

To help participants:

1. Define networking in the context of career planning.
2. Understand individual purpose and goals of networking.
3. Review the techniques of effective networking.
4. Begin to develop a networking plan.

Materials:

- Handout A: Network Building Worksheet (one for each participant)
- Handout B: Network Tracking Sheet (one for each participant)

Process

1. Use language such as the following for the introduction:

   There are often professional challenges associated with reentry. Employers may not value or understand the importance of your international experience, or your cross-cultural perspective. Your experience abroad may even be viewed as irrelevant once you have returned home. These challenges can lead to frustration and job dissatisfaction. Some returning sojourners return without a position and/or in need of a new place of employment. Accompanying spouses may have been unemployed during the sojourn and are now ready to reenter the workforce. Others returning may feel they are being underutilized, and this incites a desire for a career move.

Having an organized networking plan will be an important asset during reentry. Networking occurs both consciously and unconsciously as we interact with colleagues and friends. Relationship-building skills are essential for success in today's workplace. Returning expatriates can draw on their effective communication styles and relationship-building skills to develop networks.

Specifically, in the context of this activity, networking is defined as the cultivation of productive relationships for personal, employment, or business benefits. Your network is everyone you know who can help you in your career or personal life. The purpose of this exercise is to explore all aspects of networking: the purpose, planning, and objectives for enhancing networks that will help your career.

Networking can be fun. As you get to know people, you may discover hidden talent and new areas of interest. Your network of acquaintances, friends, and colleagues can be sources of insight, learning, expertise, and assistance.

2. Remind participants that it is important to understand the value of networking. Ask them to think of someone they know who uses his or her network effectively. This might be a boss, a customer, a team member, or a friend. Give participants a few minutes to identify how networking is adding value to that person's life. They should jot down a few ways they think the person benefits from the network and then turn to a partner and share ideas about how networking can be important. Return participants to the larger group and discuss key insights.

3. Distribute and ask learners to complete the Network Planning Worksheet (Attachment A). Then break learners into groups of three and ask them to discuss the following:

   - What have I learned so far about the people/organizations in my network?

   - Are they the right ones? Whom should I add?

   - Where am I under-invested?

   - Where am I over-invested?

4. Now prompt participants to discuss the "Dos and Don'ts of Successful Networking." Ask half of the group to identify the "dos" and the other half to identify the "don'ts." Here are some examples.

   Possible *Dos*

- Do engage in conversation. Ask people to talk about themselves, which will allow you to identify their skills, experiences, interests, and ways they might be helpful. Listen carefully to understand them, not just for ideas about how to "use" them. People who feel you care about them are more likely to offer to help you—or to say yes when you ask for help.
- Do ask what might be the best way to stay in touch (e-mail, social networking, texting, etc.) Follow up within forty-eight hours.
- Do spend time helping people. Share your advice and contacts. When you get a reputation for caring about others, people will want to be part of your network.
- Do make networking a part of your lifestyle, not just with work colleagues. The person you meet at a local coffee shop may turn out to be the best network partner you have.
- Do include social media, such as LinkedIn or Twitter.
- Do develop a systematic way of keeping track of your contacts and records of when you have had communication with them. Be clear about your career focus and what you need both short-term and long-term. Nobody can help you if you don't know what you need.

Possible *Don'ts*
- Don't ask for a job. Ask for ideas, for suggestions, for other contacts. People are happy to share information, but even if they have hiring power, most organizations have a process that needs to be followed. It is appropriate to ask about the process.
- Don't drop your contacts once you get an interview or a job; networking is a lifetime process.
- Don't use names of people for references without permission.

5. Ask both groups to report their list and together create a list of how to avoid the "don'ts" and improve/increase the "do's."

6. Encourage participants to create an action plan:
   - Ask participants to develop a list of contacts and determine how to connect with each individual.
   - Ask participants to divide the contacts into two groups:
     - Those who are most important to meeting their short-term goals.
     - Second-tier relationships or those who might be helpful but are less critical.

- Help participants set up a network management system to track their calls, contacts, and follow up. Distribute Attachment B: Network Tracking Sheet. Note that the spreadsheet can be used to keep track of communications, referrals, or actions.
- Encourage participants to nurture and maintain good relationships throughout their various networks. This will allow them to ask for a favor or help from someone, whether it is specialist knowledge or an introduction.
- Divide students into pairs so they can practice approaching someone for networking purposes. Each partner should select the individual who will be most challenged to approach and the setting in which that discussion will occur (e.g., party, lunchroom, etc.). Partners can offer suggestions for how to strengthen the approach, paying attention to words, tone, body language, etc.

Debriefing Questions:

1. Why were you interested in a workshop on networking?
2. What are some of your thoughts or feelings about networking? What is the most difficult part of networking for you? What is the easiest? Why?
3. How has this experience been helpful? Describe any new insights and/or surprises.
4. What are your next steps? How will this networking plan help you?

Debriefing Conclusions:

1. Networking can be a source of learning, inspiration, and assistance in your career planning. It can also enhance your non-work life.
2. Relationship-building is an essential aspect of networking and can be fun.
3. Having an organized network plan will be an asset for sojourners returning home.

This exercise was adapted from Susan Bloch and Philip Whiteley's work in *The Global You* (2010), published by Marshall Cavendish (http://tinyurl.com/po5xar5).

Handout A: Network Building Worksheet

Given my career goals, which people/organizations/institutions should I be including in my network?

Important Relationships: (e.g., Jacob, who is head of HR; Mary, who is the CEO of one of our largest suppliers; Mike, who is in the hiking club; Janet, who is our external auditor; host country nationals; home country colleagues)

Name	Phone	E-mail	Comments

Organizations and Institutions of Interest (e.g., alumni associations, civic organizations, sports clubs, etc.):

Adapted from Susan Bloch & Philip Whiteley's work in *The Global You* (2010), published by Marshall Cavendish (http://tinyurl.com/po5xar5).

Handout B: Network Tracking Sheet

Person	Date Contacted	Method of Contact (e.g., lunch, e-mail, phone)	Follow-Up Date	Comments

Adapted from Susan Bloch and Philip Whiteley's work in *The Global You* (2010), published by Marshall Cavendish (http://tinyurl.com/po5xar5).

Taking Leave: Pre-Departure and Reentry

Time Required:

60–75 minutes (15 minutes to introduce the Five-Step Cycle for Successful Relocation and discuss "Leaving"; 30–40 minutes for two rounds of group work; 15–20 minutes for debriefing and synthesis)

Work
X–X
X, X, X, X

Objectives:

1. To teach participants about the Five-Step Cycle for Successful Relocation
2. To heighten their understanding of challenges in "Leaving."
3. To help them normalize feelings during the leaving/detachment step
4. To provide them with techniques/tools for "healthy closure"

Materials:

- Chart paper and markers
- Appendix B: A Five-Step Model for Successful Relocation (one copy per participant)
- Index cards (optional)

Process:

1. Distribute copies of Appendix B and use that information to introduce the topic of successful relocation as a five-step process.
2. Use language such as the following to give a brief lecturette on "Leaving":

   Leaving is often a paradoxical time. On one hand, we want to know about the future and can be very excited about that, but at the same time we have the very personal challenges of letting go. (Children, especially, will worry more about the friends they will lose than about where they are going.) Make the point that in a real sense, leaving starts the minute you hear there will be a move, which becomes "the moment everything changed."

On a deeper, more personal and psychological level, the leaving stage is when we are preparing to let go of our life as we currently know it. We consciously and/or unconsciously begin to loosen emotional ties. We begin to slowly back away from personal and professional relationships and responsibilities. Feelings of confusion, anger, isolation, and so forth are likely to be experienced by the person who is leaving and also by those who will be staying behind.

Separation from our present situation is a normal and necessary part of the relocation process. Detaching is actually a self-protective strategy often used to make the leaving (and associated loss) as painless as possible. Understanding the underlying motivation and emotions associated with this separation process offers us an opportunity to choose alternative and productive ways of "letting go."

3. Ask participants to form groups of three to five people and brainstorm some answers to the following two rounds of questions. (If time allows, ask the groups to generate answers for all of the questions; if time is limited, you can list the questions on index cards and have someone draw a single question to be answered by each group.)

Round 1:
   a. How did you feel when you first got the news that you would be relocating?
   b. Have you ever found yourself bragging about or glorifying the new destination as you are preparing to leave? Or, conversely, have you found yourself saying unfavorable things? Why do you think you might have chosen one of these patterns to use during your leaving stage?
   c. After announcing that you will be relocating, have you ever felt "invisible" at work? With friends?
   d. Have you ever felt rejected, when it was time for you to leave, by those you thought were your friends? Why might coworkers become angry or frustrated with the person leaving? Why might this happen with friends?
   e. How might "unfinished business" (e.g., an unresolved conflict, an assigned task with no plan for completion, etc.) be

handled by someone who is leaving? By someone who is staying? Why?

Round 2:

Now with a better understanding of the emotions and behaviors that can be associated with the process of leaving, generate some suggestions for easing the separation.

   a. How might personal relationships be nurtured and sustained? Conflicts resolved? Why is this an important step?

   b. How can coworkers remain engaged and supportive during this time? Why is this important for the person leaving? Those left behind?

4. Ask each group to share answers and solutions to the questions.

Debriefing Questions:

1. How did you feel during the discussion of the relocation cycle? How did you respond to the information about the five steps? Was there any information that was a surprise for you? Sounded or felt familiar?

2. What happened as your group began to focus on "Leaving"? Were your group members able to easily identify and discuss experiences? Possible reasons for denial and/or avoidance?

3. How easy was it for your group to shift into suggesting strategies for healthy leaving? Share some similarities and/or differences in suggested strategies.

4. What did you learn from this activity? Which strategies or tools might you use when leaving for your next assignment? Preparing to return home?

Debriefing Conclusions:

1. International relocation can be understood in terms of a five-cycle process.

2. Leaving in the right way is an essential step to entering in the right way. Preparing for the departure with an appropriate goodbye strategy is an important step in closing out unfinished business and preparing for a smooth start at the new destination.

3. Expatriates frequently experience a sense of loss or grief for what is being left behind: friends, stimulating environment, sense of autonomy, etc.

4. Ignoring or avoiding feelings of loss, anger, grief, and so forth, and the associated separation behaviors, can have long-term consequences. It is important to recognize and normalize these feelings to prevent the loss of friendships and avoid poor job performance.

This activity has been adapted from David C. Pollock and Ruth E. Van Reken's work in *The Third Culture Kid Experience: Growing Up Among Worlds* (2009).

Reentry Debriefing: The R2-A4 Model

Time Required:

1–4 hours

Objectives:

To help participants:

1. Reflect on the experience of living internationally.
2. Heighten understanding of the reentry process.
3. Normalize the feelings associated with reentry.
4. Provide practice in talking about the experience of living overseas.
5. Plan action steps toward personal and professional integration of the international experience.

Materials:

A journal for the coaching/mentoring option. If this activity is used for individual or family coaching/mentoring sessions, participants will focus on a single stage each week, reflecting on the questions and journaling their answers. Journal insights are then the focus of each session.

Note to Trainers:
It is important to have an experienced facilitator set the tone for the session, including boundaries and expectations for respect and confidentiality. This can be a high-risk activity depending on the depth of the participants' reflection and willingness to share.

This material can be structured for use with families or individuals in ongoing coaching or mentoring sessions. It is the sequencing of this activity that is essential for maximum effectiveness. The time available for training will be the determining factor in planning the approach.

<table>
<tr><td>Work</td></tr>
<tr><td>X–X</td></tr>
<tr><td>X, X, X, X</td></tr>
</table>

The stages of this activity have an implicit structure. The sequence of the model is designed to be followed in a logical progression moving from "immediate now" to "recent past," "analysis," "perceived linkages," "desired future goals," and "action plans."

During the debriefing of each stage, participants may digress and/ or shift their frame of reference. A skilled facilitator will need to listen empathetically, and at the same time gently guide the process back to the chronological order of the activity.

Process:

1. Introduce the Six Stages of the Reentry Debrief (R2-A4 Model):

   - Stage 1: **R**eview present (present life, current feelings, concerns)
   - Stage 2: **R**ecollect past (mental archeology, past experiences, background)
   - Stage 3: **A**nalyze/Compare (linkage between past and present circumstances)
   - Stage 4: **A**ttitude Adjustment (psychological, emotional, affective, cognitive status)
   - Stage 5: **A**nticipate (future projection/goals)
   - Stage 6: **A**ction (cognitive analysis and behavior)

2. For each stage, ask participants to consider questions such as the following. (The sample questions provided in this exercise for each of the six stages in the R2-A4 Model can be easily modified or amplified for specific age groups, variation in professional background, and/or complexity of the participants' overseas experience.)

   Stage 1: **R**eview Present
   - What issues are you currently dealing with regarding adjustment?
   - How is your current life (apparently) being influenced by past events?
   - What is it about NOW that you see as being related to prior experiences? Is that good, bad, or only a fact of life?
   - What is it about the PRESENT that might be related to your entire life journey? (And most saliently to your most recent overseas/cross-cultural experience?)

- Is coming home a return to "old ways," or an unsettling combination of resuming prior patterns while attempting to integrate or retain "new ways" of thinking and behaving?

Stage 2: **R**ecollect Past

- What factors, people, places, and events shaped your past life and recent international experience?
- What is the relationship, if any, between your life before your relocation and what you actually experienced while living abroad?
- What stood out for you about your time abroad, and what were the high and low points of that period of your life? What did you enjoy most, and what negative aspects were involved?
- To what extent did you integrate into the new cultural or work setting? How successful were you in bridging intercultural barriers and various encounters with "difference"?
- What do you miss most about living abroad since you have returned?

Stage3: **A**nalyze/Compare

- How are the first two stages (present and past) interrelated?
- What influences from the past are now irrelevant (even if sad to admit), and which have the power to influence and possibly overwhelm your ongoing life?

Stage 4: **A**ttitude Adjustment

- How is your "former" self related to your "returning self"? What are the salient differences? How do you feel about it?
- Has there been too much change? Not enough? Are you feeling confused? Why? What can you control, and what do you have to ignore, suppress, or continue to tolerate?
- How are you feeling about all this now? What might you do to change or alleviate negative impacts, while integrating, separating, synthesizing, or promoting the positive impact of those interactions?

Stage 5: **A**nticipate

- Where do you see this process going? Where would you like to be or get to?
- What about the present or future do you want to change or deal with more effectively?
- What can (or should, or might) be altered that would be more satisfying or less dysfunctional?

- Given the current trajectory of your reentry, what is the likely outcome of continuing with the current pattern unchanged? Are you satisfied with that vision of the future, or are there aspects of it that you will need to deal with, immediately or eventually?

Stage 6: **A**ction (Cognitive analysis and behavior)

- How can you develop a plan to examine, change, and/or cope with current circumstances as well as consider what you must do *now* to ensure that those actions will support and align with the *future* you envision?

- What actions will help you in both your current adjustment and to reach your longer-term goals?

- Since anticipation of any future changes will be most successful when backed by a conscious plan and accompanied by appropriate and reasonable behaviors, what steps can you take to meet the need to move beyond simple cognitive recognition (self-reflection) to a more active mode (self-intervention)?

- After setting actual goals/ideals, how can you take the final crucial step, which is to begin consciously working toward implementing new behaviors congruent with your new attitudes and preferred outcomes?

- While "worrying can help," it is more immediately productive to devise a strategy based on a clear and accurate assessment of what your new realities are likely to be. It is also important to decide explicitly how you want to approach your adjustment, rather than drift along. Bottom line . . . what you *do* about your situation is as important as what you think about it!

Debriefing Questions:

The debriefing questions are built into each of the stages.

Debriefing Conclusions:

1. Living internationally may result in personal changes and preferences that can go unnoticed until the expatriate returns home.

2. Returnees may initially feel like "strangers," and it is hard for them to know what their experiences have meant to them or how they have changed without an opportunity for reflection.

3. Expatriates often experience a sense of loss or grief for what has been left behind: missing friends, feeling special, enjoying a stimulating environment, having a sense of autonomy, etc. It is important to discuss those feelings.

4. Reflection on the international experience is an important step necessary in planning new personal and professional goals.

5. Integrating the experience of living internationally into personal and professional goals capitalizes on the richness of that learning opportunity.

This exercise was developed by Bruce La Brack for the Summer Institute for Intercultural Communication course "Training for Transition" in Portland, Oregon.

45

Dancing Through Reentry

Time Required:

45–60 minutes (attribution selection and reflection 15–20 minutes; partner discussion 15–20 minutes; debriefing 15–20 minutes)

Work
X–X
X, X, X, X

Objectives:

To help participants:

1. To normalize a wide range of feelings associated with reentry.
2. To initiate reflection on personal strengths/attributes.
3. To connect "lessons learned" abroad to the reentry process.

Materials:

- Worksheet: Attributes (one per participant)
- Dancing and change quotation (use on an opening slide or chart):

    "The only way to make sense out of change is to plunge into it, move with it, and join the dance." —Alan Watts

Process:

Part I

1. Ask participants to reflect on their own reentry (or last move or job change if they have not reentered). What might/does present the greatest challenge?

2. Distribute the Attributes Worksheet. Briefly discuss the concept of living abroad as one of the best ways to strengthen or develop these attributes. Ask participants to read over the list and reflect on their time living abroad. They should circle any and all of the attributes that apply. Then ask them to select the attribute that was most helpful and that they relied on the most or the one that best defines them. They should also mark a second choice.

3. "Think about the ways these attributes help you when you were abroad." (Allow time for reflection.)
4. "Think about how these attributes might help you during reentry." (Allow time for reflection.)

Part II

1. Select a partner. (You each will have five minutes to share.)
2. Explain why you chose this attribute.
3. Describe how this might be useful during your return "home."

Debriefing Questions:

1. How did you feel as you read through the attributes? As you identified the one or two attributes with the greatest congruency?
2. What were some similarities or differences that occurred during the sharing?
3. Why might this concept be important for someone who is reentering?
4. How can you apply this information personally, to enhance the benefits of living internationally? What are the organizational applications?

Debriefing Conclusions:

1. Returning is not a predictable process. It is difficult to know what the experience has meant to the returnee and how she or he may have changed.
2. Returnees can initially act like or feel like "strangers." This is a normal part of reentry.
3. Competencies and skills acquired while living abroad are readily available to the returnee.
4. Connecting to past experiences with transition can help to ease the reentry process.

Optional Process:

Create a chart matching the Attributes worksheet. Ask participants to place a dot or an X on the chart next to their first and second choices. A discussion can then be generated about group similarities and differences.

This exercise was developed by Patricia Cassiday, Collaborative Connection, Seattle, Washington (www.collaborativeconnection.org).

Worksheet: Attributes

This is a partial list of personal attributes recognized in individuals who have been successful when working across cultures. Please review and circle the attributes that best describe you. (Feel free to add additional attributes.) Circle all that apply and then select the one or two attributes you depend on the most (or that you believe will be most helpful during your transition home).

Independent	Open-minded	Flexible
Inquisitive	Resourceful	Self-reliant
Enthusiastic	Assertive	High energy
Humble	Nonjudgmental	Creates trust
Manages uncertainty	Good listener	Responsible
Perceptive	Self-aware	Adaptable
Emotionally resilient	Balanced life	Manages conflict
Embraces duality	Risk taker	Builds relationships
Learning-oriented	People "reader"	Tolerates ambiguity
Culturally empathetic	Curious	Takes initiative
Organized	Sense of humor	Handles rejection
Spiritual practice	Problem-solver	Self-confident
Culturally aware	Resilient	Observant
Manages time	Language skills	Creative

Developed by Patricia Cassiday, Collaborative Connection, Seattle, Washington (www.collaborativeconnection. org).

46

What's on Your Plate?

Time Required:

45 minutes (5 minutes for introduction; 10 minutes for activity; 20 minutes for report-out; 10 minutes for debriefing)

<table>
<tr><td>Work</td></tr>
<tr><td>X–X</td></tr>
<tr><td>X, X, X, X</td></tr>
</table>

Objectives:

1. To explore participants' expectations and/or concerns about their transition
2. To incorporate each individual's skills and experiences into mastering his or her current or upcoming transition
3. To engage a group (or a couple/family) in sharing and mutual support

Materials:

- Large white paper plates
- Markers (enough for each participant to have a few different colors)
- Blue painter's tape

Note for facilitator: When working in languages other than English (or with speakers of English as a foreign language), explain the metaphorical meaning of "What's on your plate?" Also, this activity allows tailoring the starting question to fit a specific learning event and a specific place within this event where the activity is used.

Process:

1. Give each participant one paper plate. Distribute markers for the group to share.
2. Ask participants to think about what is on their "plate" at the moment. For example:

a. As you are preparing for your move, what are the expectations and concerns?

b. As you are preparing to go back home after your time abroad, what kind of self-discoveries are you taking with you?

c. As you are adjusting to living and working or studying in a new country, what are your main challenges?

d. As you are preparing to work on this new project, what keeps you up at night?

e. Thinking about previous changes and transitions that you experienced, what have you learned from them that will be useful in navigating your current transition?

f. Based on what you have learned in this training/coaching session, what are you taking with you that will be useful in your upcoming transition?

3. Ask participants to present their ideas in a form of drawing on their paper plates. Suggest that they should not use words unless a word or two are necessary in their drawings. (This activity is not about creating a bulleted list of points.)

4. Ask participants to put their finished plates up on the wall using the blue painter's tape.

5. Do a "gallery walk" with participants. Ask them to take turns explaining their drawings.

Debriefing Questions:

1. How did it feel to be asked to present your thoughts through a drawing?

2. What were some of your discoveries (aha moments, learning points) during the process?

3. What do you notice as you look at others' plates and hear their stories?

4. What skills and competencies do you have that are instrumental in carrying this particular plate? What skills and competencies might you want to develop or strengthen?

5. What kind of support do you have available? How do you access this support?

6. What is a main insight (learning, conclusion) that you are taking from this experience?

Debriefing Conclusions:

1. Identifying those things we have "on our plate" can help us identify how to manage them and what resources are available to us.

2. Sharing those things on our plates with others can help reduce the emotional power the issues have over us.

Notes:

1. This activity incorporates a multiple intelligence approach to learning by asking people to express themselves through drawing rather than verbally. During the debriefing it allows for a discussion of a number of important issues (e.g., operating in and out of one's comfort zone, resistance to change, communicating in a "foreign" language, etc.).

2. Sharing one's thoughts, expectations, or concerns and thus making oneself vulnerable allows for development of empathy toward self and others. When done in a group environment, this activity can lead to better mutual understanding and support.

3. Specific topic-related conclusions are driven by the topic that is defined by the original question given to the participants, so take care with the initial question(s) you pose.

4. This activity can serve multiple purposes. For example, used in the beginning of the training it can serve as an assessment of needs, concerns, skills, etc. Used at the end of the process, it serves to summarize learning or facilitate action planning.

This activity was created by Tatyana Fertelmeyster, Founder and Principal, Connecting Differences: Consulting, Training, Facilitation, and Coaching (connecting.differences@gmail.com).

47

Payoffs from Paradox!

Time Required:

60–90 minutes depending on group size

Objectives:

1. To heighten participants' awareness of cultural paradox
2. To enhance participants' ability to perceive and learn from paradoxical challenges
3. To encourage participants to develop a more cognitively complex perspective

Materials:

- Worksheet: Awareness of Paradox Assessment (one per participant)
- Notepaper
- Pens or pencils

Process:

1. Start the introduction by using language such as the following:

   Can you think of any instances during your assignment when you had to deal with contradictions or paradoxes at work or in your social life? A paradox can be defined as a statement that apparently contradicts itself and yet might be true. These are examples: "Nobody goes to that restaurant; it's too crowded" and "Don't go near the water until you've learned to swim." For this activity we are defining paradox in the following way: when a person holds or sees two contradictory points of view that are both true, and she or he must decide which point of view to act on in a particular situation.

2. Distribute the worksheet.

Work
X–X
X, X, X, X

3. Ask participants to complete the nine questions and then rank their YES responses in the order of significance. Participants should not write their own paradox yet.

4. Discuss the importance of writing the "critical incident" paradox. This can be used in this group to further insight and to enhance awareness. With the participants' permission, these incidents can be shared with the organization to better prepare new expatriates for their assignments.

5. Allow 10–15 minutes for participants to write up a factual paradox situation.

6. Discuss the critical incident paradoxes. (This can be a high-risk activity depending on the incident disclosed.) Participants can be encouraged but should not be compelled to share with the larger group.

7. Conclude by collecting the written incidents from participants who are willing to contribute to an "organizational resource log."

Debriefing Questions:

1. Were you surprised by any of the statements on the paradox assessment?

2. What did you think about the questions? About the process of writing up a critical incident?

3. What are the different ways people resolve their paradox? What lessons can we take away from paradox resolution? What skills does this involve?

4. What do you see as significant about this activity? How might you use this information in the future? How might the organization benefit from gathering this type of information?

Debriefing Conclusions:

1. When an expatriate interacts with host-culture nationals, he or she frequently encounters paradoxical situations.

2. Once the expatriate recognizes the paradox, he or she must decide how to meet the challenge in the most effective manner.

3. Holding two or more "realities" at one time requires a cognitively complex perspective. Expatriates' exposure to difference can help to enhance this skill.

This exercise was adapted from the work of Joyce Osland, professor at the Global Leadership Advancement Center, San Jose State University.

Worksheet: Awareness of Paradox Assessment

Have you ever experienced the following? Please write YES or NO on the blank line. Then rank-order the YES paradoxes/contradictions according to their significance or the importance they held for you. Assign #1 to the paradox that was most significant, etc.

_____ 1. Possessing a great deal of power as a result of your role but downplaying it in order to gain necessary input and cooperation.

_____ 2. Generally thinking well of the host-culture nationals while at the same time being very savvy about being taken advantage of by them.

_____ 3. Feeling caught between the contradictory demands of headquarters, the host-culture nationals, and the local situation.

_____ 4. Seeing a valid stereotype about the culture you live in but also realizing that many host-culture nationals do not fit the stereotype.

_____ 5. Giving up some of your home country values in order to be accepted in the other culture while finding some of your home country values become even stronger as a result of exposure to another culture.

_____ 6. Feeling at ease anywhere but not really belonging anywhere, as a result of having lived abroad for a long period of time.

_____ 7. Becoming more "world-minded" as a result of your exposure to different values and conflicting loyalties but at the same time becoming more particular in formulating your own value system and view of life.

_____ 8. Trying to represent your organization well in order to succeed but realizing the "ideal" values you act on abroad may not exist at headquarters.

_____ 9. Having freedom from many of your own cultural rules and even some of the host culture's norms but not having freedom from certain host-culture customs if you hoped to be effective.

Choose one of the paradoxes above, or another example that comes to mind. (This should be a paradox that represents one of your biggest challenges.) Write up an incident in a way that it could be shared with future expatriates; include details and facts as you prepare to answer these questions:

What lead up to the situation?   Who was involved?

What were you thinking?   What were you feeling?

What did you actually do?   What was the outcome of the situation?

If you learned to live comfortably with this paradox, please share how you were able to do that.

Adapted from the work of Joyce Osland, professor, at San Jose State University.

48

The Edge

Time Required:

50–65 minutes (5–10 minutes for introduction; 15 minutes for experiment and exploration; 15–20 minutes for small group discussion and drawing; 15–20 minutes for debriefing)

Objectives:

For participants to:

1. Experience the dissonance or disequilibrium commonly associated with change and growth.
2. Become familiar with their own natural responses when experiencing dissonance or disequilibrium.
3. Identify the kind of support that best serves them during times of dissonance or disequilibrium.

Materials:

- Newsprint
- Colored felt-tip markers
- Masking tape

Process:

1. Introduction
   - Ask the group to think about the word *edge*, and to then look for edges in the room.
   - Ask the group to identify some of the elements or characteristics of edges in the room: what are they like; what do they accomplish? As they respond, note these on newsprint.
2. Experiment and exploration
   - Ask the group to go outside and physically experiment with edges. Participants can explore edges alone or with a

partner. Give them instructions such as these: Try to walk some edges, such as a crack in the sidewalk or the edge of a curb (experiment with safe and less safe edges, but don't endanger yourself); approach the edge, look over the edge, back away from the edge; explore as many kinds of edges as you can.

- While exploring edges, participants should pay attention to how they feel as they walk the different kinds of edges.

3. Small-group discussion
- Place participants in groups of four or five, and give each group a piece of newsprint and several colored markers.
- Ask the groups to talk about and draw what they learned about their own natural inclinations when walking on edges.

Debriefing Questions:

1. Post the small groups' newsprint depictions on the wall, and give participants time for a "gallery walk" so that everyone can look at them.

2. Ask each small group to explain their depictions. Ask, "How did you feel walking the various edges? What did you learn about your inclinations around edges?"

3. Facilitate a discussion. Ask, "What good does it do you to know how you feel about edges, to know how you tend to react?"

Debriefing Conclusions:

1. Learning and growth often take place when we're on "the edge"—maybe because we're more open then to new possibilities.

2. Some people will resist moving up to edges, and others will want to leap over them. Being conscious of our natural inclinations can help us recognize when we're on an edge, when we need help, or when we can offer help to someone else.

3. It's important to know that different people (e.g., within a family or within a classroom) will respond differently to the same edge, and that even the same person may respond differently at different times.

Note: This exercise works best when either (1) participants come to the realization that this is a metaphor on their own; or (2) the idea that this is a metaphor isn't introduced until the full-group discussion. The facilitator should not introduce the activity as a metaphor.

A preliminary activity can help contextualize the metaphor for a particular subject area (e.g., cross-cultural difference) or an experience (e.g., international transitions). For example, participants are asked to work in groups to depict on newsprint the best and worst things about leaving, about staying, or about arriving new. This establishes a train of attention. It contextualizes the use of "the edge" as a metaphor, even without naming it as such, helping participants better understand their experiences and needs in the midst of international transition.

This exercise was created by Gordon Watanabe, Ed.D., Founding Partner, Personal Leadership Seminars, and Barbara F. Schaetti, Ph.D., Owner/ Consultant, Transition Dynamics and Founding Partner, Personal Leadership Seminars.

49

A Good Return

Time Required:

90–115 minutes (10 minutes for introduction; 20–25 minutes for storytelling or video; 30–40 minutes in small groups; 30–40 minutes for large-group debriefing)

Objectives:

1. To heighten participants' awareness of the reentry process
2. To normalize the feelings associated with reentry
3. To emphasize that the reentry experience is very personal (i.e., individual family members, colleagues, etc., may not experience the effects of reentry in the same way or at the same time)
4. To call attention to the positive aspects of reentry in addition to the challenges

Materials:

- Reentry stories (organizational, personal, country-specific, and culture-general) to be shared during the activity (samples are provided in the attachment; examples from your own employees, students, families, and organization will add relevance)
- Pen and paper for note-taking

Process:

1. Introduce the activity with language such as the following.
   - Many people do not expect coming home to be difficult. ("It is home, after all.") They wonder what there can be to talk about.
   - Yet people who have returned from international assignments or study abroad say that reverse culture shock can

be even more traumatic than the culture shock they went through in moving overseas.

- During this activity, you will hear stories from people who have returned home from abroad.

- Coming home is a very personal experience. What happened to others may not happen to you. Even so, you may be interested in hearing what some of these people have experienced.

- It is important to note that the *process* of reentry is not specific to a particular location or assignment. As you are listening, think about the way the experiences are similar to or different from your own.

- You may wish to have a pen and paper handy to jot down anything that comes to mind that you would like to discuss or ask about later.

2. Taking one story at a time, either the facilitator or designated participants should read the sample stories in Attachment A aloud under each heading. Then ask participants for their immediate response.

   a. Does anything in this story make sense to you? Does anything sound familiar?

   b. Were there any statements or observations you especially related to?

   c. What, in these stories, contrasted with or was similar to your experience abroad and/or upon return?

   Depending on how people answer, you may want to follow up with probing questions that make people expand on the statement they have just made:

   - Can you say anything more about that?
   - Can you give an example?
   - What makes you say that?
   - Why do you feel that way?

3. When the "immediate reaction" phase of the discussion begins to wind down, take participants through a more personal exploration. Organize participants into small groups of four to six. Provide the following sets of questions and provide time for small-group discussion.

I. *"Welcome to the New Land."* Settling into the culture abroad:

- If (country) has become home, then what does that mean about the "home" you are now returning to?
- Do you feel you made (country) home when you lived there?

- Did you think of (country) as your home, even temporarily?
- Did it ever occur to you that instead of coming home, you were leaving home?
- Did you get deeply involved in your professional assignment when you were abroad? Will you miss (or are you missing) this level of satisfaction and involvement in your new job?

II. *"Saying Good-Bye."* Deciding and preparing to leave:

- Adjusting successfully to a foreign culture often means behaving in ways that do not come naturally to you. Can you think of ways you had to behave in (country) that were not natural to you?
- Have you changed in ways you wish you had not? In ways you really like and enjoy?
- Are you ever surprised by the ways you behave now that are different from how you behaved before you lived in (country)?

III. (a) *"Welcome Home Stranger, How Was It?"* Returning home, reverse culture shock, surprise, confusion, and frustration adjusting to home:

- Are there ways you feel you don't fit into U.S. (or home country) culture?
- Have you ever been in a conversation where everyone except you knew some "common" piece of information (joke, reference to commercials, political reference, etc.)? How did you feel?
- Are there things you didn't know or couldn't remember how to do when you came back?
- Did you bring back any behaviors or habits from (country) that people in the U.S. (home country) find strange? How did they make their surprise evident to you?

III. (b) *"Welcome Home Stranger, How Was It?"* Have you found that people really wanted to listen to your stories?

- How does it make you feel when friends and family don't seem interested in what has been one of the most significant experiences of your life?
- Do you understand why they are not interested?
- Have you asked what happened in their lives while you were away?
- What does it mean if you have to keep these important experiences to yourself?

- Have you found people you can talk to about your overseas experience?
- Why might someone feel lonely upon repatriation? Do you?
- Have you experienced friends or family being surprised or even offended because you don't "seem happy" being back in your home culture? Do you understand why they might feel this way?

IV. *"Back to Life; Back to Reality."* On the professional side of reentry, how has your overseas experience "played out" back home?

- Do you feel you have a lot to offer your employer as a result of your international experience? What skills and knowledge did you acquire?
- Is your international experience going to be put to use in your new job?
- Do people in your organization understand how to make the best use of your international experience?
- Is there anything you can do to help leadership in your organization make use of your experience?
- How do you feel about not being able to use this experience? Does it feel like a failure?

Accompanying Spouse:

- What is your professional situation at this moment?
- How has the overseas sojourn affected your career path? Adversely or positively?
- Can you think of ways the overseas experience has enhanced your marketability? What can you offer a potential employer that many other candidates cannot?
- How do you see your repatriation experience as being different from that of your spouse? Do you think reentry is easier or harder for you than for your spouse?

V. *"Issues for the Family"* (*if applicable*). It appears that very young children have a relatively easier time moving since their life revolves mainly around parents and the home. Older children, whose lives have begun to revolve around friends outside of the home, find relocation more difficult. Teenagers, whose identity comes mainly from peer group association and acceptance, can have a very difficult time adjusting. Older children and teens don't have a peer group in the home country; they do not know the latest music fads, etc. Two most common issues for older children and teens are: (1) other kids think the repat kids are bragging when they talk about their overseas experience or speak another language; and (2) frequently the repat kids link up with either "inappropriate" friends (teens who are outsiders in their own school and have no peer group) or with other teens who have lived abroad or come from another country.

- How do your children feel about coming home?
- Do they have friends who seem to accept them?
- Do they have to keep their overseas experience to themselves? Is there a way for them to share some aspects of their experience?
- Is there any way to help them meet other repat kids?
- What seems to help children and teens get established in a school, neighborhood, or youth group?

VI. *"What They Gained."* This is a good time to discuss the positive aspects of the expat sojourn, as well as the positive aspects of being back home.

- What new skills, knowledge, attitudes, or experiences do you have as a result of this experience?
- How do you feel you benefitted from your overseas experience?
- What do you think you have to offer your organization (or prospective new employer) that employees who have not lived abroad are not able to offer?
- What are some things you do not miss about your life as an expat?
- What do you especially like about being back home?
- Do you think people who are members of a minority in their home culture have an easier or harder time when living overseas (in contrast to those who are in the majority)? (Remember that for many white U.S. Americans, living overseas is the first time they experience being in the minority.)
- Do you think the experience of coming home is different for members of minority groups as contrasted with majority groups? How? (You can modify this question to reflect specific groups in the seminar, such as African Americans, Japanese Americans, etc.)
- Do you think people who have lived abroad are more open to and/or more skillful at dealing with people from diverse backgrounds in their own country?
- How has your experience abroad changed your views about the minority experience in your own culture? How has your

experience affected your approach to living in a diverse society?

Debriefing Questions:

The debriefing questions are embedded in the activity.

Debriefing Conclusions:

1. Reentry is a transition process that requires time.
2. The experience can be very personal; others may not experience reentry in the same way or at the same time as you.
3. Identifying positive aspects of being home will help navigate reentry shock.
4. Other returnees are more likely to share your feelings, listen to your stories, and be sources of support.

Optional Process:

In lieu of participant stories or organizational case examples, use the video *A Good Return*, which is available at www.globalfilmnetwork. net.

This exercise was adapted from the work of Craig Storti for the video *A Good Return*, directed by Regge Life (available from www.globalfilmnetwork.net).

Attachment: Sample Story Segments

I. *"Welcome to the New Land."* Settling into the culture abroad:

When we first moved to Germany, everything was new: the currency, the telephone booths, the driving regulations, etc. After the first several months, we had found a home, understood the road signs, and knew how to use the telephone and where to go to pay for utilities (at the post office). We accepted that there were no closets and that the kitchen did not even come with a sink. It was amazing how much we learned quickly from necessity and then how it all began to feel familiar. After the first year, Germany began to feel like home.

II. *"Saying Good-Bye."* Deciding and preparing to leave:

We only realized how much we had changed while living abroad after we returned to the U.S. One example: In the U.S., good service in a restaurant is to take the order, deliver the food, and deliver the bill quickly. Good service is being attentive and checking in frequently to be sure "everything is alright." In Europe, going to dinner is an event. People expect to leisurely sip wine and enjoy conversation. Restaurants may turn late diners away because "we are full for the evening." The wait staff is careful not to interrupt conversations and rarely will come to the table unless summoned. The bill is never presented until requested. One of the first "reverse culture shock" experiences for our family came when fast and quick service met with our slow and leisurely expectations.

III. (a) *"Welcome Home Stranger, How Was It?"* Returning home, reverse culture shock, surprise, confusion, and frustration adjusting to home:

During the early 1980s there was no Internet and very limited access to English-speaking television. It was a forty-five-minute drive to see a new English-speaking film, so we saw very few movies, let alone experience the MTV generation. It was amazing how little of U.S. humor we understood. References from *Laugh In* and *Saturday Night Live* were completely lost on us. We also noticed we walked slower and spoke more softly than many of our family members and friends.

III. (b) *"Welcome Home Stranger, How Was It?"* Have you found that people wanted to listen to your stories?

I think we all agree that regardless of the setting or the generation, everyone wanted about a three-minute synopsis of the experience that ended preferably with "and it is so great to be back in the U.S.A." For the kids, if they mentioned "in Europe" or "in Germany" at school, they were met with blank stares or with side comments about being stuck-up or snobby. If you share some things you liked better about Europe, you were sometimes viewed as unpatriotic or just strange.

IV. *"Back to Life; Back to Reality."* On the professional side of reentry, how has your overseas experience "played out" back home?

Even at work, no one really wanted to know what I had learned or how it might help the company be more effective overseas. It took me a long time to figure out how to work effectively in that new German environment. I would never have figured it all out on my own. Thank goodness for my office mates who helped me understand the subtle and not-so-subtle differences and the reasons for those differences. I felt like I was returning with some really valuable insights, but no one really had time or the desire to listen. It just was not important to them.

V. *"Issues for the Family"* (if applicable).

When the plane landed in Germany, I turned to my teenage son and said, "Oh, Brian, this is my childhood dream." His response was, "It is sure not mine." Being pulled away from lifelong friends was very difficult for him, but after a few months he was able to make some wonderful friends at school and especially through sporting activities. The opportunity to travel and experience other cultures has been part of his great adventure, but he will tell you it has also changed his U.S. friendships to some degree. Not being able to share the high school stories (football games, homecoming, and proms) that these friends have in common can be hard. Also, there is no one there who can share his stories about skiing in Austria or Switzerland, or the senior trip to Sarajevo, so those stories usually go untold.

VI. *"What They Gained."* This is a good time to discuss the positive aspects of the expat sojourn, as well as the positive aspects of being back home.

Traveling abroad and especially living abroad makes you aware of the many different ways people can solve the same problem. You can never again be positive you have the one true answer, but instead you are much better at generating a number of possible options for resolving the issue. I think I am a much better listener and very, very empathetic to someone who is not a native English speaker. You will never hear me saying, "Why don't they just speak English?"

When we first were in Germany, the stores closed at noon on Saturday and nothing was open on Sunday (family day). One Saturday a month was "long Saturday," and stores were open until 5 or even 6 p.m. It took some time to get used to this, and often we were without milk, etc., until Monday. One thing I love about being back home is the easy access I have to everything. Sometimes the choices seem overwhelming, but I know I can find what I need and get it done pretty much 24/7.

Adapted from the work of Craig Storti for the video, *A Good Return*, directed by Regge Life, and available from www.globalfilmnetwork.net.

50

Job Reentry—Coming Home

Time Required:

85–125 minutes (5–10 minutes for introduction; 60–90 minutes for activities; 20–25 minutes for debriefing)

Work
X–X
X, X, X, X

Objectives:

To help participants:

1. Identify the new skills, competencies, and cultural insights gained from living abroad.
2. Explore processes to build and refresh personal global profiles.
3. Provide an opportunity to structure a road map for job reentry.

Materials:

- Worksheet: Pre-Workshop Questionnaire (one for each participant, to be distributed prior to the training)
- Chart paper and markers
- Paper and pens or pencils

Process:

1. Introduce the activity with the following questions and narration:

   - How many of you have a plan for your job reentry?
   - Have you maintained your professional and personal networks?
   - How many of you are confident that you'll have a job when you return home?

   Having a personal strategy for securing meaningful work when returning home can do much to relieve work-related anxiety frequently associated with reentry. This exercise is designed to help you map out a strategy for job reentry, and help you hit the ground running.

2. Divide the participants into groups of three. Allow time for each member to share his or her elevator speech. Group members will then provide constructive feedback, noting strengths and offering suggestions for possible improvement.

3. In this same small group, invite participants to share two or three new skills, cultural competencies, or personal insights they have acquired during this assignment. Make notes and then allow time for each group to share general themes or patterns and/or any unique or surprising findings.

4. Returning to the plenary group, introduce this SWOT analysis activity. Ask, "Given what we've just learned about ourselves, what are the *Strengths*, *Weaknesses*, *Opportunities*, and *Threats* we need to consider in job reentry?"

   Place four sheets around the room, each with one word on it: *Strengths*, *Weaknesses*, *Opportunities*, and *Threats*. Place participants in four groups, one at each of these sheets. Give them ten minutes to brainstorm as many responses to the topic as possible; then have them rotate to the next sheet, spending five minutes reading what the previous group has written and adding new ideas to the sheet. Repeat this until everyone has been at all four sheets. Now ask people to return to their original sheet, examining what has been added. Ask for observations. Point out that each group added something important to each page, so the more people job seekers consult with in their job search, the more effective they are likely to be.

5. Now give individual participants approximately ten minutes to write a half page detailing three or four key things they can personally do to manage their job reentry.

   Examples:

   - Revise elevator speech.
   - Prepare for interviews.
   - Update networks.
   - List companies I would like to work for and form an approach strategy.

6. If time allows, pair participants and ask them to share their plans for next steps. Summarize these key points, including:

   - Make sure you can articulate the additional competencies, skills, and cultural insights you have gained from working abroad.
   - Update your profile and CV at regular intervals.
   - Continuously update your profile on social media.

- Keep your networks active. Keep in touch with your contacts regularly, rather than just asking for an introduction or "favor" from time to time.

Debriefing Questions:

1. What did you think when you heard about this workshop? When you received the questionnaire? What one thing did you learn about yourself that will make your job reentry easier?

2. How did you feel sharing the information from your questionnaire? When hearing about others? During the SWOT analysis?

3. Describe any surprises you experienced during the workshop. What types of observations did you make during this process?

4. What is the first thing that you plan to do now to help yourself hit the ground running?

Debriefing Conclusions:

1. We develop new skills, competencies, and cultural insights through the experience of living abroad.

2. It is important to develop a process for continuously building and refreshing our personal global profiles.

3. Having a roadmap for job reentry can relieve much of the work-related job anxiety associated with reentry.

4. Accessing the thinking of others can strengthen your approach to job searches.

Note: Trainers should distribute the questionnaire and ask participants to complete it prior to the workshop. Trainers may also wish to put the topics (elevator speech, curriculum vitae, resumé, etc.) into a quick Internet search and provide the most current online resources for effective models. These steps will allow time for participants to reflect and arrive at the workshop with their elevator speech; a list of newly acquired experiences, skills, and competencies; and a fresh curriculum vitae or resumé.

This exercise was adapted from Susan Bloch and Philip Whiteley's work in *The Global You* (2010), published by Marshall Cavendish (http://tinyurl.com/po5xar5).

Worksheet: Pre-Workshop Questionnaire

This questionnaire is designed to help you to begin reflecting on your career choices and job reentry strategy upon returning home after an assignment abroad. It will help you begin to think about planning a road map for your job reentry. This includes:

1. Developing or updating your elevator speech.
2. Identifying skills, competencies, and cultural insights gained abroad.
3. Revising your resumé.

1. Elevator Speech:

Whether you are at an airport, at a conference, mingling with friends, or interviewing for an assignment, you have approximately sixty seconds to leave an exciting, impactful, and meaningful impression with those you come in contact with. So make those sixty seconds count.

You need to develop a compelling yet simple statement to explain what you do, and why it matters. This "elevator speech" is key to successfully prospecting at networking events as well as at chance meetings. Please write down your elevator speech:

_____

_____

_____

_____

_____

_____

_____

_____

_____

_____

2. Competencies Update:

You may not realize it, but inevitably you have developed a number of cross-cultural skills and competencies while working abroad. These new skills can enrich your value to the job market. Please take the time now to reflect on the new skills, competencies, and cross-cultural insights you have gained since your arrival. These might include: functional expertise, cross-cultural communication skills, ability to virtually work with teams across borders, etc. For example:

- I have enhanced my ability to work with others from different cultures by being more sensitive to their cultural values and understanding how to decode behaviors.
- I devised a strategy to build a supply chain for cosmetic products in Brazil and Argentina; this taught me how to identify key players and quickly uncover laws and policies that need to be attended to.
- I prepared a communication plan for building relationships with government officials in Pakistan and Indonesia, which taught me how to access specific information required to be successful.
- I have become more flexible as a result of understanding how different cultures operate and appreciating that almost every difference can be seen as an advantage if one looks for the positive.
- I recognize that even though we all speak English, much can get lost in translation.

_____

_____

_____

3. Profile and CV

Please describe your thoughts about what your next job might be and where:

_____

_____

Reviewing your responses to this question in light of the information above, please review your CV. Is it up to date? What needs to be added?

_____

_____

Adapted from Susan Bloch and Philip Whiteley's work in *The Global You* (2010), published by Marshall Cavendish (http://tinyurl.com/po5xar5).

51

Returning "Home"

Time Required:

120–145 minutes (15 minutes for introduction; 20 minutes to prepare personal stories; 45–60 minutes for work in triads; 10 minutes to record skills on flipchart, 30–40 minutes for group reports and large-group debriefing)

> **Work**
>
> X–X
>
> X, X, X, X

Objectives:

1. To heighten understanding of the reentry process
2. To normalize the feelings associated with reentry
3. To recognize and affirm core strengths and cultural competencies
4. To encourage application of strengths and competencies to "home" situations

Materials:

- Paper and pencils
- Notepaper
- Flipchart and marking pens (one for the facilitator and one for each group)

Process:

1. For the introduction, make the following key points about reentry:
   - Culture shock when going abroad is expected, and support to ease transition is frequently available.
   - Culture shock when returning home (reverse culture shock) is unexpected, and support to ease transition is important.
   - Returnees frequently have unexpected challenges and frustrations when returning home.
   - "Home" has changed, and so has the returnee.

- Reentry requires establishing new routines and relationships.
- Reentry requires reestablishing prior relationships and reestablishing trust and credibility on work teams, with former classmates, etc.

2. Invite participants to think back to their international experience with the following narration:

   Think about some of your early frustration, confusion, and discomfort. Now think about some of your personal and/or professional successes. Choose one event, which you felt particularly good about, to be shared. Describe both the event and your specific role in the event. Include:

   - A description of the event.
   - The challenges and/or obstacles you needed to overcome.
   - How you were able to accomplish your goal.
   - Any surprises along the way.
   - What you learned about yourself or others.

3. You have approximately twenty minutes to decide on the event you would like to share and write your story, including the key points noted here. (You may wish to display the key points for participants, to guide their writing. Give a five-minute warning for story completion.)

4. Ask participants to form triads for the sharing of stories. (It is suggested that family members and close friends join different triads, so they receive fresh feedback.) The triads have 45–60 minutes for story sharing and feedback (15–20 minutes per person). Ask one member to be the time keeper for the triad. Explain that as Person A shares the story, Persons B and C should listen carefully and individually record at least three strengths and/or competencies revealed (implicitly or explicitly) in Person A's story. When Person A completes the story, Person B and Person C will each share the competencies and strengths they heard in the story. Each listener will share his or her list. (Repetitions are to be expected.) After the listeners have shared, Person A will then respond with any feelings or questions he or she has about the feedback.

5. This same process is repeated for Person B and then Person C. Help triads manage their time so each individual gets a fair share and no one individual dominates the conversation.

6. Next, ask each triad to compile a list of all strengths and competencies that were identified. Record the list on the group chart.

7. Reconvene the larger group and review the charts.

- What similarities/differences appear?
- Do certain skills or competencies appear on every chart?
- Are there any surprise or unique listings?
- How might this exercise be helpful during reentry? (Participants might note that the skills they used for success in the "host" country are the same skills they can now use to support their successful reentry at "home.")

Debriefing Questions:

1. What did you think when you heard the directions for this activity? When you realized you were going to tell a personal story?

2. How do you feel now that the activity is complete? Now that you have heard the stories of others?

3. Which actions or behaviors were helpful to you as you worked with your triad? Were there actions or behaviors that interfered with your group participation?

4. What have you learned from this experience?

5. How might you apply this information to your personal or professional life?

Debriefing Conclusions:

1. Living internationally frequently results in personal changes and preferences that can go unnoticed until the expatriate returns home.

2. Returnees may initially feel like "strangers," and it is hard for them to know what their experiences have meant to them or how they have changed until they are "in-country" for a number of months.

3. It is important for returnees to share experiences and feelings. Sharing with other expatriates, even if they were located in different countries, can be beneficial.

4. Many of the strengths and competencies returnees developed or enhanced while living internationally are the same skills and competencies they can draw on when they encounter change and experience "difference" at home.

5. Reflecting on international experiences and challenges is an important step toward fully integrating the benefits derived from living abroad.

This exercise was developed by Patricia Cassiday, Collaborative Connection, Seattle, Washington (www.collaborativeconnection.org).

Expatriate Debrief

Time Required:

80–115 minutes (10–15 minutes for introduction; 15–20 minutes for work in pairs; 20–30 for small-group work; 20–30 minutes for large-group work; 15–20 minutes for debriefing)

```
Work

X–X

X, X, X, X
```

Objectives:

1. To frame individual experiences in a broader "expatriate tradition"
2. To give participants an opportunity to reflect on "lessons learned"
3. To help expatriates recognize and record important cross-cultural learning
4. To help participants explore possibilities for sharing the lessons learned with future expatriates (e.g., managers, study abroad students, family members)

Materials:

- Worksheet: Returning Expatriate Questions (one copy per participant)
  (If possible, distribute the worksheet prior to the facilitated exercise, so participants can complete it at their convenience, allowing time for reflection.)
- Chart or PowerPoint slide prepared with the questions from Step 3 and instructions and questions in Step 5
- Optional: Appendix F: The Myth of the Hero's Adventure and the Expatriate Experience
- Short clips from the first *Star Wars* film

Process:

1. Using information from the introduction of this book, from the introduction to the reentry section, and from Appendix F,

introduce the concept of reentry and possible challenges associated with the process. Acknowledge that living in another country is usually a life-changing experience. Explain that many expatriates report that one of their greatest challenges (and often biggest disappointments) when returning home is not being able to share their experience with friends and family and/or with individuals in the organization that sent them out. Using language such as the following, make these key points:

- It is not that family and friends are not interested, but the experience may just be too "different," and they are not able to relate to your enthusiasm or frustration.
- They may be interested but then quickly overwhelmed by the amount of information you have to share.
- Family and friends may even feel left out, jealous, or hurt that they were not part of this special time in your life.
- Personnel at organizational headquarters may not see the relevance of what is being shared, or may think you have "gone native."

Whatever the reasons, not being able to share what you have learned can leave returnees frustrated, confused, and misunderstood. Today we are going to have an opportunity to share our international experience with someone who can relate and is interested in hearing more. We are also going to brainstorm some ideas of how we can share our stories and build on lessons learned.

2. Ask participants to select a partner. (If debriefing with families, the partner may be chosen by role, such as another employee, spouse, teen, elementary student, etc.) Give pairs the following instructions: "Think of some memories that came up when you were completing the questionnaire and from your actual experience abroad. Move to a quiet space with your partner and share your stories using this set of questions and the answers you provided on the questionnaire." Each person should take about fifteen minutes to do this.

3. Review the following questions on a chart or PowerPoint slide:
- Where were you located?
- How long were you there?
- Did you speak the language? How do you think this affected your experience?
- What were some achievements or accomplishments you feel proud of?

- What were some of the biggest challenges? How did you handle the situation? What did you learn?

- What is the best part of being back "home"? The most challenging?

- What has this international experience meant to you personally? How do you make sense of this in the context of your present life?

4. Ask pairs to discuss any similarities, common themes, or patterns that they hear in their stories.

5. Ask participants to keep this information in mind as they move with their partners to join another pair. In this group of four, participants should discuss the similarities and differences they have discovered in their journeys. Give them the following instructions:

   - List similarities and/or differences of what you learned from living abroad.

   - List some of the greatest rewards of being "home" and some of the greatest common frustrations or challenges.

   - What are the characteristics or competencies you believe are most important for a future expatriate to develop?

   - How might you now be able to share and/or build upon your knowledge?

6. In the large group, review the questions, giving each small group an opportunity to share and allowing for large-group discussion.

Debriefing Questions:

1. How did you feel when you heard there was going to be in a class about reentry? When you received the questionnaire? When you started to reflect upon your experience? What may have contributed to those feelings?

2. What did you observe as participants were working in pairs? When you were asked to join another group? When we were debriefing with the large group?

3. What were your thoughts as you heard about the experiences of others? How do you think we can better prepare sojourners for the challenges they will face abroad? For reentry?

4. How might this experience affect your reentry? Your future international travels?

Debriefing Conclusions:

1. The individual expatriate experience makes more sense when it can be framed in the broader expatriate tradition. This is a way to make sense of the experience and normalize the feelings often associated with reentry.

2. Having an opportunity to reflect upon the expatriate experience and share the lessons learned with someone who may have had similar experience can deepen understanding of lessons learned.

3. Keeping a record of the information shared (what worked and didn't work, greatest personal challenges, preferred communication styles, cultural-bridge resources, etc.) is an asset for an organization seeking to be effective in that host culture.

4. Having an expatriate or a panel of expatriates share lessons learned with future expatriates (e.g., managers, study abroad students, and/or family members) is a valuable resource, giving credibility to the pre-departure training. This opportunity to share also respectfully recognizes the value of the expatriate's experience and expertise.

Note: The opportunity for lifelong learning is one of the principal attractions of expatriate life. Expatriates go off on a life-changing adventure where they face a variety of challenges and where they must overcome personal and professional hurtles. The myth of the hero's journey (see Appendix F) can be used to help an individual who is struggling to make sense of his or her unique experience by framing that experience into a part of a long tradition of expatriates on the "hero's path."

This activity offers a way to ease the expatriate's transition to life back home by providing debriefing sessions where participants can talk about their experiences with people who are truly interested (a rare commodity).

Worksheet: Returning Expatriate Questions

Think back to your (last) overseas assignment, and answer the following questions. (Feel free to use additional paper for responses.)

1. What did you think when you first heard you were going to _____?
2. What were the first few days like?
3. What did your family/spouse/partner think about living in _____?
4. What was your first big aha moment about the culture?
5. What was the most important thing you learned in those first six months?
6. Did you have someone who could explain the local culture to you and whom you could confide in?
7. Can you describe your relationship with your home organization (or school) while abroad?
8. What type of non-work activities did you participate in? With whom did you do them?
9. What is it like to come back home?
10. Do you think you have changed as a result of working abroad? If so, how?
11. Do you feel you get to fully use the skills you acquired abroad in your current job? Why or why not?
12. What advice would you give to a person ending a foreign assignment about returning home?
13. What advice would you give to a friend who was on his or her way to a foreign assignment?
14. What advice would you have for HR departments about handling expatriates?
15. Would you go abroad again? Why?

Adapted from the work of Joyce Osland, professor at the Global Leadership Advancement Center, San Jose State University.

Appendixes

Building a RAFT

When an individual learns they will be leaving, they begin to prepare for the move both consciously and unconsciously. The most obvious preparations include learning about the new geographic location, information about the new culture, and aspects of the new work assignment or school where they will be studying. There are many questions about living accommodations, weather, schools, access to technology, public transportation, etc. Individuals can begin arranging for the logistics of the move. What should be taken or left behind? These necessary tasks can be both exhilarating and exhausting.

On a deeper, more personal level, sojourners are also preparing for the psychological letting go of life as she or he currently knows it. Consciously and/or unconsciously, individuals begin to loosen emotional ties and slowly back away from personal and professional relationships and responsibilities. Detachment is a normal and necessary part of the transition process. It is a self-protective strategy used to make the leaving as painless as possible. The person leaving and those who are staying behind begin to sense a change. Feelings of confusion, anger, isolation, and so forth are likely to be experienced. Understanding the underlying motivation and emotions associated with detachment offers individuals an opportunity to choose alternative and productive ways of "letting go."

> "The easiest way to remember what's needed for healthy closure is to imagine a raft. By lashing four basic 'logs' together the raft is allowed to remain afloat and get safely to the other side." (Pollock and Van Reken, 1999, p. 220)

Reconciliation: As separation begins, sojourners sometimes begin to push those closest to them away. As tensions build in a relationship, there can be a temptation to just ignore them. "Since we are leaving, why bother dealing with this?" In an effort to "move on," individuals can forget the importance of the supportive relationships they spent time building. These relationships offer a sense of connectivity to the past and possible futures. Leaving unfinished business and unresolved relationships can take a toll both personally and professionally. (Reconciliation depends on a willingness of both parties to reconcile the relationship. It is a process of both forgiving and being forgiven, and it is important to make the attempt. Be aware of cultural preferences in style of reconciliation.)

Affirmation: Building and maintaining relationships depends on a willingness of both parties to acknowledge the importance of the other. Knowing we are respected and appreciated in a relationship helps enrich life. Every culture has preferences for how best to acknowledge and affirm a valued relationship. Be sure to be sensitive to cultural preference. Here are some suggestions:

Tell coworkers you have enjoyed working with them.

Tell family and friends how important they are.

Share a special picture or gift to say goodbye and thank you.

Plan to use e-mail or social media to stay connected.

Farewells: It is important to schedule time to appropriately say goodbye to People, favorite Places, Pets, and even Possessions (4 Ps) that must be left behind. If the family is moving, it is very important to include children in the farewell process. Some ideas for saying farewell could include writing notes, baking cookies, planting a tree, having a "last supper," and so forth. Graduations, "Hail and Farewell" parties, and retirement gatherings are also rituals that help to say goodbye.

Think Destination: Begin looking to the new destination. What resources are at the new location that can assist in a smooth transition? Ask questions about living accommodations, weather, schools, access to technology, public transportation, etc. Questions need to be answered so logistic decisions can be made about what to take and what to leave behind.

The RAFT concept was originally developed by David C. Pollock in the late 1980s.

(Appendix A can also be used to supplement other activities adapted from this book.)

This activity has been adapted from David C. Pollock and Ruth E. Van Reken's work in *The Third Culture Kid Experience: Growing Up Among Worlds* (2009).

A Five-Step Cycle for Successful Relocation

1. **Involvement (current life):** When we are involved, we know what is expected of us personally and professionally. We know how we fit in to the community. We have established routines and favorite places, activities, shops. We take day-to-day activities for granted. There is no need to prove ourselves or build credibility, because those around us already recognize our talents and skills. We have a social network.

2. **Leaving:** Life begins to change when we find out we are leaving. Consciously or unconsciously, we begin to loosen emotional ties as we prepare to leave. Detaching is a necessary part of the transition process and helps to make leaving somewhat less painful. Understanding the feelings and behaviors frequently associated with this step is fundamental to a smooth transition.

3. **Transition:** The transition step begins after we depart from our comfortable way of life and lasts until, consciously or unconsciously, we begin to commit to becoming part of the new community. During transition, we are unsure of how we fit in personally and professionally. Everyday life—things such as buying food, cooking, banking, driving, and so forth—can feel like an insurmountable challenge and requires enormous amounts of energy. This can be a time of chaos and possible panic when we realize the continuity of the past is gone and the present isn't all we had hoped it would be. We have a wealth of knowledge from our past experience, but here, in the new location, no one knows our history, achievements, talents, or expertise.

4. **Entering:** During this step, life begins to feel less chaotic. Our emotions can fluctuate between excitement over new discoveries and a lingering sense of "homesickness." There are days where we think, "This is going to be alright; I am actually glad I am here." This is the best time to begin working with a host culture coach/mentor. Coaches/mentors can function as

cultural "bridges," coaching you through many of the explicit and implicit cultural aspects of the new environment. A coach can help to significantly shorten the time it takes to get acclimated. (It is important for the coach or mentor to have a clear understanding of both the home and host cultures.)

5. **Reinvolvement:** When we reach this step, we have learned new ways to adapt. We are not actually "native" but are now more able to fit in and become part of the new group. We are able to stop worrying about the future and/or reminiscing about the past. We are once again living in the present. We are now becoming part of the permanent community with clear roles, expectations, and established relationships.

This activity has been adapted from David C. Pollock and Ruth E. Van Reken's work in *The Third Culture Kid Experience: Growing Up Among Worlds* (2009).

Cultural Orientations Framework (COF)

"A group's culture is the set of unique characteristics that distinguishes its members from another group."

—Rosinski, 2003, p. 20

Eminent interculturalists have identified several key cultural features, assumed to be the "right way" of doing, thinking, and/or believing within a particular culture. A cultural orientation is that inclination to think, feel, or act in a way that is culturally determined. This orientation encompasses both the visible (behaviors, language, artifacts) and invisible manifestations (norms, values, and basic assumptions or beliefs). While individuals within the culture will fall across the continuum, the cultural "tendencies" can be used in a variety of ways:

- Provide language to describe salient traits of a culture
- Assess cultural differences
- Bridge cultural gaps
- Explore new cultural choices
- Leverage cultural diversity

Here are seven cultural dimensions arranged along a continuum. There are strengths and weaknesses to each position. Where do your *preferences* lie? Please mark your preference with an X on each continuum.

I. Sense of Power and Responsibility:

Control: People have a determinant power and responsibility to forge the life they want.

Harmony: Strive for balance and harmony with nature.

Humility: Accept inevitable natural limitations.

Control	Harmony	Humility

II. Time Management:

Past: Learn from the past. The present is a continuation or repetition of the past.

Present: Focus on the "here and now."

Future: Bias toward long-term benefits. Promotes a far-reaching vision.

Past	Present	Future

Monochronic: Concentrates on one activity and/or relationship at a time.

Polychronic: Concentrates on multiple tasks and/or relationships simultaneously.

Monochronic	Polychronic

Scarce: Time is a scarce resource. Manage it carefully.

Plentiful: Time is abundant. Relax.

Scarce	Plentiful

III. Identity and Purpose:

Being: Focus on "life" itself and development of talents and relationships.

Doing: Focus on accomplishments and visible achievements.

Being	Doing

Individualistic: Emphasis on individual attributes and projects.

Collectivistic: Emphasis on affiliation with a group

Individualistic	Collectivistic

IV. Organizational Arrangements:

Hierarchy: Society and organizations must be socially stratified to function properly.

Equality: People are equals who often play different roles.

|_____|_____|
Hierarchy   Equality

Universalist: All cases should be treated in the same universal manner. Adopt a common process consistency and economics of scale.

Particularist: Places emphasis on particular circumstances. Favors decentralization and tailored solutions.

|_____|_____|
Universalist   Particularist

Stability: Value a static, orderly environment. Minimize change and ambiguity. Efficiency through systematic, disciplined work.

Change: Value a dynamic, flexible environment. Routine is perceived as boring. Effectiveness is through adaptability and innovation.

|_____|_____|
Stability   Change

Competitive: Promote success and progress through competitive stimulation.

Collaborative: Promote success and progress through mutual support, sharing best practice, and solidarity.

|_____|_____|
Competitive   Collaborative

V. Territory/Boundaries:

Protective: Protect self by keeping personal life and feelings private (mental boundaries) and minimize intrusions into your physical space (physical boundaries).

Sharing: Build closer relationships by sharing your psychological and physical domains.

```
|_____|_____|
Protective                                  Sharing
```

VI. Communication Patterns:

High Context: Rely on implicit communication. Appreciate the subtle meaning of gestures, postures, voice, and context.

Low Context: Rely on explicit communication. Favor clear and detailed instructions.

```
|_____|_____|
High Context                           Low Context
```

Direct: In conflict or delivering a tough message, get your point across clearly at the risk of offending or hurting the other.

Indirect: In conflict or delivering a tough message, favor maintaining a cordial relationship at the risk of being misunderstood.

```
|_____|_____|
Direct                                     Indirect
```

Affective: Display emotions and warmth when communicating. Establishing and maintaining personal and social connections is key.

Neutral: Stress detachment, precision, and conciseness when communicating.

```
|_____|_____|
Affective                                   Neutral
```

Formal: Observe strict protocols, rituals, and titles.

Informal: Favor familiarity and spontaneity.

```
|_____|_____|
Formal                                     Informal
```

VII. Modes of Thinking:

Deductive: Emphasis is on concepts, theories, and general principles. Through logical reasoning comes to practical applications and solutions.

Inductive: Start with concrete situations, experiences, and cases. Through intuition and creative problem solving, formulates general models and theories.

| |_____|_____| |
| Deductive | Inductive |

Analytical: Separate a whole into constituent elements. Dissect the problem into smaller chunks.

Systemic: Assemble the parts into a cohesive whole. Explore the connections between elements and focuses on the whole system.

| |_____|_____| |
| Analytical | Systemic |

Adapted from the work of Philippe Rosinski, *Coaching Across Cultures* (2003) Intercultural Press/Nicholas Brealey. (www.GlobalCoaching.pro) and (www. philrosinski.com).

Culture and Values Narrative

I. Definition of Culture

The whole that includes knowledge, beliefs, art, law, morals, customs, and any capabilities or habits acquired by one as a member of a certain group. Culture is shared by all or almost all members of a group. It is passed on from generation to generation, and it shapes our behavior and structures our perceptions.

II. Components of Culture

Culture has both visible and invisible components. Visible culture includes those things we use our senses for: what we can see, taste, feel, and hear (e.g., art, food, music, architecture, clothing, etc.).

   Invisible culture includes those things we do not see either because they are not visible (values) or because we do not think to look for them (communication styles and nonverbal behaviors) or they are outside our consciousness (assumptions).

III. "Invisible" Aspects of Culture

It is the invisible aspects of culture that create the greatest challenges, because we consider our own assumptions, values, behaviors, communication styles, and nonverbal behaviors to be "normal." When someone acts differently from us, we often judge them negatively. Conversely, when they act like us, we either do not pay much attention or we think they are okay. Either conclusion can be incorrect.

IV. Two Types of Values

A. *Terminal* values represent the goal we want to achieve.

B. *Instrumental* values are behaviors we use to get to the goal.

We can have similar terminal values and yet act the same (e.g., two people work hard to make a lot of money). For one individual, the money is used to support a terminal value of long-term security for one's family, while another person may be using the money to support a terminal value of material success for oneself.

V. Intent and Impact Are Not the Same!

We might exhibit a behavior with very good intentions, but it may have a negative impact on another person. For instance, if we call someone by his or her first name with the intent of being friendly and inclusive, and if that person has a different cultural perspective, our friendly gesture may be experienced as an insult or as disrespect because he or she expects to be addressed formally (Mr., Dr., Ms., Professor).

Similarly, someone may behave in a manner that has a negative impact on us. An Arab might ask, for example, "Why don't you have children?" Our natural inclination might be to be offended and want to say, "It is none of your business." The safest assumption, however, is that the person's intention is good. Effective intercultural skills include (a) sharing with others the impact their behavior has had on us and asking them to help us understand their intent; (b) asking about their intent without sharing the impact—which allows us to revise the impact; (c) stating our own intent before acting when behaviors can have multiple interpretations; and/or (d) seeking a wide range of interpretations for the behavior before negatively interpreting it—in other words, avoiding premature judgment.

Taken from Stringer, D., and Cassiday, P. (2003). *52 Activities for Exploring Values Differences*. Yarmouth, ME: Intercultural Press.

Stereotypes and Generalizations Lecturette

I. Stereotypes

- The word *stereotype* means "categorizing all members of a group as having the same characteristics."

- Stereotypes may or may not be based on tangible facts and can be positive (e.g., Asians are all good students) or negative (e.g., U.S. Americans are superficial).

- Stereotypes tend to be inflexible and resistant to new information.

- They can, and often do, lead to prejudice and intentional or unintentional discrimination (e.g., women are nurturing and will therefore make good nurses).

II. Generalization:

- The word *generalization* means "categorizing many members of a group as having similar characteristics."

- Generalizations are based on considerable research or many observations in a wide range of situations.

- Generalizations are flexible and open to new information.

- They can lead to increased curiosity and awareness and improved cross-cultural relationships (e.g., many women are nurturing and those who are may be good candidates for the nursing field).

III. Flexibility—The Key Distinction

The most important thing to remember about stereotypes is how inflexible they are. Once we have adopted a stereotype, whether it is conscious or not, our inclination is to believe it is right and to act on it; the stereotype thus becomes entrenched in our responses. Generalizations on the other hand, allow us a place to begin thinking, but we remain open to examining the situation from other perspectives. This process allows us to revise a generalization based on new information.

IV. The Goal

The goal is to reduce rigidly held stereotypes and encourage more use of generalizations that keep us open to new information and tend to improve relationships.

Taken from Stringer, D. and Cassiday, P. (2003). *52 Activities for Exploring Values Differences*. Yarmouth, ME: Intercultural Press.

The Myth of the Hero's Adventure and the Expatriate Experience

Hero's Journey	Expatriate Experience	Star Wars' Example
Call to Adventure	Offer of the overseas assignment (some accept immediately, others struggle to decide, some turn it down)	Princess Leia appears in a hologram to Luke Skywalker, saying "Help me, Obi-Wan Kenobi"
Crossing the First Threshold	Leaving behind their own culture to cross both physical and cultural boundaries	Luke slips past the guards and enters the bar filled with "aliens"
The Belly of the Whale	Acculturating into a foreign culture (foreign language, values, beliefs, assumptions)	Luke is lost on the Death Star and out of control
The Magical Friend	Cultural mentors who interpret the local culture and guide them through the challenges/trials	The Force and Obi-Wan Kenobi
The Road of Trials	Numerous obstacles encountered in learning to live and work effectively in another culture	Luke is trapped in the trash compactor
The Ultimate Boon	Bi-cultural perspective from exposure to cultural differences, trials, and paradox; increased self-awareness	Luke can fly without the aid of the Force
The Return	Repatriation: Readjustment to their homeland	Luke returns to visit his aunt and uncle

Developed by Joyce Osland, professor at the Global Leadership Advancement Center, San Jose State University.

References

Adler, N. J. (2010a). *Leadership insight*. London: Routledge.

Adler, N. J. (2010b). Going beyond the dehydrated language of management: Leadership insight. *Journal of Business Strategy, 31*(4), 90–98.

Adler, N. J. (2005). *International dimensions of organizational behavior* (5th ed.). Cincinnati, OH: South-Western College Publishing.

Adler, N. J. (2004). Reflective silence: Developing the capacity for meaningful global leadership. In Nakiye Avdan Boyacigiller, Richard Alan Goodman, & Margaret E. Phillips (Eds.), *Crossing cultures: Insights from master teachers* (pp. 201–218). London: Routledge.

Bennett, J. M. (1998). Transition shock: Putting culture shock in perspective. In M. J. Bennett (Ed.), *Basic concepts of intercultural communication: Selected readings* (pp. 215–223). Yarmouth, ME: Intercultural Press.

Berardo, K., & Deardorff, D. K. (2012). *Building cultural competence: Innovative activities and models*. Sterling, VA: Stylus Publishing.

Bird, A., Mendenhall, M., Stevens, M., & Oddou, G. (2010). Defining the content domain of intercultural competence for global leaders. *Journal of Managerial Psychology 25*(8), 810–828.

Black, J. S., Gregersen, H. B., & Mendenhall, M. E. (1992). *Global assignments: Expatriating and repatriating international managers*. San Francisco: Jossey-Bass.

Black, J. S., Gregersen, H. B., Mendenhall, M. E., & Stroh, L. K. (1999). *Globalizing people through international assignments*. Reading, MA: Addison-Wesley.

Black, J. S., Morrison, A., & Gregersen, H. B. (1999). *Global explorers: The next generation of leaders*. New York: Routledge.

Bloch, S., & Whiteley, P. (2011). *The global you*. London: Marshall Cavendish Publishing.

Bridges, W. (2009). *Managing transitions: Making the most of change*. Reading, MA: Perseus Books.

Bridges, W. (2004). *Transitions: Making sense of life's changes*. Reading, MA: Perseus Books.

Campbell, J. ([1949] 1968). *The hero with a thousand faces*. Princeton, NJ: Princeton University Press.

Cassiday, P. A. (2002). *Leadership in international settings: Exploring the values, beliefs and assumptions of expatriates*. Unpublished doctoral dissertation, Seattle University, Seattle, WA.

Cassiday, P. A., & Stringer. D. (2013). International assignments: Selecting, supporting and retaining high-performing managers. In Elaine Biech (Ed.), *The 2013 Pfeiffer annual: Consulting* (pp. 127–136). San Francisco: John Wiley

Deardorff, D. K. (2009). *The Sage publication of intercultural competence.* Thousand Oaks, CA: Sage Publications.

Duke, S. T. (2014). *Preparing to study abroad: Learning to cross cultures.* Sterling, VA: Stylus Publishing

Eidse, F., & Sichel, E. (2004). *Unrooted childhoods: Memoirs of growing up global.* Boston: Nicholas Brealey Publishing.

Fisher, G. (1997). *Mind-sets: The role of culture and perceptions in international relations.* Yarmouth, ME: Intercultural Press.

Fowler, S. M., & Mumford, M. G. (1999). *Intercultural sourcebook: Cross-cultural training methods* (Vol. II). Yarmouth, ME: Intercultural Press.

Fowler, S. M., & Mumford, M. G. (1995). *Intercultural sourcebook: Cross-cultural training methods* (Vol. I). Yarmouth, ME: Intercultural Press.

Gardner, H. (1998), Creativity and leadership: Making the mind extraordinary, videotape by R. DiNozzi (producer) with guidebook. Los Angeles: Intro the Classroom Media.

Gardenswartz, L., Cherbosque, J., & Rowe, A. (2010). *Emotional intelligence for managing results in a diverse world: The hard truth about soft skills in the workplace.* Boston: Nicholas Brealey Publishing.

Gundling, E. (2010). *Working globe smart: 12 people skills for doing business across borders.* Boston: Nicholas Brealey Publishing.

Hess, M. B., & Linderman, P. (2002). *The expert expatriate: Your guide to successful relocation abroad: Moving, living, thriving.* Yarmouth, ME: Intercultural Press.

Hofstede, G., Hofstede, G. J., & Minkov, M. (2010). *Culture and organizations: Software of the mind.* Columbus, OH: McGraw-Hill Publishing.

Kelly, G. A. (1963). *A theory of personality: The psychology of personal constructs.* New York: W. W. Norton & Company.

Kolb, D. A. (1983). *Experiential learning: Experience as the source of learning and development.* New Jersey: Prentice-Hall.

Kohls, L. R. (2001). *Survival kit for overseas living: For Americans planning to live and work abroad.* Boston: Intercultural Press.

La Brack, B., & Pusch, M. D. (1999). *Training for international transitions.* Paper presented at the Summer Institute for Intercultural Communication, Forest Grove, OR.

Laroche, L., & Rutherford, D. (2007). *Recruiting, retaining, and promoting culturally different employees.* Burlington, MA: Elsevier.

Leki, R. (2008). *Travel wise: How to be safe, savvy and secure abroad.* Boston: Intercultural Press.

Lewin, K. (1947). Frontiers in group dynamics. *Human Relations* 1, 5–41.

Lewin, R. (2009). *The handbook of practice and research in study abroad: Higher education and the quest for global citizenship.* New York: Routledge.

Lowney, C. (2013). *Pope Francis: Why he leads the way he leads.* Chicago: Loyola Press.

Mendenhall, M., & Oddou, G. R. (1985). The dimensions of expatriate acculturation: A review. *Academy of Management Review 10*(1), 39–47.

Mendenhall, M., Kuhlmann, T., Stahl, G., & Osland, J. (2002). Employee development and expatriate assignments: A review of the expatriate adjustment theory literature. In M. Gannon & K. Newman (Eds.), *Handbook of cross-cultural management* (pp. 155–183). Oxford, U.K.: Blackwell Publishers.

Mendenhall, M. E., Osland, J., Bird, A., Oddou, G.R., Maznevski, M.L., Stevens, M., & Stahl, G.K. (2013). *Global leadership: Research, practice and development*. New York: Routledge.

Oberg, K. (1960). Cultural shock: Adjustment to new cultural environments. *Practical Anthropology 7*, 177–182.

Osland, J. S. (2001). The quest for transformation: The process of global leadership development. In M. Mendenhall, T. Kuhlmann, & G. Stahl (Eds.), *Developing global business leaders: Policies, processes and innovations* (pp.137–156). Westport, CT: Quorum Books.

Osland, J. S. (2000). The journey inward: Expatriate hero tales and paradoxes. *Human Resource Management, Summer–Fall, 39*(2&3), 227–238.

Osland, J. S. (1995). *The adventure of working abroad: Hero tales from the global frontier*. San Francisco: Jossey-Bass Publishers.

Osland, J. S. (1990). *The hero's adventure: The overseas experience of expatriate businesspeople*. Unpublished doctoral dissertation, Case Western Reserve University, Cleveland, OH.

Osland, J. S., & Bird, A. (2000). Beyond sophisticated stereotyping: Cultural sensemaking in context. *Academy of Management Executive 14*(1), 65–87.

Paige, R. M. (1993). On the nature of intercultural experiences and intercultural education. In R. M. Paige (Ed.), *Education for the intercultural experience* (pp. 1–19). Yarmouth, ME: Intercultural Press.

Paige, R. M., Cohen, A. D., Kappler, B., Chi, J. C., & Lassegard, J. P. (2010). *Maximizing study abroad*. Minneapolis: University of Minnesota.

Paige, M., & Vande Berg, M. (2012). Why students are and are not learning abroad. In M. Vande Berg, M. Paige, & K. H. Lou (Eds.), *Student learning abroad: What our students are learning, what they're not, and what we can do about it* (pp. 29–60). Sterling, VA: Stylus.

Pollock, D. C., & Van Reken, R. E. (2009). *The third culture kid experience: Growing up among worlds*. Boston: Intercultural Press.

Rosinski, P. (2010). *Global coaching: An integrated approach for long-lasting results*. Boston: Intercultural Press.

Rosinski, P. (2003). *Coaching across cultures: New tools for leveraging national, corporate, and professional differences*. Boston: Intercultural Press.

Schein, E. H. (1992). *Organizational culture and leadership* (*2nd ed.*). San Francisco: Jossey-Bass Publishers.

Simens, J. (2011). *Emotional resilience and the expat child: Practical tips and storytelling techniques that will strengthen the global family*. United Kingdom: Summertime Publishing.

Stewart, E. C., & Bennett, M. J. (1991). *American cultural patterns: A cross-cultural perspective*. Yarmouth, ME: Intercultural Press.

Storti, C. (2011). *Culture matters: The Peace Corp cross-cultural workbook.* Washington, DC: Peace Corp Publishing.

Storti, C. (2007). *The art of crossing cultures.* Yarmouth, ME: Intercultural Press.

Storti, C. (2001). *The art of coming home.* Yarmouth, ME: Intercultural Press.

Stringer, D., & Cassiday, P. (2009). *52 Activities for improving cross-cultural communication.* Boston: Intercultural Press.

Stringer, D., & Cassiday, P. (2003). *52 Activities for exploring values differences.* Yarmouth, ME: Intercultural Press.

Trompennaars, F., & Hampden-Turner, C. (2011). *Riding the waves of culture: Understanding diversity in global business.* New York: McGraw-Hill.

Vande Berg, M., Paige, R. M., & Lou, K. S. (2012). *What our students are learning, what they're not and what we can do about it.* Sterling, VA: Stylus Publishing.